SOUTHERN THOUGHT AND OTHER ESSAYS ON THE MEDITERRANEAN

Southern Thought and Other Essays on the Mediterranean

FRANCO CASSANO
Edited and translated by
Norma Bouchard and Valerio Ferme

FORDHAM UNIVERSITY PRESS

New York 2012

Copyright © 2012 Fordham University Press

Originally published as *Il pensiero meridiano*
by Editori Laterza, 1996

All rights reserved. No part of this publication may be
reproduced, stored in a retrieval system, or transmitted in
any form or by any means—electronic, mechanical,
photocopy, recording, or any other—except for brief
quotations in printed reviews, without the prior permission
of the publisher.

Fordham University Press has no responsibility for the
persistence or accuracy of URLs for external or third-party
Internet websites referred to in this publication and does not
guarantee that any content on such websites is, or will
remain, accurate or appropriate.

Fordham University Press also publishes its books in a
variety of electronic formats. Some content that appears in
print may not be available in electronic books.

Library of Congress Cataloging-in-Publication Data

Cassano, Franco, 1943–
Southern thought and other essays on the Mediterranean /
Franco Cassano ; edited and translated by Norma Bouchard
and Valerio Ferme.
p. cm.
Includes bibliographical references and index.
ISBN 978-0-8232-3364-9 (cloth : alk. paper)
ISBN 978-0-8232-3365-6 (pbk. : alk. paper)
ISBN 978-0-8232-3366-3 (epub)
1. Thought and thinking—Europe, Southern. 2. Thought
and thinking—Mediterranean Region. 3. Europe,
Southern—Social life and customs. 4. Mediterranean
Region—Social life and customs. I. Bouchard, Norma,
1960– II. Ferme, Valerio, 1961– III. Title.
BF441.C297 2011
909'.09822—dc22
2011008430

Printed in the United States of America
14 13 12 5 4 3 2 1
First edition

CONTENTS

v

ACKNOWLEDGMENTS

The editors wish to thank the publishing houses Editori Laterza for granting the right to translate the 2005 version of *Il pensiero meridiano*, the essays "L'Europa e il pensiero meridiano" and "Sapere cardinale" from *Paeninsula: L'Italia da ritrovare* (1998), and Mesogea for the chapter "Contro tutti i fondamentalismi: Il nuovo Mediterraneo," from *Rappresentare il Mediterraneo: Lo sguardo italiano* (2000). Words of gratitude go to Franco Cassano for his generous assistance at all stages of this work and to Martina Di Florio Gula for her invaluable editorial skills and meticulous attention to detail.

TRANSLATORS' INTRODUCTION: ON FRANCO CASSANO'S *SOUTHERN THOUGHT*

Norma Bouchard and Valerio Ferme

In 1996, with the publication of *Southern Thought*, which we present here in the English translation with four additional essays, Italian writer Franco Cassano became widely recognized as one of the most important voices in the contemporary Italian and European intellectual scene. In this engaging and provocative book, which moves effortlessly between the fields of sociology, political science, philosophy, cultural anthropology, and literature, Cassano offers a critique of normative models of modernization derived from Eurocentric and North Atlantic paradigms while claiming the right for autonomous paths to modernity for the Mediterranean and the Souths of the worlds, the so-called Global Souths. Thus, *Southern Thought* not only exemplifies a brilliant critique of Occidentalism but represents a valiant attempt at restoring agency and dignity to the heritage and legacies of Southern civilizations and cultures.

Born in 1943 in Ancona, Italy, Cassano currently resides in the city of Bari where he is a professor of sociology in the Department of Political Sciences at the local university. His writerly career began in 1971 with the publication of a study on classic works of social and political theory, *Autocritica della sociologia contemporanea. Weber, Mills, Habermas* (1971). This book was followed by an edited collection of essays on Marxism, *Marxismo e filosofia. 1958–1971* (1973); and a study on Hegel and Weber co-authored with the philosopher Remo Bodei, entitled *Hegel e Weber. Egemonia e legittimazione* (1977). In 1979 Cassano published *Il teorema democristiano*, a study on the impact that the Christian Democratic Party (DC), Italy's main ruling party from 1944 to 1992, had on postwar Italian society and politics. This study was well received by the scholarly community and even reprinted once. However, Cassano's research would soon take a different—and, by Cassano's own admission—more fruitful path by moving into a decidedly interdisciplinary direction.

Convinced that "the idea that truth as the dowry of a single discipline (be it philosophy, poetry and literature, sociology, anthropology, biology, psychology, etc.) is ridiculous, a corporate delirium,"[1] Cassano embarked on what he calls the practice of disciplinary "sconfinamento," or trespassing,[2] all the while maintaining a solid grounding in the fields of social and political sciences. He not only began studying the new sociology of science, spending time at the University of Edinburgh and publishing on the topic,[3] but by 1983, with *La certezza infondata* (1983), his research had successfully "trespassed," to use his own words, into the fields of philosophy and hermeneutics. In *La certezza infondata*, Cassano argues for the impossibility of establishing criteria of falsehood and truth within the social sciences, embracing instead the notion of symbolic universes introduced by Peter L. Berger and Thomas Luckmann in *The Social Construction of Reality* (1966), that is, sets of culturally and historically determined beliefs that lend legitimacy and plausibility to our thoughts and values, including our theoretical models and explanatory systems, but whose validity remains contextual. As Francesco Giacomantonio recalls, *La certezza infondata* made a considerable impact on the field of the sociology of knowledge as testified by the references to Cassano in what is arguably Italy's most important dictionary of sociology, *Dizionario di Sociologia* (2004).[4]

If the antifoundational approach to the social sciences of Berger and Luckmann was central to Cassano's concerns, so were the weaker hermeneutics that traversed meditations on difference and alterity by Jacques Derrida, Michel Foucault, and other continental philosophers skeptical of essentialist philosophies of History. These interests led to the publication of two works, *Approssimazione. Esercizi di esperienza dell'altro* (1989; 2003) and *Partita doppia. Appunti per una felicità terrestre* (1993). As the title suggests, *Approssimazione* provides a wide range of phenomenological readings of social reality—from sexual difference to conceptions of age—not in order to arrive at a final truth and absolute knowledge but, rather, to enter into a dialectical relationship with other symbolic universes. *Partita doppia* is animated by the same nonfoundationalist approach as *Approssimazione*, but its importance resides in the way Cassano's concern with the ambivalence and complexity of reality is applied to a discussion of modernization and the Mediterranean, themes that will become central in *Southern Thought*.

In *Partita doppia*, Cassano argues that, whereas in the wisdom of antiquity human relationships were conceived as a game producing gains and losses, winners and losers, modernity holds the optimistic belief that through economic, industrial, and technological innovation it will be possible to put an end to the competition over limited resources by teaching mankind to produce goods rather than appropriate them through violence. However, for Cassano the development promised by modernization has not proved to be a solution. Instead, despite economic, industrial, and technological advances, hierarchies, discriminations, and exclusions endure or, as the title of one of Michel de Montaigne's essays cited by Cassano puts it, "The Profit of One Man Is the Loss of Another."[5] Yet, Cassano's argument in *Partita doppia* goes beyond the mere critical unmasking of modernity's grand narratives to probe the ambivalence and double-sidedness of human experience. In the essays that constitute the volume, Cassano explores the opposite, contradictory beliefs of victors and vanquished, victimizers and victimized, saints and inquisitors, fanatics and ironists across a wide range of disciplines, from art to literature, philosophy, sociology, anthropology, political science, and more. Cassano does so to train thought to look at the world from many different angles and to inhabit opposite point of views, in order to reach the awareness that human experience constitutively implies double or even plural legitimacies that it is our duty to maintain and foster. In this strong position against the single, absolute word in the name of reality's constitutive pluralism, we can also find the beginning of Cassano's reflection on the Mediterranean and the Global Souths that will be at the center of *Southern Thought*. Indeed, Cassano concludes *Partita doppia* by proposing a return to Europe's often repressed Mediterranean roots, as a way to rediscover the space of an irreducible diversity that has historically resisted the imposition of unifying and totalizing visions of cultural, religious, ethnic, and economic plurality. But Cassano's reflection on the Mediterranean in the closing pages of *Partita doppia* and in *Southern Thought* also needs to be understood within the contexts of the revisionist interpretations of Italy's "meridione," or South, which were carried out by "neo-meridionalismo," and the theoretical perspectives opened up by postcolonial and subaltern studies.

In the eighties, a new discourse about Italy's South began to emerge in the work of scholars clustered around the Istituto Meridionale di Storia e Scienze Sociali, a center founded by Piero Bevilacqua and Augusto Placanica in 1986. A body of revisionist interpretations of Southern Italy was published in journals such as *Studi storici*, *Quaderni storici*, and especially in *Meridiana*. These interventions articulated a research agenda that wished to break free of a "meridionalismo" that, *mutatis mutandis*, from Leopoldo Franchetti, Sidney Sonnino, and Pasquale Villari to Francesco Saverio Nitti, Giustino Fortunato, Gaetano Salvemini, and Guido Dorso, was predicated on the assumption of Southern Italy as a homogenous periphery examinable only within the framework of historical and social backwardness and stagnation. By contrast, in the work of "neo-meridionalisti," a new image of the South emerged to demonstrate the region's vitality or, as Morris describes it, the ability to produce "a set of 'rational' responses to human (e.g., societal) and physical (e.g., climatic) factors . . . in response to changing conditions."[6] Thus, for example, the latifundia estates,[7] long considered relics of feudalism, were shown to have developed a considerable degree of flexibility and dynamism to counter the volatility of markets.[8] Along similar lines of inquiry, other examples of Southern backwardness, such as family networks and patron-client relationships, were described as sophisticated anthropological formations fulfilling a social rationale specific to political and social conditions in the South. Besides reassessing the dynamism of Southern economies and societies from the nineteenth century all the way to the post–World War II era, the "neo-meridionalisti," following the lead of Franco Venturi, reconstructed how, with the sixteenth century shift in Atlantic and Mediterranean geopolitics, an entire discourse was produced, a discourse that combined geography and climate with racial and biological determinism to explain the perceived backwardness and lower levels of civilizations of the Southern populace and, ultimately, to reify cultural difference in a most resilient conceptual framework. It should also be noted that much of the discourse analyses of "neo-meridionalismo" derived significant impetus from the work of Edward Said whose *Orientalism* had been published in 1978, followed by the equally influential *Culture and Imperialism* (1993).

The impact of the work produced by the "neo-meridionalisti" on Cassano's rethinking of the Mediterranean cannot be overestimated since it represents a much needed answer to over a century of studies on the South from the perspective of the region's backwardness and stagnation. At the same time, it is also crucial to note that Cassano is very aware of the limits of this revisionism. Specifically, many of the analyses by "neo-meridionalisti" remain trapped within hegemonic concepts of modernity, progress, and development. As a result, the South continues to be described from the ideological perspective of the North. For example, this occurs when the economy of latifundia estates is praised within the context of classical capitalist principles of economic rationality and maximization of profitability or when family networks and patron-client relationships are reevaluated within modern bourgeois models of civic culture.

By contrast, Cassano's rethinking of the South not only departs from Northern ideological constructs but also seeks nothing less than the reversal of the North-South relationship: "not to think of the South in the light of modernity, but rather to think of modernity in the light of the South" ("Introduction: For a Thought from the South") In his work, the South is no longer a belated, imperfect, incomplete and not-yet North, but the space of a differential, autonomous identity to be recovered and rediscovered.

> Thinking the South thus means that the South is the subject of thought: It does not have to be studied, analyzed, and judged by an external thought,

but it must gain back the strength to think of itself on its own terms, to recapture decisively it own autonomy.

Southern thought basically means this: Give back to the South its ancient dignity as the subject of thought; interrupt the long sequence whereby it has been thought by others. ("Introduction: For a Thought from the South")

Precisely because Cassano restores the specificity of the South and its position as an autonomous subject of representation, the South becomes a critical resource to question the real achievements of Western modernization while probing the system of values that legitimized it, namely Eurocentric Occidentalism: "[T]he South does not simply constitute an imperfect and incomplete stage of development, but rather a different way of seeing that aims at protecting its own autonomy vis-à-vis the developed world, while deconstructing its symbolic arrogance" ("Prologue: Parallels and Meridians").

Although Cassano's departure from "neo-meridionalismo" permeates *Southern Thought* in its entirety, it is perhaps best illustrated in the part of the volume titled *"Homo currens."* Here Cassano does not seek to uncover the signs of hidden forms of Southern modernization but, rather, to assess modernization itself. Although Cassano makes it clear that his perspective should neither be interpreted as "a defense of traditional versus modern society" ("Prologue: Parallels and Meridians"), nor as an expression of "leniency toward localism, the muddy playing with one's own vices that has correctly led some to call the South an 'inferno'" ('Introduction: 'For a Thought from the South"), he chooses to align his voice with those of political theorists and cultural critics who are skeptical or at least cautious about global modernity. Evoking intellectuals ranging from Paul Virilio, David Harvey, Zaki Laîdi, James Gleick, and Lothar Baier, to Thomas H. Eriksen, Michael Blayr, Carl Honoré, Serge Latouche, and Immanuel Wallerstein among others, Cassano explores the darker side of modernization by describing human consequences initiated by classical capitalist modernity and continued in post-Fordist economies: the radical individualism of experience; unlimited consumerism and unrestrained competition; the perception of human sociality as an intolerable boundary; and even the compromising of democratic principles by following capitalist principles to their bitter consequences. Cassano acknowledges that some individuals might flourish in the regime of modernization, but the vast majority of people do not. In the global reach of the post-Fordist era, forms of neocolonialism are resurging in the name of progress in science, technology, and economy, leading to the exploitation of human beings and human labor, the despoliation and destruction of nature, and the integration of the rich diversity of human cultures into a Western hegemony. For Cassano, such standardization of experiences and ways of life within the law of a single, normative model of modernity does not lead to a global emancipation. Instead, it benefits only a tiny minority while millions are transformed into human waste and wasted human lives.

It is at this juncture that Cassano's reflection meets the interpretative contexts of postcolonial and subaltern studies in a shared effort "to decolonize the mind,"[9] to "provincialize European thought,"[10] and to move "beyond Northern epistemologies,"[11] by probing the foundations of a system whose enabling, universalizing fictions legitimated—and continue to legitimate—a model of planetary dominance over humankind and natural resources. Among such foundations, Cassano locates idealist philosophies of history, such as Hegel's, where ethnocentric and teleological perspectives combine with the experience of difference as a limit that must and can be overcome through incorporation of the "Other" in one (Western) "self." In his revisiting of *Lectures on the Philosophy of History* (1837), Cassano acknowledges that in Hegel's work the Mediterranean exists "as 'central point' and 'axis of the history of the world,' 'navel of the world' where Greece, 'the most shining beacon in history,' lies" ("Albert Camus: The Need for Southern Thought"). However, for Cassano, Hegel's idealism ultimately conceives of this center as a stage to be surpassed in a historical movement toward the North of Europe: "Without any hesitation, Hegel states: 'Indeed, Europe is absolutely the end of world history, just as Asia is its beginning'. . . . All of history must proceed North, toward the West, to finally flow into the highest spiritual density concentrated in the ethical power of the State" ("Albert Camus: The Need for Southern Thought").

But besides questioning a vision of historical progress as a path toward the North as *Abendland*, the land of the evening and thus of a presumed "maturity," Cassano also examines the foundations of Occidentalism through geophilosophical categories in order to demonstrate, once more, the embodied nature of Eurocentrism and, with it, its untenable claims to universality. In the footsteps of Carl Schmitt, the author of *Land and Sea* (1954),[12] in *"Homo currens"* he describes how at the center of Occidentalism and its quest for dominance are two fundamentalisms: the fundamentalism of land and that of the sea.

The fundamentalism of land is rooted in totalitarian forms of belonging, such as ethnicity, culture, language, and especially place. But the fear of mobility and of encountering the other that the fundamentalism of land implies is not resolved by replacing it with the fundamentalism of the sea. Indeed, the unstoppable liquidity of the Ocean leads toward utilitarian individualism and toward aberrant forms of freedom that do not know the restraint of limits and the importance of returns. It is the moment when the figure of Captain Ahab of *Moby-Dick* replaces that of the Greek Ulysses, a *homo viator* whose travels, limited to the Mediterranean by the Pillars of Hercules, always implied a return: the journey-as-*nostos*. More damagingly still, the lack of limits and restraints of the fundamentalism of the Ocean has led to the darkest pages of the Western system of planetary dominance: the colonization of the continental Americas and of the Caribbean, Africa, the Middle East, and Asia; and the neocolonial formations of the present era, where the same tradition of Eurocentric Occidentalism currently legitimizes the new world order of the post–Cold War, of which the war in Kosovo and the American response to the events of 9/11 are, for Cassano, but the latest expressions.

> The first gesture of Columbus, after he lands in the "Indies" and kisses the ground, is to baptize the island he has just touched, foisting on it the name of San Salvador. The metaphor of discovery removes the Other from the stage, along with its gods, names and rights. . . . What was colonialism if not the division of the planet in many provinces of Europe, the contempt for and domination of the other? Who can forget maps from the early twentieth century, where the vast majority of non-European peoples were under the control of Old World empires? Who can forget that Angola was Portuguese; Congo, Belgian; the Antilles, Dutch; India, British; and Algeria, French? But Western fundamentalism did not end with colonialism. Far from dying out, it has begun to write another page of its long story with the passage of planetary primacy from old Europe to young America. Obviously it had to be another form of fundamentalism, one that was compatible with the demise of colonialism. ("Thinking the Mediterranean")

However, the reactions that Occidentalism elicits can be just as devastating as Occidentalism itself. Indeed, in several passages of *"Homo currens,"* Cassano, borrowing categories developed by Arnold Toynbee's *A Study of History* (1947), contends that opposition to Occidentalism leads to two paths: the one of the Zealots and the one of the Herodians. While the Herodians undergo a process of deculturation that leads them to assume the West as a model, the Zealots embark in a reactionary search for identity to maintain their integrity as a subaltern culture. For Cassano, the recent rise of Islamic fundamentalism is akin to a response by the Zealots even though, in the sixties, Middle Eastern countries such as Egypt, Algeria, Syria, and Iran had chosen, like the Herodians, a Western path of modernization. When this path failed, many embarked in the path of the Zealots, in a shift that demonstrates how fundamentalism is often the effect of the disastrous uprooting brought about by modernization.

> *We can say, then, that fundamentalism is not the expression of the essence of Islamic culture.* . . . Its prevalence is not the expression of a culture suspicious

of modernity, but the *effect of the relationship*, of the deeply asymmetrical
nature of the relationship between the West and those nations, and of the
refusal to pursue avenues that have ended in failure. ("Thinking the
Mediterranean").

Despite such an assessment of the global consequences of post-Fordist
modernity and of the Occidental episteme that gives it a foundation, Cassano's *Southern Thought* does not translate into an abdication of sociopolit-
ical and cultural agency. On the contrary, it articulates a new discourse on
the Mediterranean and the Global Souths that should not be seen as a
gesture of regressive Southern identity politics.[13] Instead, it ought to be
conceptualized more in the terms articulated by Dussel, that is, as a "project of liberation of a periphery negated from the very beginning of modernity."[14] But the liberation of this periphery as the repressed "Other" of
Atlantic Europe also means that Cassano's Mediterranean is both a geographical entity encompassing Eastern, Western, Northern, and Southern
Mediterranean shores—and a such an area of interactions and exchanges
to recover or uncover—and a metaphor whose referent is the Global
South(s): the Caribbean of Edouard Glissant and the Asia of Homi
Bhabha, Gayatri Chakravorty Spivak, Ranajit Guha, Gyan Prakash, Amar-
tya Sen, and Dipesh Chakrabarty; the Latin America of Walter Mignolo,
Boaventura de Sousa Santos, Anibal Quijano, and Edgardo Lander, and
the Northern and the Sub-Saharan Africa of Mohammed Arkoun, Nelson
Mandela, Wole Soyinka, Aminata Traoré, Chinua Achebe, and Ngugi wa
Thiong'o, among many others.

> But luckily the South that is worth listening to is very diversified. One
> cannot but think of the Latin American South, the South of the Western
> world, a South we all know through some great figures in politics, music,
> sports, and literature. . . . There is also the South of hybridity and *métissage*,
> the whole of the Mediterraneans of the world, which has a decisive role in
> shaping a path that moves away from every cultural and national fundamen-
> talism: a South that stretches from America to India.
>
> Finally, there is the African South, a South that, despite its recent great
> voices . . . cannot avoid sinking into suffering and the inability to make
> itself heard. ("Prologue: Parallels and Meridians")

Such connections between the Mediterranean and the Global Souths
are not meant to elide differences and asymmetries among Mediterranean
shores nor minimize the magnitude of Asian, American, or African colonization. Rather, these connections seek to establish a transnational dialogue
among peripheral zones that, despite their differences, share some com-
monalities; because the Mediterranean, like Asia, Africa, the Caribbean,
and Latin America, is one periphery among many other peripheries; it is

the South of Northern Atlantic culture, the margin of Europe, the "Other" of the West, an "Orient" among other "Orients." In the words of Cassano,

> Southern thought explicitly claims for itself the connection between a South, the Italian one, and the Souths of the worlds. This is done not to establish equivocal identifications and assimilations, but to oppose the tendency to think that the emancipation of the Italian South can be read as a separate question, enclosed within the boundaries of a national or continental state, and blind to its connections with the outside. ("Prologue: Parallels and Meridians")

Yet, like Asia, Africa, the Caribbean, and Latin America, the Mediterranean is also a resource, a subaltern archive of values and traditions that Cassano locates in a number of unsuspected sites.

> The image of the Mediterranean thus is turned upside down: It no longer is something that preceded modernity and its development, as its degraded periphery; instead, it becomes a deformed identity that must be rediscovered and reinvented through its links with the present: no longer an obstacle, but a resource. ("Against All Fundamentalism: The New Mediterranean")

In "Going Slow" (Chapter 1 in Part I: "Mediterranean"), these values range from slowness, contemplation, and conviviality to reflections on the Mediterranean reality of exchange, hybridization, and plurality. While for Cassano values of slowness, contemplation, and conviviality have kept the South from reaching the conquests of North Atlantic modernity, they have also screened it from its pathologies. Otherwise stated, in a manner that is not dissimilar to the articulations on various forms of slowness provided by the writer Milan Kundera, the filmmakers Wim Wenders and Werner Herzog, and cultural theorists Paul Virilio and A. O. Hirschman, these values should not be dismissed as impediments to development and progress but ought to be conceptualized as examples of resistance to the excesses of capitalist and especially post-Fordist modernization. Next to the recovery of values such as slowness, contemplation, and conviviality, Cassano evokes another dimension of the Mediterranean heritage: its history of networks and connections between cultures, societies, and ethnicities, stretching from Western Europe and the Sub-Sahara to the Middle East all the way to the Indian Ocean and the Asian steppes. Cassano frequently recalls how, over the course of its millenary history, the Mediterranean Sea, which is a body of relatively calm and navigable waters surrounded by the nearby shores of three continents—Europe, Asia, and Africa—has enabled peaceful trade and commerce but also violent conflicts. As a result, a great deal of hybridization and exchange has taken place between cultures, societies, and ethnicities stretching from Western Europe and the Sub-Sahara to the Middle East all the way to the Indian Ocean and the Asian steppes: "That it was a sea of different shores not far from each other made it navigable from the start. On this sea between lands, the Other was never a huge distance away, beyond the gap of the Oceans, but could be reached in few days of navigation. In the names and bodies, in the histories, the Other has always been present" ("Thinking the Mediterranean").

Despite its constitutive hybridity, however, the Mediterranean is also an area where various groups have sought to impose their unifying and totalizing vision on cultural, religious, ethnic, and economic plurality, from the Roman Empire to the rise of Islam, from the Crusades and the Reconquista to the development of European Atlanticist modernity from the eighteenth century onward, when European monarchic state-systems evolved into the modern states, leading to an even greater rigidity by way of juridical borders and confines regulating the inside from the outside, the native from the foreign body. Cassano's intent, however, is to conjure the repressed history of pluralism of the Mediterranean periphery, to recover the Mediterranean heritage of networks, hybridities, and shared spaces, and, through it, oppose History's totalizing claims.

> In the course of the centuries, this sea has witnessed invasions, forced conversions, and abuses of power; but every time the claims of one land over others has worn itself out and has ebbed, just like the sea's undertow. The Mediterranean, as a sea *between* lands that does not belong to any of them, is a *communal sea*. This belonging to everyone and to no one is an obligation to mediate, to hold lands together. The memory of abuses of power must be transformed into the creation of a common homeland capable of adding to the beauty of places and to the resemblance between places and bodies, a harmony that is strong, self-assured, and capable of translating the knowledge of the border into permanent immunity against all fundamentalisms. ("Thinking the Mediterranean")

It should be noted at this juncture that Cassano's notion of the Mediterranean as a place of exchange and connections does not imply a facile endorsement of the historical creolization of the basin. By creolization Cassano intends the intercultural spaces of hybridity and *métissage* theorized by Frantz Fanon, Edouard Glissant, Homi Bhabha, Kwame Anthony Appiah, Paul Gilroy, Françoise Lionnet, Arjun Appadurai, Néstor Garcia-Canclini, among others. To Cassano, as well as to a number of recent critics of hybridity and *métissage*, such as Prabhu, these concepts often obscure the real inequalities and the conflict-ridden aspects of interconnectedness. By contrast, his notion of interconnectedness is one that does not hide tensions, inequalities, and the asymmetries of power among cultures. But besides disclosing the fluid Mediterranean cartographies of intertwined and entangled histories and cultures, of patterns of creolization, contamination, and crossovers between North and South, East and West, a fundamental component of Cassano's recovery of the Mediterranean heritage is also his revisiting of the culture of ancient Greece, a culture whose keen awareness of limits and borders has often been forgotten in late modernity. As discussed in the chapter "Of Land and Sea," this is a culture that attracts the author of *Approssimazione* and *Partita doppia* because it does not seek the certainties of the *epos*, but welcomes differing point of views. Pondering its origins, Cassano resorts to a geophilosophical explanation to describe how the fractal geography of the Aegean was crucial to the development of ancient Greek thought. The presence of land bordering—and thus limiting—water, and of water bordering—and therefore containing—the liquid expanse of the sea, was internalized by ancient Greek culture, allowing it to avoid the fundamentalism of land and sea that Cassano has located as the central aspect of the quest for dominance of Occidentalism. In his words,

> The Aegean Sea and the Mediterranean . . . limit themselves to separating lands; they set a distance that is never the excess of the ocean; they are a strong discontinuity between lands, but not their relinquishment without bearings. This distance that, especially for the ancient sailor, could be great and fearsome, is not, however, an abyss and the sea does not drown into the ocean. It separates from the motherland but does not lead one to repudiate it. The Pillars of Hercules fix in the Greek imaginary the gap between the sea bound by lands and the endless extension of the ocean. ("Of Land and Sea")

Precisely because it internalized the idea of the border between land and sea, the Greek cultural imaginary developed the awareness of the ineluctable existence of difference. This was a difference that could—and did—alternatively lead to exchanges and coexistence as well as to confrontations and conflict, but that ultimately evaded fixed attributes of language, culture, and ethnicity, and the unbridled, limitless liquidity of the Oceanic expanse: "This sea, which is at once external and internal, inhabited and waded into, this sea-as-border interrupts the rule of identity, forces one to accommodate division. Here land, with its obsession for fixity, assuredness, and appropriation, clashes always against a boundary" ("Of Land and Sea").

Greek polytheism, tragedy, and philosophy exemplify, for Cassano, the most significant achievements of this cultural imaginary, as each allows for the legitimacy of many points of views. In the polytheism of Greek religion, for example, Dionysus implied Apollo: The many gods existed as competing particularities, engaging in conflict and interaction but never making claims to universality. Tragedy involved the irresolvable *agon* between dramatic characters, such as occurs in Sophocles' *Antigone* between the discordant truths of Antigones and Creon, or in Aeschylus' *Prometheus Bound*, where the Titan is both right and wrong. Philosophical thought developed the *dissoì lógoi*, the practice of arguing both sides of an issue, which foregrounds the discursive frailty of wanting to own the ultimate truth and is so well exemplified in the speech between the Melians and the Athenians, from Thucydides' *History of the Peloponnesian War*. In this work, the objectivity of the historian, Cassano notes, "is an example of the tragic diverging of perspectives whose gap the logos cannot bridge" ("Of Land and Sea"). But internalizing the physical borders of its geography also allowed Greek thought to realize that limits should not be trespassed, as we see in the Greek myth of the Homeric Ulysses, the traveler who returns home. When trespassing did occur, Greek thought unfolded into the greatest of crimes, the *hubris* that led to the destruction through one's *nemesis*.

Here it is worth noting that, throughout his recovery of the Greek cultural imaginary, Cassano often reflects on the misuse of its legacy, which was either forgotten or actualized *if* and *when* its components could be used to reaffirm a universalizing Occidental episteme: "When the need for empire begins, all the wealth contained in that knowledge begins to vanish and the only part that can save itself is the one that can be capitalized in a universal (and universalistic) domain" ("Of Land and Sea"). Focusing on the misuse of this tradition, Cassano detects in Nietzsche a return to Greece and the South only as a step leading to the limitless, boundless expanse of the Ocean, as it is described in *The Gay Science*;[15] while in Heidegger he locates a reterritorializing of the Ocean that completely erases the sea, thus allowing only the telluric dimension to endure.

> Heidegger's, therefore, is not *the* philosophy, but the complete reterritorializing of philosophy, a metaphysical hand that tried to hold within itself all of philosophy, while wishing to elide the sea, and the relationship with tragedy and the nonbeing of truth. This is the fundamental limit of Heidegger's philosophy, its being sucked into the Hearthland, far away from the corruption of any sea, of any border. ("Of Land and Sea")

Nietzsche and Heidegger, then, come to represent, respectively, the fundamentalism of the sea and that of the land, misunderstanding the more enduring significance of the Greek humanistic heritage. Other philosophers in the post-Nietzschean tradition, such as Gilles Deleuze and Félix Guattari, are equally unable to recover the specificity of Greek thought. For Cassano, the "nomadology" of Deleuze and Guattari is a more contemporary form of de-centeredness that, just as is the case for Heidegger, misses the complexity of "the knowledge born in Greece" ("Of Land and Sea"). Indeed, the forgotten side of the Greek heritage exemplified by these philosophies continues to lead the West toward the aberrations of Occidentalism, by eliding the tension and contradiction—in one word, the dialectic—that used to be a fundamental component of the Greek heritage, and which helped temper the tendency toward excess and lack of moderation. It is precisely because Cassano seeks to recover the buried dialectical dimension in Western epistemologies that he devotes a section of *Southern Thought* to two writers whose life and work exemplify what he calls "the friction of thought": Albert Camus and the Italian poet, narrator, and filmmaker Pier Paolo Pasolini.

The Algerian-born, French writer Albert Camus, as he is discussed in "Albert Camus: The Need for Southern Thought," is a thinker of friction who questions not only the teleology of Christianity, Marxism, and the philosophies of History in post-Kantian ideology, but upholds values that are no longer current in modernity, such as a Donquixotesque notion of honor. He is thus praised by Cassano for his "ability not to follow the flow of the river, to remain standing while everyone else reasonably takes a seat in the armchairs of the present, being outdated not as a sign of affectation but of friction that accompanies another way of being of the mind" ("Albert Camus: The Need for Southern Thought"). However, Camus is also important for Cassano in how he revisits Greek culture. In 1937, against a background marked by dictatorship, empire building, and racism, Camus delivered the lecture "The New Mediterranean Culture" (1937) on the occasion of the inauguration of the *Maison de la Culture* in Algiers. He not only targeted the aggressive ideologies that were seeking to establish the superiority of one culture over another, but sought to counter them through a humanistic foundation of tolerance and respect for the other as it is posited in Mediterranean civilizations. Camus would further expand his ideas on the Greek Mediterranean in two essays from the 1940s, "Prometheus in the Underworld" (1947) and "Helen's Exile" (1948); but it is in the politico-philosophical essay *The Rebel*, a text written after two worldwide conflicts, that Camus's writings more forcefully pitted Mediterranean versus Northern epistemologies. In the last section of *The Rebel*, titled "Thought at the Meridian,"[16] Camus called for a recovery of the repressed values of the Mediterranean heritage: the balance and equilibrium between extremes; the awareness of final limits and boundaries; the primacy of values internal to human beings and no longer originating from a philosophical system exterior to them; the respect for nature; and the affirmation of the present through the fraternity and solidarity of the human community against the promises of a distant, teleological future.

   Like Camus, Pasolini offers Cassano the opportunity to meditate on difference as a positive site of engagement for the de-centering of Western thought in the essay "Pier Paolo Pasolini: Life as Oxymoron." Using the author and filmmaker's life and writings as a point of departure, Cassano discusses how the Italian writer's sexual diversity acts as a catalyst to question the centrality of certain Western imperatives, but he also accounts for Pasolini's evolving thoughts on politics, fatherhood, and the sacred in order to chart an existence lived always under the sign of the oxymoron and in a nondialectical resolution. For Pasolini, to remain in the oxymoron means much more than to be tied to his diversity, condemning oneself to its simple and infinite repetition. It means instead to exalt and superimpose the many forms of antithesis and contradiction, to look for and be open to those forms with feverish and inexhaustible eagerness, to live a life far from those that found a home in it and judge the world from that vantage point, even when this home is the uncomfortable and painful one of "diversity." Thus, Pasolini becomes an emblem of the contradiction that is necessary to make relative the claims of the final, absolute word, and, in this sense, Pasolini emerges as a fully "southern" writer and, like Camus, the bearer of a critical thought necessary to oppose hegemonic epistemologies and normative paradigms.

The emergence and consolidation of new geopolitical realities that followed the fall of the Berlin Wall have not diminished the relevance of Cassano's work. Instead, Cassano's ability to scrutinize the politics and economics of present capitalist modernity have become common currency in intellectual discussions of neoliberal globalization, neocolonialism, and the challenges posed by global modernization. Moreover, the complex realities that have emerged amid the tensions of post-Maastricht Europe (especially as they pertain to religious, ethnic, cultural, and economic divides) continue to render Cassano's reflections on culture current. Indeed, in his vision of the Mediterranean as the heritage of unity in difference lies the possibility of reimagining a context of cultural exchange wherein coexistence and fruitful, creative dialogue might finally become possible. But equally significant is his articulation of the Mediterranean within the Global Souths, since here resides the possibility for the emergence of a truly transnational civil culture and public sphere, one that, as Schulze-Engler has cogently written,[17] can come about only by drawing on the global cultural ecumene. And while Cassano's vision remains, for the moment, a cultural and political hypothesis, it carries with it the need to fulfill an incomplete yet very necessary project while testifying to the continuing vitality and legacies of the Mediterranean and the Souths of the world.

As a result, over the years *Southern Thought* has ceased to be the title of a successful book to become an umbrella concept, used to describe the cultural practices of those who question the rigid cartographies of an Occidental, imperial modernity while striving to reconceptualize and reimagine the South beyond the gaze of Northern epistemologies. Cassano himself has continued to expand the intuitions contained in *Southern Thought*, and we have thought it necessary to provide the readers with a glimpse into these further elaborations of his thought. We have therefore appended four additional essays to the original text: "Europe and Southern Thought" and "Cardinal Knowledge" from the 1998 volume *Paeninsula*; "Against All Fundamentalisms: The New Mediterranean," from *Rappresentare il Mediterraneo: Lo sguardo italiano* (2000); and "Thinking the Mediterranean," which Cassano wrote specifically for this volume.

The centrality of the Mediterranean as it relates to Europe is examined in the essay "Europe and Southern Thought," where it is presented as necessary to counter the fundamentalism of an Atlantic Europe, a Europe that has forgotten its Mediterranean dimensions to embrace only the North Atlantic, Oceanic expanse.

> Europe . . . becomes a world power when its gravitational center shifts from the Mediterranean to the Atlantic; when, as Carl Schmitt points out . . . the sea turns to its advantage the relationship with the land, accepting no boundaries and becoming ocean. The breach and eclipse of the Mediterranean coincide with the wane of moderation, and the rise of sea-based fundamentalism in complete opposition to land-based fundamentalism. The flowing of the sea beyond every boundary, its absolutization, marks the birth of modern economy, the unbridled freeing of technology, universal uprooting and total nomadism, and the disappearance of every return route, as man becomes a ship always at sea without moorings. It is the end of the coast, of the port, of those points where land and sea come into contact creating boundaries and thus knowing and limiting each other. ("Europe and Southern Thought")

Similarly, the essay "Cardinal Knowledge" makes a case for the importance of limits to counter essentialist tendencies, but does so through a playful style where Cassano draws on the stereotypes of North, South, East, and West to provide a spiritual topography of human characteristics engendered by the four cardinal points. Here too, he concludes by affirming the importance of contradiction and unresolved dialectic to prevent the prevailing of one cardinal knowledge over the others.

> The cardinal points are four, and they all live inside each of us. We must prevent the establishment of their fundamentalism, the rise of some as criterion and means of evaluation for the others, the ridiculous expectation

that one of them might think of itself as the universal cure. We must be the center in the only way this is possible today: as a crossroads, as the ability to play each cardinal point against the fundamentalism of the others. ("Europe and Southern Thought")

In "Against All Fundamentalism: The New Mediterranean," Cassano explores Italy's relationship with the Mediterranean from the Unification of 1860 to the postwar economic miracle, focusing on the different construction of the Mediterranean by the governments of the Liberal State, Fascism, and the Republic, first as a sea of colonial and imperial conquest, later as the "antimodern demon" that Republican Italy must overcome to fully participate in a Westernized vision of the world.

The disavowal of the Mediterranean is not simply the disavowal of the Other, of those who live beyond the sea. It is also the disavowal of the Italian South and of Italy itself, a loss of awareness of one's own specificity, a diseased relationship that Italians have with themselves. In Italy, the emphasis on modernity and on the construction of European unity has translated into an authentic "passion for the North"; in the obsessive and repetitive hammering away of the idea that the only right way to be European is to cleanse ourselves of all our "Southern" vices and temptations to become "Northern" European. Wherever the fundamentalism of "the modern" rules, not only are the Mediterranean and the South a black hole, but even Italian identity becomes an illness that must be cured. ("Against All Fundamentalisms")

Cassano concludes this essay by arguing for the rediscovered centrality of the Mediterranean and the Italian South that has emerged with the end of the East-West bipolar divide and praises the work of writers, philosophers, musicians, and filmmakers who are reimagining a new cultural space "far away from official and institutional channels, which are . . . about to choke on the rhetoric of modernity" ("Against All Fundamentalisms").

Finally, the last essay, "Thinking the Mediterranean," explores points of contact and dialogue between cardinal points and the conditions that are necessary to deconstruct absolutizing perspectives and the clashes of civilization that they engender. With pointed references to the West and the Arab-Islamic world, Cassano makes it clear that "the exchange of meaning between two cultures must take place in both directions, aimed both at teaching and learning. *It is neither a universal truth defined by the strongest nor a relativistic closure of cultures within themselves, but the complex construction of a polyphonic universal.*" Here Cassano also dialogs with Mohammed Arkoun, Fatima Mernissi, Leila Ahmed, and Tariq Ramadan, among others, exemplifying his own practice of intercultural exchanges. The essay concludes by reaffirming the importance of the Mediterranean as a *pluriversum* resisting all reductions *ad unum* and, we should add, summing up Cassano's entire reflection on Southern thought, from the homonymous book and essays that grow from it. In his own words:

> The dialectic that the Mediterranean teaches is much more complex than the linear movement of evangelization, even in its lay and secularized form. Its universalism is not dogmatic and a priori, but syncretic and a posteriori; it is a universalism that is always imperfect and lives on translations. . . . It does not ask to burn one's roots, but to renew them through the encounter with the other. . . . And today more than ever, the world requires that future chapters be written together, drawn from different forms of knowledge and wisdom. The world needs Moderation, that noun that keeps us away from the intoxication that lives within every fundamentalism, intoxication that leads it to forget that where we end the Other begins, and that no one among us can ever claim the exclusive right to God's word. ("Thinking the Mediterranean")

On publication, *Southern Thought* received much critical acclaim from the scholarly community and the public at large. The many positive reviews of *Southern Thought* testify to its success: Among them, suffice it to recall the praise of reviewers writing for *Linea d'ombra*, *L'Unità*, *La voce repubblicana*, *La gazzetta del Mezzogiorno*, *Il manifesto*, *Liberazione*, *Puglia*, *Altreconomie*, *Il Sole 24 Ore*, *Il Mattino*, *Conquiste del lavoro*, *Gazzetta del Sud*, *Avvenire*, *Il Secolo XIX*, *La Repubblica*, and *Agorà*. But Cassano's accessible and jargon-free prose also rendered the book appealing to the larger public, making *Southern Thought* one of Italy's best-selling books, as the 1998 ranking by *Tuttolibri*, in the newspaper *La Stampa*, reports. Similarly, *Southern Thought* did not fail to attract the attention of readers outside of Italy and was translated into French (*La pensée méridienne*, Editions de l'Aube, 2003), Spanish (*Pensamiento meridiano*, Losada, 2003), and Japanese (Kodansha, 2006). Because of its success, the publisher of the original 1996 volume, Editori Laterza, reissued it in 2003 and in 2005. Cassano, as mentioned earlier, has continued to develop his thinking in his later writing, including *Mal di Levante* (1997), *Paeninsula. L'Italia da ritrovare* (1998), *Rappresentare il Mediterraneo: Lo sguardo italiano* (2000), *Modernizzare stanca: perdere tempo, guadagnare tempo* (2001), *Homo civicus. La ragionevole follia dei beni comuni* (2004), and the monumental *L'alternativa mediterranea*, which was edited with Danilo Zolo (2007).[18] In addition, he has continued to contribute essays to major journals and newspapers, including *Micromega*, *Democrazia e diritto*, *Rassegna Italiana di Sociologia*, *Il Mulino*, *Meridiana*, *Nord e Sud*, *Vita e pensiero*, *Pluriverso*, *Iride*, *Critica Marxista*, *Altrove*, *Cinecritica*, *Thesis Eleven*, *Cahiers du MAUSS*, *Eutropia*, *Democrazia e diritto*, and *Rive*. To this impressive scholarly activity, one needs to add editorial positions in *Rassegna Italiana di Sociologia, Democrazia e diritto,* and *Paradigmi,* as well as the direction of the Interdepartmental Center of Peace Studies of the Università di Bari, and the presidency of Città Plurale, an association devoted to intercultural dialogue, humanitarianism, and international human rights.

To conclude, a final word on this English translation, which, given the impact of Cassano's work, is long overdue. As mentioned in the beginning of this introduction, *Southern Thought and Other Essays of the Mediterranean* provides the English reader with an edited and annotated translation of the 2005 edition of Cassano's *Southern Thought,* which includes the prologue "Parallels and Meridians" to the original text of 1996. *Southern Thought and Other Essays of the Mediterranean* also comprises a prologue by Cassano that was specifically authored for this translation, as well as the already mentioned additional essays ("Europe and Southern Thought" and "Cardinal Knowledge" from *Paeninsula* (1998); "Against All Fundamentalism: The New Mediterranean" from *Rappresentare* il *Mediterraneo: Lo sguardo italiano* (2000); and "Thinking the Mediterranean," written specifically for this volume) that help flesh out the arguments that Cassano had originally presented in *Southern Thought.* Throughout our work as translators and editors, we have been in contact with the author to ensure that the text corresponded as closely as possible to the ideas and wording of the original.

The basic idea for writing *Southern Thought* is very simple. It has been many centuries since the South has spoken in the first person because others have been speaking in its place. The civilization that has been speaking for and representing the South is the one that, during these centuries, has become dominant, the civilization of the world's North-West, in whose eyes the South is, at best, synonymous with a backward society and a perverse mix of misery, repression, and superstitions. According to this perspective, the South's only possibility for redemption is to become North, to erase, as quickly as possible, its difference, to free itself from a culture that, like ballast, prevents it from reducing its disadvantage and embark on the path toward progress.

The theoretical program of *Southern Thought* is therefore very clear: to deconstruct this image; to interrupt the long historical sequence during which the South has been thought by others; and to give it back its ancient dignity as subject of thought. In other words, *Southern Thought* originates from the conviction that the South is much more than a simple not-yet-North, that it represents an autonomous and different point of view, and that today more than ever such autonomy enables us to gain a critical perspective on the direction that the world has taken in the era of globalization and hegemonic liberalism. The South does not just represent the past but also offers useful suggestions for the future: It is another point of view on the world, a voice that today, more than ever, we must learn to hear.

The core of the dominant expression of modernity is, indeed, the hurried one of *Homo currens*, the man who has become an appendix of the production machine that he built, but which has now escaped his control: Those who stop or slow down are lost. This world, far from being the best of all possible worlds, is ruled by the fundamentalism of business, which turns the expansion of markets and profits into every aspect of life in an unquestionable and unrelenting absolute. Such an obsessive competitive pressure, which ranges from the workplace to consumerist practices, unleashes a growing acceleration of our experience that deeply transforms it. One of the crucial arguments proposed by *Southern Thought* resides precisely in its radical, critical distance from the pressures of competition in all spheres of life. In a world where acceleration seems to have become an inevitable destiny, there needs to be a voice that is not afraid to forcefully affirm that some essential dimensions of experience are in grave danger: Indeed, acceleration transforms and mutilates love, education, thought, and relationships between people, as well as their relationship with the collectivity and with nature.

In a world where the dominant rule is *cursus omnium contra omnes*,[1] two processes that are only apparently contradictory affirm themselves impetuously: on the one hand, the radical individualization of experience; on the other, the fragmentation of individual identity. Thus, even the difficulties that are born of structural conflicts are transformed into individual problems, and life becomes a game we are always condemned to play by ourselves. For its part, the acceleration of experience destroys even the feelings of delay and duration. The endless request for innovation and the tyranny of urgency bombard the individual (*in-dividuum*, that which should not be divisible), causing him to split into many elementary particles, each without connections to the others. If, with the advent of modernity, the past had already lost its force, today even the future seems to have disappeared from the horizon, and humankind remains prisoner of a present that, having undone all ties, has become *ab-solutus*.[2] The crisis of those cultural mechanisms that allowed one to transcend the here-and-now (so that one could bring the future into the present with the offer of promise, commitment, and hope) encloses the individual in a kind of ethnocentrism of the moment, but at the same time increases his loneliness and expands feelings of contingency and fear. Those who have broken every tie with the world constantly fear its sudden return as catastrophe.

If the South has begun talking about itself again, it is because North-Western thought appears to have lost its self-control and moderation. The crisis that we are experiencing shows unforgivingly that not only were some banking investments "toxic," but so was the whole system, unable as it is to slow down and forced each time to increase the measure of its speed. After all, hadn't Oswald Spengler already found in *Faust* the mythological core of the West? As a result, it is the crisis itself that makes room for voices that seemed to have been silenced forever, buried under the seal of backwardness. Never as now does the triumphalism of those who, like Francis Fukuyama, had seen in the fall of socialism the beginning of a unipolar world seem so far away, falsified as it is by the irony of that same history whose end it had announced.

But we must immediately clarify that the defense of an autonomous Southern point of view does not wish to counter the fundamentalism of the North-West with a Southern one that is equal and symmetrical to it. The intention of this book is not to replace the fundamentalism of speed with one of slowness, but to return humanity to its mastery over time. The research project that inspires *Southern Thought* wishes therefore to reintroduce our thinking to a multiplicity of perspectives, and to damage every monologue and every attempt to replace the pluriverse of cultures that suggest that one of them might provide us with a universal framework. To think that God entrusted truth to a single people, religion, or culture is, on top of it, a blasphemous claim that lessens the quality and the authority of God. Contrary to what fundamentalists of every ilk argue, no form of life holds the monopoly on perfection: whoever spans a culture without prejudices realizes that, within it, lights alternate with shadows, and assets and liabilities must coexist within its accounting books.

This is the reason why exchanges and dialogue between cultures, especially when they are based on equal dignity, are the only way for humanity to move forward. And this is also the reason that the Mediterranean plays a crucial role in the perspective of Southern thought. Today's dominant vision of history sees in the Mediterranean only a sea of the past, a small sea full of glory but destined to be surpassed by the immense spaces of the oceans and by the power of technology that makes them traversable. Yet, it is precisely its being located in the middle—an imprint fixed in the name Medi-terranean itself—that today makes this sea a place that has a crucial and important meaning. Certainly, the Mediterranean has always been crossed by conflicts, but it is also the sea where, from the beginning, people have mixed their languages, histories, and genetic patrimonies. The Mediterranean "we" is a "we" full of others, where the dream of every purity and ethnic cleansing is a criminal delirium that, as we have already seen, leads to a spiral of slaughter.

There is, however, one particular aspect of our time that makes the Mediterranean a sea of crucial importance. It is the long liquid border where the world's North-West and South-East meet and confront each other. It is not by chance that in his *The Clash of Civilizations*, Samuel Huntington made one of the cleavage lines that divide and set civilizations against each other pass through this sea. This is the dominant representation of the Mediterranean: a frontier of the Western empire that is a seismic and insecure area. Yet, the vision I propose here is radically opposed to this image: Far from being periphery and frontier sea, the Mediterranean can be a sea of connections, peace, and dialogue, not a remote province of the Atlantic empire but the starting point to overcome all fundamentalisms and allow civilizations to meet.

For this vision to become reality, however, the dialogue must be taken seriously, everyone has to respect the logos of the other and all partners in this encounter—therefore the West as well—must recognize and fight their own fundamentalism. Only this attitude can trigger reciprocity and a spiral of collaborative behaviors and friendship. Africans portray their relationship with their European colonizers through two different masks: One shows the African with large ears and a small mouth; the other shows the European with a large mouth and small ears. The European is the one who teaches, while the other, having nothing to say, is forced to listen. It is the portrait of every colonialism, even the postcolonial one, and a fundamentalism that plagues the West. Those who think they are the exclusive owners of truth and seek to convert all others to it do not work toward building a universal culture but toward its contrary, the abuse of the weaker by the stronger. Thus, a culture that wishes to be universal is not the work of a single maker but is only the result of a many-handed construction and of an exchange that does not erase identities but asks each to be open and offer its contribution to the well-being of mankind and of the planet.

The ambition of the perspective that I am proposing here is to reorient the spatial and temporal coordinates upon which the North-Western vision of the world rests. It is not an easy perspective, but it is the only one that can reopen the door to a shared future. This venue also allows me to clarify the relationship between this perspective and the movement that has been labeled postcolonial studies. The path of *Southern Thought* has been, in many ways, parallel to, but also autonomous from this movement, which is very broad and internally varied. If it is true that there are many authors and themes in common, and that we can find points of convergence with some of the proponents of that movement, it is also true that the vision that characterizes this book did not originate in postcolonial India but in the plural dimension that accompanies the history of the Mediterranean. This book, which was first published in Italian in 1996, has been translated into a number of languages but not in English, the lingua franca that facilitates the largest circulation of ideas. It is probable that the dissemination of ideas that are at the core of the postcolonial critique has contributed to the interest in the theoretical path here presented.

I am therefore very happy that Fordham University Press has decided to bring the book to a North American public. All of this would not have been possible without the constant encouragement of Norma Bouchard, who translated and edited the book with Valerio Ferme, and who has faced with serene determination all the challenges that a work of this sort entails, helping me with her observations and advice. I also cannot but thank those who, in time, have shown interest in my work, such as Walter Mignolo, Roberto Dainotto, Claudio Fogu, and Artemis Leontis.

I hope that the book will meet with the approval and answer the questions of readers of a country that, having exhibited great vitality, is trying, at this very moment, to move from fear toward hope.

Bari, July 1, 2009

Since its publication in January 1996, *Southern Thought* has elicited a wide range of responses, from unconditional approval to suspicious opposition, from requests to translate its categories into concrete political terms to expressions of ironic skepticism. Many of its arguments have also been simplified and those who have analyzed the thesis of the book did not always examine it in all of its dimensions.[1] It is possible that this tendency toward simplification resulted from the fact that the author, focused on the theses he was proposing, did not seek to render explicit (because he considered them self-evident) the threads that connected the theoretical underpinning of this book to the ones that precede it and to the international debate. That assumption was probably mistaken and herein lies the main aim of this prologue: to reconstruct the intersection of arguments formulated in *Southern Thought* so as to allow the discussion to continue on more precise foundations.

The one who writes has not arrived to the South and to Southern thought from a "we" or a sudden passion for identity, but from the category of the "other," from a meditation on the shadowy side of every identity. In others words, the strongest motivation for reclaiming the value of the South came from a rebellion against its representations by dominant culture and the inadvertent forms of racism found in many of its variants, even those that are beyond suspicion of being so and politically correct. Faced with the haughty obtuseness of these representations, and an arrogant universalism that is not accustomed to being questioned, choosing the South was an attempt to take the side of the other even before taking the side of the self, a theoretical reaction to a characterization presented in such a negative and caricatured manner that it could not be true. Indeed, such a conclusion was coherent with the entire path that preceded *Southern Thought*; a path that began in the early eighties with a critique of the philosophies of history and with an interest in dissonances and residues, in that dust that dominant reason hides under the carpet to remove the possibility of other ways of life and experience. For the one who writes, that decade was, more than a period of mourning, a feverish season of reading and thinking away from beaten paths and disciplinary enclosures, a tour of the world highly recommended for those who are intellectually complacent, those who never abandon their conceptual cells. Already at the end of the seventies I enjoyed Philip Dick's *The Man in the High Castle* even before having seen and loved Ridley Scott's *Blade Runner*. As is well known, that book, which has become more than just a science fiction classic, suggested that the outcome of the Second World War had been reversed. It seemed to me that Dick was teaching us, as few have done, to discover the ambiguous and complex relationship that we have with "truth." The result of this was, against the grain of prevailing bigotry, a specific curiosity for "revisionism" and an attention to the effects that power relations exert over the structure of the dominant cultural field.

The winners, after all, can always count on obliging intellectuals, and thus know full well how to impose their reasons, how to remove from the official version of history the ambiguity that traverses its depths and that only on rare occasion rises to the surface. However, this sensibility was different from the one that is normally attached to the adjective "revisionist," because here the losers are many more than those that are dear to our home-grown polemics: They are all those who cannot hire lawyers, those we do not know and do not speak about, they are the so-called "Muslims" described unforgettably by Primo Levi in *The Drowned and the Saved*.[2] Today, many have made a career out of revisionism; but what rendered it respectable and engaging years ago was precisely that it went against the tide. The "revisionism" that asserts itself today is the opposite of what it was in the past: It is the adaptation of historiography and cultural politics to the new winners, to the relations of powers that have emerged after the fall of the USSR. It is precisely for these reasons that the torch of "revisionism" is now being passed on to others even though few have realized it.

Therefore, my path to the South did not originate from the desire to reclaim "a tradition that needs to be restored in its integrity," but from a systematic distrust of capital letters and the subservience that is paid to them, and the conviction that no identity can claim to have a privileged relationship with the truth and be authorized to colonize others. I was coming to the South from the systematic deconstruction of arrogance, from the belief that every discourse is full of perverse effects but also of tricks to hide them.[3] Drawing me to the South, even before and even more than the fact of living there, was a constant attention to the "weak" points of every "strong" discourse, the choice to maintain the world free and open, the will to defend its multiplicity against the wish of the victors to enclose it in their uni-verse.

This is why it is difficult to understand *Southern Thought* if one does not realize that, within it, the two dimensions of separation and mediation intersect. On the one side, there is the need for rupture and for reclaiming the autonomy of the South, the need to tear down the false neutrality and universality of dominant representations. On the other side is the defense of cultural multiplicity and diversity, the conviction that the future will be plural or not at all. Each of these positions needs to learn something from the other: The claim for autonomy must avoid the trap of identity fundamentalism, while mediation must avoid being confused with the passive recording of existing power relationships.

Today we are confronted with a great imbalance, a formidable lack of moderation, and every day we discover the existence of abysmal differences among the conditions of the people of the planet. The reestablishment of moderation can come, as Pier Paolo Pasolini teaches us,[4] only from a great jolt, from a force capable of creating a new equilibrium. In the majority of cases, categories of rupture and mediation are mutually exclusive: The aim of this book is to elaborate a kind of intersection between them that might enable us to handle the complexity of the task. I will try to reconstruct this effort by examining some of its dimensions, dimensions that will be discussed separately for the sole purpose of analytical ease. In reality, they function and have meaning only when considered together.

Autonomy

The first, essential step of *Southern Thought* rests in the decisive and radical assertion of Southern autonomy. As written on the book's original dust jacket, the goal of the project is to "give back to the South its ancient dignity as subject of thought, to interrupt a long sequence in which it has only been thought by others." The South is not a not-yet, it does not exist solely in the perspective of becoming other, of escaping horrified from itself to imitate the North with a delay of twenty or one hundred years, and thus probably never. The first step toward autonomy resides precisely in the awareness that the future cannot be an eternally incomplete and failed chase.

The fundamental theoretical move is therefore to upset the hierarchy implicit in this temporal gap through a radical subversion of perspectives: the South as an autonomous point of view, rather than the not-yet-North. It is not by chance that a similar move is also proposed by Boaventura de Sousa Santos who sees precisely in the epistemology of the South the core of a critical utopia that animates the World Social Forum.[5] It is also not by chance that Walter Mignolo bases his *Geopolitics of Knowledge*[6] on the creation of a thought from the borders (*Border Thinking*), the only one capable of thematizing "colonial difference," the discontinuity of power and epistemology between the Northern core of the planet and the ensemble of populations from its peripheries. Indeed, this theoretical gesture is also similar to the one that gives birth to *Subaltern Studies:*[7] Every autonomy is born of relativization or, to say it with Chakrabarty, from provincializing the dominant symbolic universe,[8] and neutralizing its claim to centrality and uniqueness. A South that goes back to think of itself autonomously, that refuses the passive, belated, and impossible imitation of the North, completely reverses the dominant representation. The first move, then, is to unhinge the concept of time that informs this representation, since, by reducing every difference to the simple category of backwardness, it cuts off every thought that seeks to create a different theoretical field.

The transformation of one's relationship with places, the bringing into focus a horizon that is at the same time farther away and closer to the habitual one, goes hand in hand with this changed concept of time. Southern thought explicitly claims for itself the connection between a South, the Italian one, and the Souths of the worlds. This is done not to establish equivocal identifications and assimilations, but to oppose the tendency to think that the emancipation of the Italian South can be read as a separate question, enclosed within the boundaries of a national or continental state, and blind to its connections with the outside, especially those with the Southern shores of the Mediterranean.

Every idea about the future of the South and its development needs to be matched with the specificity of its geographical location and culture. "The key"—I said then—"lies in re-considering the places, in the double meaning of having consideration for and thinking anew about them." Reconsidering the places meant first of all to reexamine the geographical map, to expand our vision beyond national borders, to discover new connections, proximities, and distances. In other words, it was an attempt to give wider scope to the way one discusses the South of Europe and of Italy, while attempting to situate them in the context of the international theoretical debate. But to reconsider the places also meant to transform our cognitive and affective relationship with them. No development can be based on the contempt for and auctioning of places, starting with the industrial rapes of modernity all the way to the postmodern ones of tourism. To reconsider our places means to care and respect them, and to rebuild, through *pietas*,[9] our shared public properties, those properties that belong to everyone and are vehicles of identity, solidarity, and development. In short, the driving idea was the redemption of the South, its abandoning marginality to proceed autonomously. This idea fulfilled the widespread need of Southerners to change the negative image of themselves and of their land while trying to define another, new, and positive one that might instill hope and confidence, and allow them to face the challenges of the future.

It is probably here, at the intersection between a new theoretical context and a widespread need, that we can find the reasons for such strong reactions to the book. Some judged this convergence as dangerous, as if the appeal to the pride and desire to reclaim the South proposed by the book revealed an obscure connivance with Southern "vices," a sort of separatism of the South. For some narrow minds, the word pride can seem rhetorical and insidious, but it is quite easy to understand that it designates not only *amor loci*[10] but also confidence in one's abilities, and the will to accept challenges without the aid of interested tutors. Thus understood, pride is the main productive force because it generates unsuspected energies and leads one to break with a long-held habit of passivity. Pride shows that passivity is not an ontological and immutable state of the South, but derives from subordination, from having internalized a feeling of marginality and having resigned itself to the role of history's spectator. It is an addiction to the lack of autonomy and a dependency on others, and the unhealthy behaviors that result from them. The vast majority of so-called Southern "vices" are not, as some people conveniently believe, a prerogative of the South but are the outcome of a long marginalization from History[11] and of the passivity and cynicism that derive from it.

There is nothing that is farther removed from Southern thought, then, than the attribution to Southerners of the attitude that the Prince of Salina ascribes to Sicilians: "The Sicilians never want to improve for the simple reason that they think themselves perfect."[12] In its radical claim for autonomy, Southern thought not only is stern toward the South as it exists in reality, but in many ways it constitutes its most radical negation because it pushes toward action and openness. The idea of autonomy that informs it is rigorous and demanding, suited to a South that aims at changing itself by changing the relationship between Italy, Europe, and the Mediterranean. If today one can raise an objection to that perspective, it is perhaps to its titanic ambition, a will that leads to underestimate the existing disproportion between the project's ambition and the forces capable of carrying it forth. This issue is open to discussion. What instead is fanciful and unacceptable is the accusation of indulgence of old Southern vices; an accusation that is founded more on the inertia of old stereotypes than on the actual reading of the book.

Ida Dominijanni has found, in the theoretical move that seeks to establish the autonomy of Southern forms of representation, analogies with the direction taken by thinking about gender difference.[13] It is an astute and pertinent observation. Just as female experience is not an inferior and imperfect form of its male counterpart, but rather a different perception of the world that critiques the false neutrality of male dominance, so the South does not simply constitute an imperfect and incomplete stage of development, but rather a different way of seeing that aims at protecting its own autonomy vis-à-vis the developed world while deconstructing its symbolic arrogance.

It goes without saying that this movement does not represent a defense of tradition, just as thinking about difference, which claims the autonomy of the female point of view, does not coincide at all with the idealization of the traditional role of women. In both cases we are not faced with a defense of traditional versus modern society, but with a critique of the false neutrality and universality of dominant cultural models. The danger that Southern thought might turn into an apology of tradition can appear credible only to those who, acting from within the paradigm of one-dimensional thought, think that everything that does not belong to their miserly monotheism of profit ("you shall have no other development before me") coincides with an idealization of the past rather than with a broadening of the future and an expansion of the possibilities contained within it, as well as with an increase of freedom.

If a critique can be leveled at that interpretation, it pertains perhaps to the theoretical privilege it seems to assign exclusively to thinking about gender difference. To reclaim the value of a difference that is discredited by the dominant symbolic power is a move that accompanies many forms of rebellion, one of those doors that open onto a new history and establish a discontinuity with regards to the old one marked by subordination. One need only consider the recent history of the twentieth century and the struggle for colonial emancipation that led first to reclaiming the value of négritude and then to its severe critique; or the lengthy discussions concerning the existence of a Latin American identity and its traits. It is not by chance that the theme of the contradictions of identity traverses postcolonial studies. But if one recognizes that this symbolic deconstruction is common to many radical claims of autonomy, perhaps a better strategy is one that facilitates the exchange of experiences so that each learns from the others, without privileging a specific one as the original. We should also underscore a significant difference between the theoretical move of Southern thought and the critique of Orientalism highlighted by the work of Edward Said.[14] Said's contribution to the critique of forms of symbolic dependency is very important. Cultural domination, Said tells us, is always accompanied by a representation of subaltern culture that reproduces its subjection: It is a representation that emphasizes its difference and, by chaining it to exotic and seductive forms, ends up denying it any autonomy, maturity, or ability to rule itself. Certainly one aspect of the dominant image of the South corresponds to the paradigms of Orientalism: It is the one that continuously swings between its representation as a tourist paradise and as an archaic and Mafia hell, between desperation and abuse on the one side and the desire for a dream-like drift and loss of self on the other. This temptation, it should be noted, surfaces not only in more conventional representations but also in sophisticated and "alternative" ones. It is a particular image of the South—always "minor and prophetic," irreducible to any normalization through meaning and representation—that captures its subversive force, but also appears to enclose it in a spiral of negation that feeds upon its own impotence.[15]

Said's contribution is certainly valuable in helping to build the autonomy of those who have long been in a subaltern position. But perhaps we should add that, in the case of the South, symbolic subjection passes also, and especially, through its definition as a space of backwardness and underdevelopment, as an unfinished version of the North. Symbolic dominance plays out around the imposition of a specific conception of historical time. Here cultural differences lose meaning and value, and are transformed into temporal gaps, into a hierarchy based on how closely they approximate the paradigm of perfection: the North-Western civilization of the world. Probably, both the topic (the literary texts and the Orient) and an Enlightenment-like distrust for the category of difference stirred Said away from critiquing how the category of progress and the consequent flattening of every civilization on a single temporal scale have created a normative and homologizing model that, especially in the second half of the twentieth century, has structured the symbolic dominance of the West in a much stronger and pervasive manner than the exotic exasperation with its diversity.

It must finally be remembered that the notion of autonomy that characterizes the proposal of a Southern thought cannot be, when applied to the Italian Mezzogiorno,[16] but a broad notion that helps bring into focus a much larger geopolitical and geoeconomic context.[17] The marginalization of the South has very distant origins: To overcome it means to conceive political equilibria and the relationship between Italy, Europe, and the Mediterranean very differently from how they are conceived today. The Italian South is, first of all, a periphery that the national-state has tried to cure through state intervention. Now that this state intervention is no longer practiced, and the solidarity between different areas of the country has been drastically reduced by the liberal forces of globalization, the apology for a limited notion of autonomy is, for the South, a dangerous illusion. State intervention was compensation for a peripheral placement. A limited degree of autonomy runs the risk of leading to the acceptance of a subaltern position that has no remedy, and of leaving the Mezzogiorno defenseless in the greater game of cold secessions. Any optimism that comically mimics the gestures of strong areas is destined to fall apart in the clash with real processes.

There is thus a "greater" autonomy to reclaim, and the specificity of the Mezzogiorno must certainly not be erased, but reclaimed with geopolitical intelligence. This requires, first of all, a courageous imaginary, a theoretical horizon capable of creating autonomous foreign policies very different from the ones followed so far. The protagonism of civil society, the renewal of public life, the institutional transformations and the politics of development will never succeed if they do not clearly establish that, in order to make the South a new junction of a euro-Mediterranean network, it is indispensable to articulate how to emancipate Italian and European foreign politics from their status as Atlantic fiefdoms.

Slowness

Reclaiming the value of slowness, which happens especially in the first chapter and in the second part (*Homo currens*) of the book, is one of the topics that struck readers the most, splitting them between a vast majority of people who agreed and a minority of dissenters who found, in the praise of slowness, echoes of a reactionary ideology idealizing a South that has never existed and whose charm we are best rid of as quickly as possible.

I will not remind us here that the praise of slowness is not the exclusive monopoly of Southern thought, since it occurs in the work of many writers and artists who are often far removed from the South, at least geographically.[18] More simply, that praise was meant to increase the awareness that the identification of progress with acceleration destroys forms of experience that are precious and indispensable for mankind. The idea that traditions are reducible to a mixture of superstition and repression is an unforgivable banality, the logical consequence of a hasty and arrogant gaze that is certain to have something to teach others and nothing to learn from them. Among many others, Gregory Bateson has had the merit of teaching us how to understand traditions as the repository of ecological wisdom and as the awareness of limits, an archive that was subsequently dissolved by the expansive triumphalism of modernity.[19] An impartial and unprejudiced gaze would realize that there are experiences that rapidly deteriorate or even disappear with an increase in speed: from loving and caring for others to meditation; from education to conviviality and all the other activities and qualities that, in order to exist, need a longer breathing time to use the oxygen of duration. The absolutization of speed produces a grave deformation or mutilation of experience, and what is lost is often replaced by something that still has the same name but is only its terrible caricature. A speedier love is one you pay for; and a sped-up education presupposes that we might fit in a time of our liking the sedimentation of knowledge.

Fast food[20] accommodates at the same table, one next to the other, the gazes of strangers focused on their own lonely conclusions. Even the locus of *cum-vivere* loses the *cum* and becomes a nonspace traversed by solitary atoms.

Undoubtedly speed increases some abilities while creating new ones. At the same time, it reduces others: it gives us the world, but contemptuously discards a part of it. We do not wish to reactively build a fundamentalism of slowness, but, here too, it is a matter of exploring the ambivalence of speed and discovering that real progress occurs only if we are allowed to use a multiplicity of times. The dangers caused by *homo currens* do not result from speed but from its absolutization, from its identification with progress. The arrogance and vacuity of the so-called "single thought" are revealed precisely on this point: Everything that does not fit within prede-termined parameters is assigned to a temporal resistance of sorts and to a past that refuses to end, before being labeled as nostalgia. To those who point out that the expression "single thought" is grossly polemical and reductive, because it erases the differences that inhabit it, one can calmly answer that we see the narrow-mindedness of that thought at work right here, in a concept of historical time that, by positioning the West as the necessary destination of all progress, labels as regressive every alternative to the dominant form of life. Those who mistake the defense of slowness for a form of nostalgia do so because they have already restricted the field of possibilities to a pure continuation of the present, to existing power relations and to the mechanisms that are at work within them. And this is the precise reason they restrict the world.

Certainly, the speeding up of the world did not begin today, but coin-cides with the origin of modernity itself, which ties even its etymology (modo = now, at this moment) to the endless production of the new, to "that which has value now," and to the awareness of the novelty of the present. Koselleck locates the defining trait of modernity precisely in this growing distance between experience and expectations: One no longer needs the past to guide the action that is now in tune with the future.[21] And Luhmann reminds us in clear terms that the temporization of com-plexity is the distinctive trait of modernity.[22] Such acceleration, however, follows a geometric progression and grows into an avalanche.

Indeed, capitalist modernity itself has known several stages character-ized by a growing acceleration that leads it to pulverize all obstacles: It is what Zygmunt Bauman has described as the passage from solid to liquid modernity, from heavy to light modernity.[23] His metaphors are clear: The spatial pervasiveness of water and the volatility that accompanies lightness show clearly that every form of duration is under attack. Even the perma-nence of ruins that, by enduring and lasting into the present, remind us of our transient nature, faces a crisis. As Marc Augé writes, "Future history will no longer produce ruins. It does not have the time for them."[24] All it will produce is waste, beset as it is by the present perfect of its metabolism. All the counterweights to acceleration, even the modern ones, are thrown away as ballast, and the history of modernity itself is shaped by a harsh and prescriptive philosophy of history: All that restrains the acceleration of profit, the dissolution of social molecules in the competitive dispersion of the market and in boundless individualism, has to be satisfied as if it were a law of nature.

Richard Sennett[25] has highlighted how this growing acceleration produces a corresponding difficulty in defining the calculability of the future, as it increasingly shortens the time frame on which action can rely. In other words, we are facing a radical modification of the classical parameters of modernity itself, parameters that were founded on a spatial extension of time and therefore on its calculability (one need only think of the models of Weber's rationality, but also of Norbert Elias's reflections on time).[26] If, in classical modernity, the future still guided the action, in liquid modernity our breath shortens, and the present conquers center stage.

The liberalistic drift of global capitalism and the centrality of its financial structure cause a narrowing of the temporal horizon: They render the present absolute and sacred, as the only certain and empirically verifiable horizon of experience, in a truly explicit "tyranny of urgency"[27] that reduces to shreds the stability of every expectation. Geometric progression deconstructs the fundamental forms of classical modernity, which are too rigid and "terrestrial" to move in the oceanic space of liquid modernity. It is what many have defined the crisis of the nation-state confronted with the enveloping and deterritorializing dynamics of globalization. The structures that in classical modernity had offered—albeit with some side effects—protection, permanence, reliability of expectations, medium-term and long-lasting benefits, and notions of a collective interest, face a time of crisis. This is why the liquefaction of modernity coincides with a growing individualization of experience[28] and with the freeing of the individual from all social duties, which are now perceived as unacceptable limitations on one's increasingly radical and intolerant freedom.

The increasing collapse of the structures that provide safety and reliability does not pertain only to the growing decline of public institutions: The tyranny of urgency influences economic behaviors as well. Managers themselves, in order to achieve brilliant results that will grant them promotions in the job market, squeeze dry not only the workforce but all the industrial plants, whose life span and efficiency they end up compromising. As Robert Jackall has demonstrated,[29] those who follow in leading a company that was run by a successful manager face huge problems, because surely their predecessor has built his fortune by "drugging up" the plant and maxing out every one of its activities. After all, it is not surprising that, faced with financial conjuring tricks and the hall of mirrors' games that characterize them, measures of control become increasingly difficult to sustain. Since the latter are entrusted to the market and to agencies that compete among themselves, they become more and more unreliable, favoring the proliferation of behaviors that bend the rules and "pump up" the accounting books.[30]

Today, those who speak of slowness do not look back but are concerned with problems in the present that will become even greater in upcoming years.[31] We cannot forget, for example, the observations by Agnes Heller concerning the damages that acceleration inflicts on social memory, and the loss of intergenerational knowledge and openness to the complexity of the world that derives from this mutilation. The centrality of profit erodes memory because "interest needs only a short-term, not a long-term memory, and certainly not a cultural one," as it "does not believe in repetition, it is anti-ceremonial."[32] Where everything can be continuously renegotiated there is no place for memory, since it becomes an impediment, a nuisance, and a limit to freedom of movement that needs, in order to be absolute, to dissolve, as if it were an archaic bond, all the "*cum*," both in time and in space.

The consequences that the process of acceleration of new capitalism has had on human beings have been superbly studied by Sennett in *The Corrosion of Character*. Quality of life, its security, and even its being recognized in time are progressively being lost, and a fragmentation of identity without remedy has begun. To be sure, there are those who are capable of living well in this perpetual movement, which requires that everyone become a skilled surfer. Sennett writes that Bill Gates, for example, "seems free of the obsession to hold onto things. His products appear and disappear with the same rapid speed."[33] Indeed, he is a master of innovation and a perfect surfer. But "mobile" individuals are only one segment of society; on the others weighs the nightmare and very often the reality of failure.

The "temporal regime" that says "down with the long term" and increasingly diminishes trust, also produces a precise hierarchy: "Irreversible change and multiple, fragmented activities might be the natural habitat of the new regime's masters . . . , but they disorient their servants."[34] Even more dramatically Bauman states: "Nowadays it happens that some people easily move in and out of an area, any area, while others watch helplessly as the only area they belong to is taken away from under their feet."[35] We might add that today the process is so advanced that it is not only the powerful who "move out of the area," but the weak ones as well, human beings escaping from repression and depression, the migrants of the entire world.

To sum it up, turbocapitalism has thrown off all ballasts to run faster and faster, but the weights it discharges are the elementary structures of social relations, the reliability that renders individuals and institutions trustworthy, preventive antidotes against all anomic drift. Probably among these discharged ballasts are many precious social resources that only a critique of the despotism of acceleration would allow to list and recuperate. Once more, it is not a question of returning to the past. We are not dealing with a banal regret for an out-of-fashion modernity, but with the need to choose between tagging along a destructive drift and another possibility. It is a matter of enriching the future, of not resigning ourselves to the idea that it must be dominated by cathedrals of waste (the hidden underside of the rhetoric of innovation). In these dumping grounds reside not only millions of human beings but also patterns of relationships and experience that are precious for a more just and wiser world, a world freed from the delirium of Faust and capable, as Peter Handke does, of singing of enduring time.[36]

Last, allow me one more observation. In a society dominated by the fundamentalism of speed, democracy constitutes an unbearable waste of time, another of the patterns of experience that, authoritatively stamped with being "post," it seems we should consign to the past. Yet, the most precious gift of our tradition is precisely the habit of discussion, this wasting time that we see at play even just by leafing through Plato's *Dialogues*. There, the different protagonists chase each other day after day, giving life to discussions on all sorts of topics, from love to virtue, from government to justice. Socrates can conclude these discussions only provisionally because they are virtually infinite. These limitless discussions, wherein Habermas locates the legitimate foundations of the institutions of modern democracy, are a terrible waste of time vis-à-vis the parameters of *homo currens*; but they are absolutely indispensable to rebalance our societies at a time when communicative action seems to have become a simple sidekick to the unlimited dominion of instrumental action, and every pattern of communication appears to have been colonized by profit. It is difficult to think of unlimited discussions without presupposing large swaths of time, without seriously allowing for what Hirschman calls commensality:[37] the coming together of those who discuss in some public space or public square, be it a physical or a virtual one. In all likelihood democracy presupposes a temporal a priori and cannot be achieved at whatever speed. When the speedometer exceeds a certain speed, democracy no longer rules but becomes the handmaiden of a new master, a simulacrum of itself, part of a machine that not only leaves the stragglers afoot but increases their numbers and resentments by the second.

To reclaim the cultural autonomy of the South is thus not the beginning of a separate battle, but the articulation of a crucial need that is not the exclusive prerogative of the men and women of the South. It means to question our form of modernity, and to consider the difference between it and other paths that are not delivered to the primacy of competitive obsession and the dominion of economic illusion. It also means to articulate an idea of Europe independent of the reading that reduces it to a backward and evolutionarily inferior stage of the United States. Having arrived in Europe a little more than a century ago, the African American writer W. E. B. Du Bois wrote: "Europe modified profoundly my outlook on life and my thought and feeling toward it. . . . I had been before, above all, in a hurry. I wanted a world, hard, smooth, and swift, and had no time for rounded corners and ornament, for unhurried thought and slow contemplation."[38] If Europe wishes not to lose itself and seriously aspires to create an autonomous identity, it has much to learn from its South and the South in general.

Mediterranean

It is precisely on this point that reflections about the South meet the sea that lies between the lands, the Mediterranean. A sea that, though it is very ancient, has a hard time showing up on geographical maps, because it is pushed to the margins by the centrality of continents and appears only at their borders: the South of Europe, the North of Africa, and the West of Asia Minor. In the view of atlases it almost always occupies only the role of border and backdrop, a blue frontier that separates one land from the others, alluding to them and their distance. To reform this gaze means to place the Mediterranean centrally, to think of it as a connection that, without negating its ancient patterns, wants to differentiate itself from them in a basic way, becoming a connection that is capable of moving beyond the epoch of nation-states that many call "early" or "first modernity." Very few things are more powerful than gazes; very few things naturalize and neutralize hierarchies more than they do. To start demanding their reform is therefore not a dream, even though, in order to think about it, we must let the imagination fly forward as happens more often and more easily to writers, musicians, and film directors.

The long drift of the Mediterranean toward the margins was, at the time, but the cartographic repercussion of the ascent of a new kind of force and power: an imperious Northern and Atlantic modernity, cast toward the oceans, that tore the world away from the past and its old centrality (though it is difficult to imagine this power without empires and colonies, or the subjugation of other people and the Souths of the world). But this new gaze is not a restoration, a banal reconquest of the center: This gaze is not the victim of any nostalgia.

Here too one can see the difference between the past and the future. What is relevant today about the Mediterranean is precisely its status as border, interface, and mediation among people. Its centrality does not wish to return to the center ancient lands, and reassign ownership of that sea to someone. The Latin expression *mare nostrum*, hateful in its proprietary sense, today can only be pronounced if one accepts a slippage of its meaning. The proprietary subject of that adjective is not and cannot be an imperial people that expands and absorbs the Other within itself, but the Mediterranean "we." This expression will cease to be deceitful only when it will be pronounced with conviction and in many languages at once.

Mediterranean today means putting the border, that line of division and contact between people and civilizations, center stage. It does not reveal a nostalgia for an old youth, for a "grandeur" that always produces, as Simone Weil has taught us, tragic results. Instead, it is the fulfillment of maturity, the moment when we completely acquire the awareness of our finitude. We do not go to the Mediterranean to seek the fullness of our origins but to experience our contingency. The Mediterranean shows us the limits of Europe and of the West. It is on the Mediterranean that the North-West world encounters the South-East. And this is the reason that today it has, once more, become crucial. If the Mediterranean were a sea of the past, as many say it is, it is difficult to understand why the fleet of the United States, the symbol of the Atlantic empire, moves about restlessly in its waters.

But gaining awareness of this delicate and complex contact requires a precise way of looking at the past, wherein traces of blood, landings by invaders, conversions and slaughters, and imposing one's name on or destroying other people's cities are all rescued by a new *koiné*. The Mediterranean is an irreducible pluriverse that does not allow itself to be reduced to a single verse. Its value rests precisely in this irreducible multiplicity of voices, none able to smother the others. The land-based exteriority of the continents is there to remind us that their difference cannot be eliminated and that the coexistence we must build cannot be founded on a single law. No sunshine will hand us the keys to a process that we must build ourselves.

In this fraternal narration of the past, tendentious as they all are, but finally worthy of this sea's multiplicity, the abuses of power are transformed into communication, exchange, and coexistence. After all, the Other has not landed for the first time on our shores. On the contrary, if once upon a time it landed looking like a master, now it arrives hidden in the belly of ships, a clandestine escaping from old masters, but perhaps already in the vise of new ones. In a land where many others have arrived, there is no monolithic and pure "we" to defend from the snare of the Other. It is sufficient to scroll through the list of names in any city's phone book (and not just Southern ones), or to look back a few generations at our very own history, to discover contaminations, arrivals and departures, that restless genetic mobility that Edgar Morin and Predrag Matvejevic[39] have reminded us turns the many people of the Mediterranean—and luckily not only them—into incurable mongrels, into the antithesis of any purity, integrity, and fundamentalism: Our "we" is full of Others.

It is also through this irredeemable impurity that our civilization acquires the awareness of its contingency and must face the most important of choices, the choice between the fear and the demonizing of the other and a more mature and complex vision that turns the perception of one's finitude into the beginning of a new history. On the Mediterranean, the old continent redeems itself of its Eurocentrism and discovers that its own finitude is not an obstacle but a resource, a path to the future. It is not by chance that the margins have entered philosophy after the decolonization of Algeria thanks to Jacques Derrida,[40] a Jewish *pied-noir* born in that land. The Mediterranean's greatest significance resides precisely in its ability to transform our limitations into a common advantage, a tragic memory into the fight against all fundamentalisms.

There is more than one fundamentalism, even though it is easy to think that they all fit one mold, that of the turban and the suicide bombers. Indeed, what else is fundamentalism if not a growing and active ethnocentrism, the pretense to export one's values by annulling the difference of the Other? Fundamentalism is disturbed and tormented by someone else's difference, which it considers an evil to be cured, an inferior state to be redeemed and canceled. But if this definition of fundamentalism is plausible, today its most dominant form is the fundamentalism of the West. The other fundamentalism is a reactive one: It is the choice of militarization on the part of cultures that feel under attack. To think of beating it by strengthening one's own fundamentalism means to suggest pain as therapy and to initiate the perverse spiral of conflict among civilizations.

One must counter this perverse spiral—a self-fulfilling prophecy that creates its own premises by allowing to come true what initially was false— with a reverse spiral, one equally capable of creating its own premises. The Mediterranean is the possibility of this reverse movement: a deconstruction of fundamentalisms, and a demilitarized reading of one's own tradition capable of triggering in the others equally new readings (this is where the prophecy creates its own premises!). This is how cultures, rather than gravitating around an immutable essence and an imaginary and homicidal purity, can attempt to open themselves to the other, selecting from the present but also from the past every opportunity for friendship, collaboration, and contamination. It is a desire to recapture the tradition of the Mediterranean as a bridge between civilizations, transporting it from the metabolism of secular times to the historical ones of politics, triggering the more active and constructive energies on both shores.

The demilitarization of identities wishes to pluralize societies by nourishing their internal multiplicity and therefore making them freer. The lay culture we need is a much more inclusive structure than the one we customarily designate with that adjective. Traditions become monolithic only in times of conflict. In reality, they are complex and manifold structures, permeable and subject to different interpretations, which depend, first of all, on the relationship that every tradition has with the environment that surrounds it and, second, on its relationship with other traditions: In order for one of them to relinquish its fundamentalism, it needs not to feel threatened. Thus, a lay culture cannot be born out of a military imposition but grows side by side with the complexity of a tradition and the emergence, within it, of multiple voices and subjects, and with the difficult construction of their coexistence and training in pluralism.

All of this goes beyond a simple discussion of methods. The demilitarization of cultures means that the developed world must acknowledge that even where it has not yet arrived there exist patterns of perfection. The desert is not the not-yet of the water, an imperfection that will be eliminated by the rescuing arrival of technology. The desert is a key location for many regions and many cultures: To reduce it to a symbol of backwardness is a monstrous demand. For those who make this equation (and there are many), one might use the reproach that Wittgenstein made to the positivist anthropologist James G. Frazer: In his ability to understand spiritual matters he is much more savage than his savages.[41]

A crucial dimension of the Mediterranean derives from its hosting diverse civilizations: the ability to enliven and bring together many people, interweaving not only their languages and faiths but also their concepts of time and rhythms of life. Development and civilization are not only on one side, with backwardness, barbarity, and indigence on the other. The difference between the lands is not a time lag or a hierarchy of values, but a spatial gap that should not be overcome through a linear transition (i.e., "progress") from a "backward" to an "advanced" state. It is not a temporal transition, but a transfer, a translation. These realities exist at the same time and have equal dignity. Rather than playing into the homicidal hands of the hierarchy game, those who live among the civilizations of the Mediterranean rime would do better to favor their contact and exchange, and promote their richer and most promising forms. We must put a stop to the fundamentalism of the continents, and it is up to those who live on the border to do so, because they have been more exposed to the Other since time immemorial.

Obviously this entire process requires that we think of a new relationship between Europe and its South, both the internal one and the one across the sea; it requires an extended plurality of voices, the demise of the *vallum*,[42] and the construction of bridges, and that the Mediterranean people unite their voices onto a new stage, free from their subjection to others. If Europe succeeds in understanding that this match not only pertains to it but can also help its own constitution as subject, we will have achieved a significant result.

Perhaps the world is not inhabited by a single Mediterranean, because there are many places where, for centuries, civilizations have met and hung in the balance between conflict, coexistence, and contamination. But this is a vast and complex whole that stretches from Edouard Glissant's Antilles[43] to the India that has spawned the research of Homi K. Bhabha[44] and Gayatri Chakravorty Spivak.[45] This multiplicity of loci of intersection is further grounds for a possible broadened fraternity, and it would be useful to recognize these correspondences, bringing into focus differences but also affinities. Samuel Huntington sees in the Mediterranean only a fault line, a line of division between civilizations.[46] But the cleavages between civilizations that he proposes should not be taken too seriously because his maps of Europe and of the Mediterranean are dominated by an Atlantic gaze. Those who are not in awe of Huntington's premises have another vision, geography, culture, and politics.

Moderation

The suggestions in *Southern Thought*, however, do not exhaust themselves in the defense of pluralism and multiple perspectives against the imperial expansion of a single culture. After all, as I have already tried to show, even a simple coexistence between cultures is never the result of their petty juxtaposition. For them to coexist, it is necessary that traditions privilege those representations of themselves that thematize coexistence, relegating to the background the more aggressive ones, such as the fundamentalist calls for purity that present every contact with the other as a danger. In other words, one presupposes that traditions, though they start from different and irreducible premises, be endowed with a reflexive capacity, the first antidote against the awful temptation to label as "evil" what is only discordant with their premises. The construction of this ability constitutes the clue for a modest and plural universalism, which does not result from the imposition of one tradition onto all others, but is the "premise-promise" for a minimum common patrimony, a many-handed, delicate, and unstable construction.

The perspective that *Southern Thought* tries to define, which is centered in the concept of "measure," aims at something more than a minimal understanding between cultures. Indeed, it is necessary to take another step and try to translate one into the other: a worthy, but difficult and impervious effort since something, and at times a lot more than just something, is lost in translation. But every appeal to the sacredness of translation needs to be carried much further than a simple methodological exercise. This is not about going on a sightseeing tour inside the culture of the other but about taking it seriously and learning something from it. The flaw of every fundamentalism lies in the obsession to bulldoze everywhere new tarmac for the airplanes of power. An earnest idea of universality cannot mean only the expansion of one's self but also implies learning, receptivity, and knowledge. The concept of "moderation" is crucial precisely because it requires that we distance ourselves from the linear concept of time that prevails in the way the West sees itself.

The idea of "moderation" alludes in fact to a criterion of equilibrium that rescues thought from the mythology of progress. History can take many different paths without any guarantee of an upward outcome. On the contrary, if one forces a situation beyond its moderation, one runs the risk of catastrophic outcomes. This swinging back and forth clashes completely with the fundamentalism of the West and its hard-and-fast conviction that the problems and tensions that are born from its expansion must be dealt with only by increasing the treatment's dosage.

This behavior reveals a true passion for excess, while moderation presupposes that none of the extremes be considered absolutely positive or absolutely negative. Indeed, behind the fight against all fundamentalisms lies the idea that each subject of this polarity has something valuable to say, and that the wiser stance, when faced with an imbalance, is to go in the opposite direction.

In *Southern Thought*, I propose a broad but precise criterion of comparison, a notion of "moderation" as a point of equilibrium between two opposite fundamentalisms: the one of land and the one of sea. If land grounds identity, common belonging, and the social contract, the sea illustrates, by contrast, the idea of departure, the pointing of the bow on a freely chosen route, the adventure of individual freedom. In the chapter "Of Land and Sea," this reconstruction is brought to its extreme consequences, as I try to span, along the filigree of this opposition, the history of European thought. For this reason, though it is clearly influenced by Carl Schmitt's great short classic, *Land and Sea*, the solution I propose here is very different from his "earthly" nostalgia, from a faithfulness to the land that turns into a demonization of modernity's opening phase, into a closure to the other that always runs the risk of transforming the *hospes* into *hostis*.[47]

The importance of freedom and of one's emancipation from a total bond with the land emerges in Joseph Brodsky's harsh polemic against the Orient and the earthly nightmare that he describes in "Flight from Byzanthium": "Though in Athens Socrates could be judged in open court and could make whole speeches—three of them!—in his defense, in Isfahan, say, or Baghdad, such a Socrates would simply have been impaled on the spot, or flayed, and there the matter would have ended."[48] But right next to this danger there exists the opposite one: the anomic drift of an individualism without moderation, constantly bent on itself and on its own present, so that it stops at the bank of life only to withdraw and never to make a deposit. Brodsky himself discovered this in the last years of his life, leaving a record of it in a bitter "letter on post-communism."[49] Without making deposits, one cannot withdraw anything unless stealing from others. This is the Oceanic drift, the nomadism of an "I" imprisoned in its own instantaneous ethnocentrism, which is horrified by any ties, including promises made to others and to oneself just yesterday, a pathology that is exactly symmetrical with totalitarianism.

It is against this background that today we can probably examine the opposition between East and West, freeing it from the spiral of ethnocentric reprisals. The West narrates the history of individual freedom, the narrative of the "I" who traverses the world experiencing it. By contrast, the East narrates the importance of what comes before us, of social cohesiveness, of all that surrounds the adventure of the "I." The risks of a perverse polarization are clear: on the one side the anomie and the drift of limitless privatization, a Waste Land traversed by monads endowed with technological prostheses proportional to their income; on the other one, the equation between freedom and deviancy, detentions without legal representation, public executions, and perhaps the greatest humiliation: the request made of the condemned to acknowledge their guilt before dying. It is the opposition between individualism and holism, unchecked liberalism and "Asian values," between an "I" that does not recognize anything outside itself and a "we" that is omnipotent, implacable, and repressive. On the one side the stranger lying on the ground, face first, who is searched to determine whether he has the right to be helped and cured; on the other side, a "caring for others" that does not recognize the pronoun "I," and labels even the smallest emergence of freedom an expression of dissidence or defeatism.

If one accepts the plausibility of my depiction, if the metaphors of land and sea describe recognizable phenomena, one can perceive the first indication of what I mean by "moderation." Different traditions must not only reject their reciprocal demonizing but must learn something valuable from each other. Indeed, each reminds the other of the secret costs of what it holds dearest, the unofficial accounts it hides. This is why the relationship with the Other is so difficult. In the image the Other has of us, lies often something we have repressed: our hidden and uneasy sides, the accounting books that we do not wish to show.

Every tradition remains and cannot but remain itself, but if it is pushed into a journey, it can come home having learned much and thus re-read its own history in a new way, valorizing something that it once knew but has since forgotten. Differences remain but can now host other points of view and all have taken a step not toward a unilateral universalism but rather a complex one traversed by a multiplicity of pathways. To describe this phenomenon, Raimundo Panikkar uses the image of a mountain climbed from different paths:[50] None is the "true" one, since every mountain has many. Yet, when we meet at the top and discuss our paths there with others, we do not return to base camp the same as we were when we started the ascent. We will each have a different image of the mountain, including how to reach the top, and perhaps our paths are destined to cross later.

This reciprocity is not just a methodological abstraction; it can help the East make room for freedom, and the West to thematize the dimensions that transcend the *hic et nunc*[51] of the individual. Besides, as we have already mentioned, this learning process almost never coincides with the grafting of unknown elements from the outside, with the import of exotic marvels. Instead, it often leads to valorizing paths that have been previously marginalized or rejected, ways of thinking that have been forgotten, but still exist or once existed. Just as Amartya Sen tries to reconstruct traces of an Indian lay culture,[52] so in our own symbolic hemisphere there are previously marginalized or rejected perspectives that transcend the solipsistic anxiety of individuals turned upon themselves. Is it by accident that one of the founders of thinking about difference, Luce Irigaray, for years has been reflecting on the contamination between East and West?[53] Or that ecology proposes to superimpose the circular concept of the equilibrium of the ecosphere onto the linear one of discovery and conquest? And, faced with the arrogance of a fundamentalism of freedom that increases all distances, do we not sense a revival of an old, out-of-favor word, equality? Is not precisely in this revival that the more interesting interpretative key for the West rests? Rather than obliterating community, should the West not support its democratic creation, one where freedom does not help to exalt but to reduce distances between human beings in order to give new life and meaning to what they have in common?[54]

Only then do we discover that not only one West or East exists, but that each is plural, holding within itself many possibilities; and that instead of the old polarity-opposition there are paths capable of crossing each other. The expression "Asian values"[55] can be pluralized and diluted because the East is not only the Confucian tradition but many others, from Buddhism to Hinduism and Taoism. Likewise, the West is not only the extreme West, but the United States and Europe, and America is a continent that needs to be described in the plural. This is where one meets the path of Post-colonial Studies and the dissemination of subjects that it produces by breaking old and new monoliths. Perhaps it is also possible to see in the emergence of these new developments the push for a tradition that would be constitutively plural, the tradition that leads Salman Rushdie to say that India is founded on a nonsectarian philosophy and that Hindu culture is unthinkable without Mumbai, "a metropolis in which the multiplicity of commingled faiths and cultures curiously creates a remarkably secular ambience."[56]

This discussion, however, cannot be limited to the East-West axis, but must account for the North-South one that in the debate over Asian values seems to have disappeared, even if Singapore sits on the Equator. But luckily the South that is worth listening to is very diversified. One cannot but think of the Latin American South, the South of the Western world, a South we all know through some great figures in politics, music, sports, and literature. This South has also other voices that can help us look at the world from a different perspective. Suffice it to think of Enrique Dussel and Aníbal Quijano,[57] who help us read the obscure side of modernity, the basic role that colonial domination has had in the construction of European centrality and identity. The result is the emergence of another history, a narration very different from the predominant ones, little known in our hemisphere but essential to balance our vision of the world, to rattle old commonplaces. There is also the South of hybridity and *métissage*, the whole of the Mediterraneans of the world, which has a decisive role in shaping a path that moves away from every cultural and national fundamentalism: a South that stretches from America to India.

Finally, there is the African South, a South that, despite its recent great voices, from Nelson Mandela to Wole Soyinka, from Chinua Achebe to Ngugi wa Thiong'o or Aminata Traoré, cannot avoid sinking into suffering and the inability to make itself heard. Yet, the feebleness of the voice of the South is one of the planet's greatest problems. Even before helping the South, the North should try to create some silence and begin listening to the voice of the South, because, among other reasons, it returns to us a surprising image of ourselves. It becomes then impossible not to see that the hidden side of the debate between East and West over "Asian values" is the quest for power. Those who support "Asian values" seem unconcerned with the excesses of technology but only wish to acquire it to rebalance, if not to turn into one's favor, the axis of the world. It is not by chance that reclaiming those values originated in countries that were undergoing a long phase of economic development. The opposition West-East and thus the discussion over *Asian values*[58] (human rights versus social cohesiveness) is a contest over who must rule the world.

The path of the South changes this game, bringing into play forgotten elements. It is a path that does not lead to the quest for power, but the need to distribute equally among all the inhabitants of the world the benefits of technology, which instead are today, above all, an instrument of division. The South proposes the problem of justice, not the quest for power; a concept of life that does not seek to dominate nature and other cultures, but to live in harmony with both. The suffering, marginalization, and silence of the South are the suffering and marginalization of justice. Currently, the most dramatic and "unfashionable" issue is that of a more equitable and supportive world, of a planet that, instead of chasing the wealthiest countries' income and GDP, should succeed in pausing to distribute differently its riches, freeing itself from the Faustian obsession that pushes to search for water on other planets rather than seeking, protecting, and sharing it more equitably on earth.

In trying to define, through the example of theater, the difference between Western and African cultures, Wole Soyinka compares Western creativity to a locomotive that at every station picks up the most different suggestions, intoxicated every time by a new discovery. This rhythm coincides with a "series of intellectual spasms that, especially today, appears susceptible to commercial manipulation." The West has thus completely abandoned something that for African theater remains, by contrast, essential: a "culture defined as man's knowledge of fundamental, unchanging relationships between himself and society and within the larger context of the observable universe," "one culture whose very artifacts are evidence of a cohesive understanding of irreducible truths."[59]

The idea of a deep cohesion between man and the world, common to many African writers, does not foresee the emergence of the subject onto a world disenchanted and reduced to simple object of domination, but rather keeps man away from the hubris of power. Here, as well, another concept of historical time matters: We are not facing the prehistory of the West but the possibility that it might regain at least some of its lost wisdom. This distancing by the South from the epics of the chase could reactivate, both in the West and the East, those forces that do not divinize power but know how to live the relationship with the other openly and hospitably. There exists a gentle European tradition, the one represented by Montaigne but also by the forgotten side of Enlightenment: the one that emerges from the gaze of Micromégas, the letters of Usbek,[60] or Giacomo Leopardi's gaze that looks over the infinite disproportion between us and the universe.[61] They all remind us of our common frailty and insignificance; foreground the limitations of our point of view; and practice a grammar that is different from the one of expansion and power. Those who, searching the sky, see only the probe on Mars are like that idiot who, facing the person who points at the sky, can see only her hand.

Let me conclude with the words of Ryszard Kapuściński, a man who traveled the whole planet, witnessing its horrors and injustices. The *Shadow of the Sun*, his book devoted to Africa, begins thus: "More than anything, one is struck by the light. Light everywhere. Brightness everywhere. Everywhere, the sun"; it ends with a chapter that describes the day of a small Ethiopian village, in whose center rests the generous and cool shadow of a large mango tree. The entire community gathers around this tree, finding protection, making decisions, narrating, schooling itself, and waiting for the arrival of the evening. Africa had this delicate balance, this "perfection" built by using nature's hiding places. It has been devastated by the power of the Europeans who conquered and raped it, and completely redrew its borders, reducing Africa to "a thousand situations, varied, distinct, even contradictory" (323).[62] In the South, the fundamentalism of Western civilization shows itself in its entirety. It is a civilization of expansion and conquest that sees in the sky only its own power so as to avoid seeing the frailty of mankind and the injustices that traverse our home on earth.

Southern thought is on the other side of the world. If the South must gain back its ability to speak, it must focus on justice and create the awareness that no certainty can base itself on such ruthless inequalities. May I be forgiven the repetitiveness, but redundancy is necessary in one's closing remarks. We must react to a great disequilibrium with a great push in the opposite direction. Today, those who want balance must come forth and compensate the imbalance by going to the other side and trying, as Ngugi wa Thiong'o proposes, to "move the centre of the world."[63] Moderation, therefore, is not caution or a banal "middle ground," but a complex and courageous construction that seeks to save the multiplicity of life forms, giving back to each, with a single act, its value and completeness.

Southern Thought and Other Essays on the Mediterranean

Introduction:
For a Thought from the South

To rethink the South some preliminary observations are in order. The most important is that we must stop thinking of its pathologies simply as the consequences of a lack of modernity. We must reverse our point of view and believe that in the South of Italy, with all probability, modernity is not extraneous to the pathologies that, even today, some think it should cure. In other words, to begin thinking of the South we must even consider the hypothesis that, normally, we would discard a priori: Is the modernization of the South an imperfect or insufficient modernization, or is it not instead its only possible modernization, its one real modernization?

Releasing modernity from its responsibilities and considering it always and only as a solution leads to two complementary mistakes that build on each other. On the one hand, one relies on a therapy that often aggravates the pathologies; on the other, one suppresses from the start the possibility of reversing the relationship: not to think of the South in the light of modernity, but rather to think of modernity in the light of the South. Thinking the South thus means that the South is the subject of thought: It does not have to be studied, analyzed, and judged by an external thought, but it must gain back the strength to think of itself on its own terms, to recapture decisively its own autonomy.

Southern thought basically means this: Give back to the South its ancient dignity as the subject of thought; interrupt the long sequence whereby it has been thought by others. This does not mean showing leniency toward localism, the muddy playing with one's own vices that has correctly led some to call the South an "Inferno." On the contrary, Southern thought must conceive the South with rigor and toughness; it has the duty to see and fight, *iuxta propria principia*,[1] the devastating auctioning that Southerners themselves have made of their own lands. In this auctioning off, in this vulgar and chameleonic entrance into modernity, two dominant facets of the South have emerged: the South as tourists' paradise and as mafia nightmare. These two facets, antithetical on the surface, are instead complementary because they represent the legal and illegal aspect of the South's subaltern participation in development, at its borders, where the seductive models that fan out from the capitals of the North-West fall apart and become deformed. Having exhausted twenty years ago the enlightened belief that one could uniformly spread industrial civilization to the South, we have witnessed in the years that followed the marginal complementarity of the South to development. One has modernized by putting everything on the market and rendering the obscene systematic, prostituting land and environment, public places and institutions. Social mobility has expressed itself in perverted ways through the growth of underworld and criminal activities that have created emerging elites where wealth could not be achieved by legal means. This destiny is shared by all the Souths of the world, which pay for joining (when one can talk of "joining") in the fragile and dirty areas of wealth through a real prostitution of significant quotas of their population. The root of this complementarity lies here. On the one hand the South is outside of development, the ideal vacuum of vacation: the Mediterranean of the Club Méditerranée, exotic paradises on special discount for the crowds of mass tourism, the South as backdrop for the outdoorsy month enjoyed by the wealthy mobs of industrial civilization. On the other hand is the chameleonic selling out of its ruling classes, their systematic corruption, an extortionist wiliness that is more refined and chameleonic among its higher strata, more violent and blatant among the lower classes. Something about the ancient rage has remained in the latter, but the ancient egalitarian push has drowned in the generalized anomie, in the loss of reference to another way of life.

A thought from the South, a South that thinks the South, wants to achieve the maximum autonomy from this gigantic mutation, to set evaluation standards different from those that hold forth today, to think of a different ruling class and a different grammar of poverty and wealth, to conceive the dignity of a different way of life. A thought from the South must no longer think of the South or the Souths as lost and anonymous peripheries of the empire, places where nothing has happened yet and where one repeats, belatedly and shoddily, opening nights that have been celebrated elsewhere. The desert was not set aside with the motorized idiocy of the Paris-Dakar in mind. It was the foundational site for a part of our spirituality, for divine passages, treks and fasting, temptations and fears. It was much richer when caravans crossed it than it is today, as the racetrack for consumerist imitators of the foreign legion. Only a dull mind can conceive the desert as a "not-yet" of development, something to fill up, to develop for tourists, to "normalize." These roots, these places that resist technology, are even more important for Southern thought. Indeed, from the reverse point of view, Southern pathologies are not the result of a deficit of modernity; instead, they are the symptoms of an infection that grows from the center of the system, the warnings of the new and one-dimensional ferocity of "turbocapitalism."

For Southern thought to exist, one South need not be isolated from the other Souths as if it were an embarrassment. Epistemologically the South, with its sluggishness, with time and space that resist the laws of universal acceleration, can become a resource; therefore, the connection between the Souths rescues thought from those places where nowadays it likes to relax and sit in comfort, from the gravitational forces of modern conformity. But Southern thought is not just an apology for the South as a sunny, oriental, and ancient land; it is not the rediscovery of a tradition that must be restored to its integrity. Southern thought is the thought one feels welling inside where the sea begins, where the shore interrupts all land-based fundamentalisms (especially those related to commerce and development), at a time when one discovers that the borderland is not a place where the world ends, but where those who are different come into contact, and the relationship game with the other becomes difficult and real. Indeed, Southern thought was truly born in the Mediterranean, on the coasts of Greece, with the opening of Greek culture toward conflicting discourses, toward the *dissòi lógoi*.[2] In the beginning, there is never just the one, but two or more. We can never reunite the two in one: No universalism will ever succeed at it. We must just ensure that the two do not go their separate ways to the point of wanting each other's destruction; we must ensure that they keep talking to each other even when the translation becomes difficult. This is not the pursuit of an equivocal equidistance; nowadays, arrogance is on the side of those who think that the world's destiny resides in development. The others, when they do not sell out, fight back, often with the ferocity that is born of fear. The side that must take the first step back and stop choking the other, that must accept other ways of living is, primarily, the side that has embraced the monotheism of technology by giving up a multiplicity of ways and the infinite names of God. Southern thought finds its roots here, in the resistance embodied by multiple voices, ways, and dignities; in the capacity to transform into resources those things that, in the primitive view of development, seem to be only ties, limits, and vices. It must protect its familiarity with those forms of life that are motionless, slow, and stratified, and that allow us to create richer relationships than through a telematic connection to the whole; where instead of the grandiose protection of technology there exists the equally grandiose protection of religion. Against the monochrome of speed, the thousand colors that one can only perceive when life slows down. Against the incontinence of "real time," the value of physical and cultural distance from others, the misunderstanding of their pride, the difficulty to comprehend them, the risk of drawing close.

Southern thought gathers and protects all those lifestyles wherein something exists that allows us to defend ourselves from the infinite secularization that severs all ties. It tries to find even in the sacred—as happens in Pasolini—the capacity to resist commercialization as the unstoppable law of our future.[3] Yet, precisely because it was born on the sea, Southern thought is not extraneous to modernity and knows that they share some of the same roots. But because, contrary to modernity, it has not lost the gift of moderation, Southern thought tries to prevent modernity from becoming one-dimensional, and to defend it from the numerous historical choices that seem to reduce it to an example of the perpetual and unstoppable motion of Monsieur le Capital. Modernity is free to look disparagingly at Southern thought, pigeonholing it reassuringly in categories that describe it as privileged exoticism, embryo of extremism, and apology of marginality. At least this is what it has done in most cases, since modernity haughtily believes that it possesses multiple dimensions and that it can always carry within itself all of its projects and dreams. But now that it has freed itself from any counterweight, shackled evermore by the rhythm of hoarding and swallowed up by its growing acceleration, it has begun ditching those dreams one by one as if they were deadweight. To gather ways of living that are "other" does not mean only preserving types of existence that are different from the dominant one on a planetary scale, but it also means safeguarding modernity from spinning itself in a spiral without exit and from getting lost in the high seas. Southern thought generously gives modernity the "chance" to show that it has restraints on board and that it can find within itself selective chains that are not the "winning" ones but are capable of blocking the fetishism of development. Southern thought is well aware of the choked suffering caused by the incense of tradition and has not ceased to embrace equality (an idea whose origins it knows something about). Yet, it demands that those who profess to love equality know that it is delicate and difficult; understand the world's dual nature and the relationship between emancipation and uprooting; and choose the proper way to equality, not the one already mapped out by structural tendencies.

Conversely, Southern thought is not stupidly exclusionary (how many Northerners have dealt with this!), nor does it rest on a comfortable, land-based income. The meeting between land and sea is not an idyll that recomposes itself: It is not stillness, but the difficulty of staying in one place; it is not a return to uncomplicated identities, but the discovery that, beyond development, many resources that had been discarded turn out to be useful. Nowadays, Southern thought exists in scattered and sometime sickly forms, and we must learn how to look for it: One can find it in our internalized Souths, in an act of folly, a silence, a pause, a prayer of thanks, in the clumsiness of old people and children, in a brotherhood that knows how to avoid connivance and *omertà*[4] in an economy that has not reneged on social bonds. One can find it in feelings generated by multiple home-lands, where one substitutes for the simplicity of yes or no the many veils of truth, where beauty is once more a reward for one who has spent much time searching rather than the right of anyone who is willing to pay for it; where the difficulty of bridging distances and the weave of interdictions are not just absurd repressions but also obstacles to the fanaticism of own-ership and consumerism, and the starting point for stories and fantasies that guide our way.

On the other side of the fence, then, do not live only the past and nostalgia, but the future as well: Southern thought has the duty to show this continuity between past and future without disparagement or resent-ment of the present. The autonomy from modernity is not given by insults or anathemas, but by a perception of the desperation that wafts in its depths, by the substitution of meaning one notices in its inability to escape acceleration. It is this awareness that allows us to see richness in ways of life we thought were obsolete: There cannot exist a thought that does not feed on a way of life, or at least on the dream of one.

The essays in this volume (which collect the work of the past few years[5] but have their origins much further back in time) only wish to blaze a trail, to point out a working direction. Their common thread is the attempt to lay the foundations for Southern thought, whether one does it directly (as happens in "Of Land and Sea" and in "Thinking the Frontier"), or by leaning on the work of those (Pasolini and Camus) who tried otherwise to think autonomously and against the grain of modernity's own mytholo-gies. Many signs seem to indicate that this effort to found/rediscover a Southern thought is not just wishful thinking. We have experienced simi-lar motivations to the ones elaborated in this book in many conversations, in the hopes of the young and in the desire to start anew of those who are not. This common feeling emboldens us to render explicit this proposal, to seek places and people with whom to confront ourselves and through whom to verify its reliability. The bet on which everything hinges is that the South can think of itself, can look at itself with the strength of a knowledge that, in some ways, it already possesses. The key lies in reconsidering the places, in the double meaning of having consideration for and thinking anew about them. The bewilderment is great, but maybe the escape route is, as in the purloined letter, right in front of our eyes, in something we have always known but have never dared say.

PART I

Mediterranean

CHAPTER I

Going Slow

Thinking on Foot

We must go slow like an old country train carrying peasant women dressed in black, like those who go on foot and see the world magically opening ahead, because going on foot is like leafing through a book, while running is like looking at its cover. We must go slow and love the pauses that enable us to see the road we have covered, feel the weariness conquer our limbs like melancholy, and envy the sweet anarchy of those who invent their journey at a moment's notice.

We must learn to be on our own and wait in silence, happy, every so often, just to rest with our hands in our pockets. Going slow is bumping into dogs without running them over; it is naming trees, corners, and streetlights. It is finding a bench and entertaining our thoughts within, allowing them to surface according to the street we are on like bubbles that float upward and, when they are strong enough, allowing them to burst and mingle with the sky. It is to elicit involuntary rather than planned thought, the result not of goals or our will, but a necessary thought, the kind that emerges on its own, from an agreement between mind and world.

Going slow is stopping on the promenade, on a shore, on polluted cliffs, on a hill burnt by the summer, going along with a boat's wind and zigzagging to move forward. Going slow is to know the thousand differences in our lifestyle, the names of friends, the colors and the rains, the games and the wakes, the shared trusts and the slanders. Going slow are the stations in between, the stationmasters, the old luggage and the toilets, the gravel and small gardens, people waiting at grade crossings, an old cart and its young horse, a scarcity that is not ashamed, a public fountain, eyes hiding in the shade of shutters. Going slow is to respect time, inhabit it with few things of great value, with boredom and nostalgia, with boundless desires sealed in one's heart and ready to explode or pointed toward the sky because pressed by a thousand prohibitions. Going slow is to ruminate, imitating the infinite look of oxen, the patient wait of dogs. It is knowing how to fill one's day with sunset, bread, and oil. Going slow means having an armoire for every dream, with big stories for little travelers and the applause of theaters for mediocre actors. It means a bus worn out by an upward climb; desire expressed through looks; few words, and those capable of living in the desert; the disappearance of the multicolored crowds of goods; and the renewed greatness of what is necessary. Going slow is being provincial without despair, sheltered from conceited history, inside pettiness and dreams, far away from the main scene and closer to every secret.

Going slow is everyone's ability to be a philosopher, living at a different speed, closer to beginnings and ends, where we experience life at its fullest, either as it begins or as we take leave from it. Going slow means stepping down without hurting ourselves, not drowning in the emotions of the industrial world, but being faithful to our senses, tasting with our body the earth we cross. Going slow means thanking the world, allowing it to fill us up. There is more life in walking ten kilometers on foot than in a transoceanic route that drowns you in the loneliness of its planning, a gluttony that cannot be digested. We are much more open to others when we look at a dog, a school's release, an appearance on a balcony, or when we watch people playing cards in the darkness, than by flying, faxing, or internet surfing. This slow thought is the only thought; the other is the thought that allows us to run a machine; the thought that increases its speed and flatters itself into believing it can do it in perpetuity. Slow thought will offer shelter to the refugees from fast thought, when the machine will start trembling evermore and no knowledge will succeed in muffling its tremor. Slow thought is the most ancient earthquake-proof construction.

From now on we must walk, think on foot, look slowly at the houses, find out when their crowding becomes vulgar, and hope that beyond them we might once more see the sea. We must think the moderation that is unthinkable without going on foot, without stopping to observe the droppings of other men who flee in fast cars. No wisdom can come from the removal of waste. It is from this waste, from its accumulation, from the world's industrial shit that we must start anew if we want to think the future. The speedy, the planners, the conventioneers, the journalists hungrily devour the world and think they are improving it. Slowness knows how to love speed, can appreciate its transgressive power, desires even as it fears the desecration contained in speed (what complexity is raised by this contradiction!); but the desecration effected by the masses has none of the sacredness that still nests itself in sacrilege, it is impiety without value, a universal right to outrage. No experience is more stolid than mass speed, than an unacknowledged desecration.

The Infinity of the Sea

Today we can live in a city by the sea without being able to see it, just as someone crossing, selling, and buying the sea can also manage not to see it. So please, when we finally talk about the sea, let's not ask the political economy for the permission to speak (as is fashionable nowadays): What we must talk about is something that comes before business. We must talk about the emotional bond with the sea, the sea we learned about without science, but only by living near it, like an older relative, like the house where we were born, a neighbor, a silence, a solitude, or a morning. The sea we rediscover when we feel we are suffocating, because we surprise ourselves in a land surrounded by lands. The sea is, first of all, meditation, an impersonal voice that transforms, maybe because of a strange Italian assonance between *mare* and *-are*,[1] every verb into an infinitive, a sky redoubled and turned earthy, a wrecked wall, a freed border, a horizon that reminds us of something precisely because it escapes us. From this line of escape emerges the anxiety one experiences when arriving alone in a land by the sea. Every pier offers the temptation to sail, to leave, to chase—without being able to grab it—the utopian line of the horizon: This is where a richer and more dramatic relationship with the land is born. We are no longer hostages of a landscape, of a bell tower that helps us find our bearings, but chokes and holds us like a ball and chain. The sea enables a breakthrough that opens the mind to the idea of leaving, to the experience of a betrayal that makes faithfulness more uncertain but also more valuable and complex; that invents nostalgia, the inward pain and longing for one's homeland that is the companion of every traveler. It makes every human being a foreigner and every foreigner a human being, turns separation into companionship, allows more than one soul to inhabit us.

On the open beaches, the sea gives itself freely to all, like an easy and unfaithful girl, even when a voracious stupidity tries to imprison, marry, lock it away, and give it the paranoid fixity of ownership. The villas on the coast, small and large rapes of cement that would like to bind the sea, illegal above and beyond every law, display the obscene garishness of ownership. Rather than being a commodity, rather than being for us, the sea is for itself, it is a different form of life, which, just a few steps away, flits around a bread crumb fallen in the water. Down below toss about conflicts, hierarchies, the differences between nomadic lives and the still gaze of plants, the subordination of shoals and the free loneliness of hunters: There among the differences in light and temperatures living equally perfect lives are the creatures of the abyss and those of the surface.

From the sea arrive ungrateful guests, the drama, flight, deceptions, and dreams of stowaways. It is a better hiding place and ridicules the coastguard men, swallowing without pity or guilt the desperados. Its cruelty is like that of death, true and inevitable. One can die from the punishment of the storm and in a beautiful day of sun. There is a silent lesson to be learned in the great and fearsome negligence of the sea, in the dark or sun-filled way it swallows us, in its knowing how to welcome and shelter the agonies that descend to its silent floor: school of thresholds that comes before any philosophy.

But we know little of its joys if, in the deep blue of its high seas, we have not encountered schools of dolphins, the friendship of these borderland souls, both wiser cousins and successful divine experiment. We know little of ourselves if we have not felt our skin's eagerness to enter the sea, its slow reconciliation with water, its consent to be owned by it and, letting go, float on it. Our body discovers a world when it accepts to entrust itself without fear to the flow of the surf, when gazing at the sky, lying flat on the sea, we listen to the sound of its resonant womb, accepting to belong to it with filial trust. In this exercise, in the intimacy with the grammar of water there is an ancient wisdom, the hint of possibilities of a different era. Without the infinity of the sea we drop to the bottom, sucked in by the vortex of our anthropomorphism, no longer the heteronomy that comes from the whims of the wind, the mood of waves, and the volatility of clouds, but only the narrow, always narrower instances of our desire. We drown the sea to silence its voice, to drown all its infinitives in the obsessive and egotistical crowd of personal pronouns, the broken and varied tenses of human beings. When progress will have proudly surpassed the "age of the sea," verbs in the infinitive will no longer exist, but only those tenses that are compatible with our communal litigiousness.

Southern Secularization

Are we truly richer? Or rather, are we really as rich as the money indexes suggest? Possibly, but side by side with the age-old poverty that never abandons us, there is a less raw and brazen poverty, a poison hidden in the foods, an unbalanced diet that disfigures and makes us all poorer. Let's look at how our parties end: how much paper, how much trash we heap. Let's observe the external signs of what our freedom has become. It is made of continuous acts of appropriation and of exclusion of others from our private possessions: our childhoods were filled with public places, with beaches and fields where we were happy without locking ourselves in small enclosures, where the paradoxical search for *mass distinction*, for an obsessive *privacy*, had not yet destroyed coasts and hills. The ability to exclude others was the privilege of the truly rich, and our freedom has become a paradoxical and inflated pursuit of that model. The harsh truth that a stock character like Fantozzi[2] reminds us of is the squalor that is born out of this pursuit, the misery and humiliation contained in the dream of imitating the wealthy. This emulation has caused the death of our gatherings and of collective solidarity, the transformation of the "public" into a residual entity, in something where one dumps, with ever diminishing scruples, the wastes of our private appropriations. And, as the poverty and veritable squalor of public spaces have become increasingly unbearable, so have we more and more hidden behind the locked doors of private spaces.

Freedom and happiness have come to be equated more and more with the exclusive care of our private well-being, with the warmth of our domestic spaces: Even as public, open spaces deteriorate, we can always decorate our balconies, and perfume and purify the air inside our homes and cars while making it unbreathable outside; we can listen to sermons against consumerism between TV commercials, and go far into the night for serious programming, bewildered refugees in a world where thought is seen as the intermediate state between depression and repression. We can ensure that politics becomes an ever more thrilling show and ever more distant from calling into question anything about our life. So we have called the great clearance sale of all that transcends our own private good modernization, secularization, or laicization. Here is the aporia of wealth: our increasingly more comfortable, fast, and noiseless cars all go at a snail's pace over the same filthy spots on roads filled with potholes. We will certainly not catch up with the rich who always manage to exclude others, but we will have learned to think like them, losing even the pride of not being like them.

Together with public spaces, even the gifts of beauty and courage are shrinking. Behind a church squeezed between train tracks and the sea in the periphery south of Bari (but maybe every Southern city has a place like this), there is a road named for the martyrs of July 28, 1943, youths killed because they celebrated the fall of Fascism. It is a bleak place, covered with condoms and syringes, a stone's throw from the sea; a sea that could even be pretty but, as if it had been insulted, refuses to be so. That's where we banish this uncomfortable courage, far away from the eyes and the heart, to avoid its hanging over us. The heroes of other cities are easier to deal with because they are remote. Those of our city are much more disturbing: They suggest that even here heroism might be possible. Downtown, meanwhile, we flock to the streets named for ministers, the city's notables, those who have adorned with fame their wealth and power, almost as if to humiliate even after their death those who have dared go against the gravitational pull of the world. It is for this reason that, even within our comfort, we experience a lack. We lack courage, that opening virtue that makes possible the new: the new that is real, not the plastic one; the poor and original one, not the one that knows only how to grab, buy, and conquer. And it is courage that allows us not to be wronged and to rebel; that makes us tell truth to the power of greased-hair bosses, blue cars, sweaty hands, cornerstones, parades, commemorations, gofers, cell phones, and obscene rituals in which one blesses the shamelessness of power.

In that same city where we celebrate this marginalization, in this same city of ours we are all poorer in beauty, because we have become accustomed to the ugly, to the rape of our coasts and of our theaters. The fiction we celebrate is no longer inside them, but outside. Those theaters feign to exist and we participate in the fiction; we pretend that they exist. We do nothing, we are too smart, too wise, too ancient to be outraged, to chain ourselves down, to yell, to protest. To protest is expensive. As a result, we increase the amount of fiction: Aren't we all pretending not to see? But can we continue not to see, to increase the amount of fiction? And doesn't the spiral of this fiction remind us of the ruble, which was only worth something in the Soviet Union, but was practically impossible to exchange for other currency? Is it not indecent to talk about our wonders and history while we continue to coat every product in plastic, increase the number of waste dumps, poison the sea, build houses, and avoid silence—those moments when everything holds its breath and we can finally start listening? This fear of silence, this *horror vacui*, the loss of the ancient mastery to handle intervals, the moment when nothingness becomes life and we lose ourselves, this flight from respite, and the fear of losing ourselves are what make us lose our way, make us swap meaning for a trade, the grace of beauty for the obsession to lock it up in the padlocks of ownership. Beauty has withdrawn (we "have exiled beauty," as Camus would say),[3] and it will continue to withdraw if we keep chasing it, believing in its infinite reproducibility; it will only resurface as the result of a pilgrimage, when one will risk much to know it, when it will be the discovery that comes at the end of a transformation. The voracity of the masses destroys it precisely because they think it is a right one can obtain simply by paying for it.

We lack shared public properties because they can result only from widespread doses of courage, of respect for beauty and for the places from which we cannot exclude others. We will all be richer when we stop growing our own private bounty and instead restore roads, beaches, and gardens for everyone, when we are cured of the obsessive search for separation and distinction. Then beauty will return to visit us. It is impossible to take power away from salesmen if we cannot figure out the difference between the experience of the world and its purchase on super discount.

CHAPTER 2

Of Land and Sea

No wave combs the sea
And settles in the steady path.
Here is the thought that comes
Like a bird in its freshness,
On the sail of each slight wing
White with the rising water.
Come, you are to lose your freshness.
Will you drift into the net willingly,
Or shall I drag you down
Into my exotic composure.

DYLAN THOMAS, "No Thought Can Trouble My Unwholesome Pose"

Greece: With the Sea in Mind

What do the sea and epistemology have in common? Is the relationship between land and sea purely accidental, or is it rather a determining and underrated factor for the birth of Greek culture? And, if this relationship exists, what is the meaning of the sea for Greece, for Greek philosophy and thus for philosophy in general? What are its effects on us today?

My hypothesis is that there exists a structural homology between the geographic configuration of Greece (and in particular the relationship between land and sea) and its culture. This is certainly not my discovery, nor an original statement. I will only try to develop some ideas following in the footsteps of those who, more authoritatively, have made this claim.

In describing the geographic environment of Hellenic civilization, Arnold J. Toynbee states: "The central and main thoroughfare of the Hellenic World was always a waterway. . . . The cradle of Hellenism was the basin of the Aegean Sea," which "provides excellent maritime communications. While it is laborious to travel across the country from one little plain to another over the steep and rugged mountains that separate them, many of the plains have a window on the wide world in consequence of their dipping below the sea's surface." Therefore, it is a setting that "grants an easy apprenticeship in navigation,"[1] a skill whose absence establishes, as Jacob Burckhardt reminds us, the fundamental difference between the despotic culture of the Asian state and the democratic one of Greece.[2]

As Gilles Deleuze and Félix Guattari note, "Greece seems to have a fractal structure insofar as each point of the peninsula is close to the sea and its sides have great length."[3] The sea divides, but at the same time offers an easier avenue of communication than the mountains. Helmut Berve in the introduction to his history of Greece, tellingly titled *Land and Sea of the Greeks*, remarks: "South of Thessaly, no place is further than 60 kilometers from the sea."[4] And Hegel, talking about the "character of the Greek spirit," notices that it "grew out of the soil of Greece, a coastal territory which encourages individual autonomy."[5]

Clearly the Mediterranean is the Greek sea, but the Aegean even more so, as a sea that, with remarkable intensity, reveals within itself those characteristics that, on a grander scale, apply to the Mediterranean. After all, isn't Aigaios close in etymology not only to Aigeus (the legendary king), but to *eggeios-eggaios* ("from and within the land"), just as *mesogaios* ("between lands") is the Greek name for the Mediterranean? An archipelago between three continents, with islands placed like stones on which to hop from one continent to the other: Europe Minor that continues into Asia Minor.

Thus, from the beginning Greece exists on the borderland and internalizes it, a place of meetings and clashes, where war, commerce, voyage, and exploration alternate and overlap to the point of becoming indistinguishable. A land incapable of closing itself off, a society open and of borders, a "fluid city,"[6] doomed to experience and contain within itself relationship and conflict; a great land precisely because it is a minor, coastal land, far away from the solipsism of continents.

This is not an apology for the sea. Indeed, if it is true that, in its libertarian urges, the sea weakens every tie by escaping ownership, it is also true that when it overflows its borders the sea transforms this weakening of ties in a planetary uprooting: Against the earth's fundamentalism stands the fundamentalism of the sea, which pushes toward nihilism and the uncontrollable unleashing of technology.[7] When the sea is transformed into an ocean—that same sea that Hegel still sees as a challenge that enriches and begets the Soul and detaches man from the fixity of nature, flinging him into History—it becomes a place without shores, an absence of land that spills into an integral dependency on technology. Indeed, only technology can offer (artificial) forms of stability and protection in a world that, founding itself on the perennial mobility of the sea, is fully deterritorialized and has renounced every home and root. Oceanic freedom is possible only by becoming completely dependent on technology, on the unlimited development of the technological form of the world.

The Aegean Sea and the Mediterranean, instead, limit themselves to separating lands; they set a distance that is never the excess of the ocean; they are a strong discontinuity between lands, but not their relinquishment without bearings. This distance that, especially for the ancient sailor, could be great and fearsome is not, however, an abyss, and the sea does not drown into the ocean. It separates from the motherland but does not lead one to repudiate it. The Pillars of Hercules fix in the Greek imaginary the gap between the sea bound by lands and the endless extension of the ocean.

The maritime distances of the Aegean and the Mediterranean open the possibility of relationship and contact, even if they are savage and terrifying. This sea is mainly (but Greek language has three names for sea) *pontos*, arm of the sea, bridge that unites yet maintains the distance from the Other who remains separate, on another shore. In this interval that connects, in this distance that correlates, one finds the jealous safekeeping of one's autonomy and the ease of conflict, but also, close to them like a body's skin, the rejection of every fundamentalism.

From the start, the problem lies in the rapport between differences (with their complex, adversarial, and often tragic dynamics). This sea, which is at once external and internal, inhabited and waded into, this sea-as-border interrupts the rule of identity, forces one to accommodate division. Here land, with its obsession for fixity, assuredness, and appropriation, clashes always against a boundary; here, from the beginning, the confusion between a city's control and the owner's power has always been more difficult to solve.

This is due to the penetration and mediation of the sea, to its capacity to preserve and bridge differences despite their at times irresistible resistance, to build confederations that only the great common enemy (the Persian Empire) can soften. And this not only in the relationship between different poleis, but also within each, or at least the ones whose inhabitants carry within them the sea and are stirred by the restlessness of those who know that there does not exist only one horizon, country, or accent. Inside a polis, each citizen carries the foreign within, and unity is immediately more difficult, more complex; it requires a longer journey. Polytheism, tragedy, and philosophy do not disagree on this point: All three know the legitimacy of multiple points of view, the difficulty of their coexistence. They all presuppose an archipelago, the extraordinary extension of the coast and the pervasiveness of the sea, even if moderation comes to life in very different ways in the three: out of the free interaction of a variety of divine powers; out of the repercussions that catch up with every hubris; out of the fragility-humanity of a dialogic solution, and the artificial and conventional space of the logos.

Thus, there is one side of Greek philosophy that is the child of the Greek sea. But there is also another one that removes and erases this origin, a side that will keep growing more powerful, pushed as it is by the desire to rescue its outcomes from the uncertainty caused by the back-and-forth between land and sea, by the duplicity of the coast. It is not by chance that Plato looks with suspicion to the sea and to the transformation of the *immobili opliti* into sailors:[8] The sea prevents the closing of the circle, even the polished, reflexive one of philosophy. The polis is unthinkable without the restlessness and the complex loyalty embedded in the double nature of those who live by the coast. Without the sea, power quickly runs the risk of falling into the hands of a despot or of the philosophers; the opening in the horizon caused by the sea ensures, at the same time, that no knowledge can be condensed in one final thought, and no power can become fixed in the immobility of personal ownership. Greek philosophy meets its reason but also its limit: It discovers itself as part of something that comes before and explains it.

On the Line That Divides

It is not by chance that this plural knowledge came into existence in a land whose vocation, by reasons of geography and history, is the coexistence between opposites: from the enigmas of clashing divine wills to the harsh and irreducible friction of tragedy, to the refined and civilized one of philosophy. Therefore, we have to ask what happens when philosophy removes itself from this background, from its contiguity with tragedy, from the places where, right from the start, unity is a problem, and where, for this unity to occur, it must cross a distance that is constantly re-creating itself.

Athens, it has been said, is a "city of two souls." It is this difficult unity, this constant starting anew of knowledge, that has spurred Derrida (in the wake of Heidegger's "philosophy is Greek in its nature")[9] to affirm that "the founding concepts of philosophy are primarily Greek, and it would not be possible to philosophize, or to speak philosophically outside this medium."[10] The adventure of the logos started on the Greek sea: "The Greek miracle . . . is the impossibility for any thought ever to treat its sages as 'sages of the outside,' according to the expression of Saint John Chrisostomus."[11]

Philosophy is thus understood in very precise terms: No word is so out-of-bounds, uncontaminated, or vertical to establish the legitimacy of its monopoly. As Nietzsche says, "Other people have saints; the Greeks have sages."[12] But this unusual opening toward knowledge and the love of it is

precisely the "Greek miracle." Deleuze and Guattari speak of Greece as
the place where philosophers find a favorable environment to create what
will become philosophy. Again, this idea originates with Nietzsche, who
notices repeatedly that only among the Greeks is the philosopher not an
accident or a comet.[13] Philosophers are foreigners who in Greece are hon-
ored for their knowledge and find the willingness toward partnership,
friendship, and opinion. This is what Greece is all about, even more than
philosophy. It is the welcoming that finds its origins in the love and discovery of the agon and of competition;[14] the familiarity with the *dissoì lógoi*,
with clashing gods, with the abundance of unexpected outcomes that originates in every act; the ability to handle major conflicts among equally
justified perspectives; and the precocious inclination to feel the tragic
nature of every choice, in direct contrast with every adoring and subaltern
outlook.

The Sages, like the Magi, land in the Greek colonies of Asia Minor
from the Iranian plateau. But when they arrive on the Aegean coast, the
verticality of their words slowly sinks; their perspectives lose their hierarchical rigidity and slide onto one plane: The sea turns horizontal a knowledge that was vertical; it forces the fixity of the land to deal with the
incessant and endless motion of the waves. As the mystics descend from
the mountains, from the meditation of the oracles, as their word descends
toward the horizontality of the sea, accepting to walk on the roads, to feel
plural, questioned, disavowed, contested, the Greek miracle takes place.
Philosophy and the sea interrupt the autarchy of the lands; they force out
of esoteric circles revelations that the rarefied air of high peaks occasionally benumbs, and break the idea of a unique and undisputable center.
They turn truth into a horizontal fact, a matter that depends on discussion
between men. Plutarch has Hepimenedes say in "The Obsolescence of
Oracles" that the navel of the world is neither at Delphi nor elsewhere:[15]
Philosophy begins when the oracles wane, when the sanctuaries slowly
migrate toward the sea. The enigma does not disappear, but the duty of
argumentation begins: The urban-civil fabric that emerges from Plato's
Dialogues reveals a mobile and curious society, used to travel and discussion, a horizontality of knowledge that welcomes everyone to the *agon* of
discussion. What kind of humanity is the one that, distancing itself from
the certainties of the *epos* and from the warm unity that opposes every
community to its enemies, embraces instead tragic heroes and a form of
civic representation where human actions meet unsolvable dilemmas?
What strange humanity is the one that roams and mills around in the
Dialogues, where interminable discussions carry into the night and move
from house to house stretching for days; where new characters come on
stage repeatedly and so many questions and answers crowd upon each

other? What humanity could ever be the one that Socrates gathers around himself, a humanity that believes that everything is questionable and that people can argue, agree or disagree? What is this unstoppable undertow of the logos, its incapacity to stop?

For Popper and Havelock,[16] the poleis, the sea republics, Athens, and the sophists originate the idea that truth is revocable, thus giving birth to liberal thought or nature, what is called liberal temper. This is correct, but too plain, because the subjectification of truth is an issue much more complex than even the wonderful practices invented by liberal culture.

To attempt to explain the difference between the idea that there is more than one truth—truths that might be in conflict with each other—and the procedures that were gradually invented to control and recompose their multiplicity *ad unum*, we will draw on the authority of Santo Mazzarino. In defining the originality of the "Greek spirit," it is difficult for him to overrate the role of a brief writ of sophist origin, the *dissoì lógoi*, which centers on the awareness of the relativity and diversity of customs.[17] Mazzarino believes that, without being aware of the at times irresolvable multiplicity of perspectives of which that writ is an extraordinary document, it is unthinkable to conjure the distancing of "scientific" historiography from myth, the style itself of Thucydides. The famous dialogue between the Melians and the Athenians is an example of the tragic diverging of perspectives whose gap the logos cannot bridge.[18] Here we can see the limits of Havelock and Popper's point of view: The diverging of perspectives described with scientific detachment by Thucydides is not solvable by philosophy's logos. Not only does the disagreement between the Melians and the Athenians remain such at the end of the dialogue, it is only resolved by the Athenian empire's use of force, by the destruction of Melos. The scientific nature of Thucydides' gaze does not attempt to justify the Athenians: It has not eliminated the tragic, and it does not give in to the temptation to recompose the conflict. Herein lies the danger of trying to explain Greece through its philosophy or at least through post-Socratic philosophy, of reducing its experience of the conflict to one that can be tackled by discursive solutions. Greek culture contains and at the same time exceeds philosophy, because the latter always chooses to soften, remove, and recompose the chasm created by the inconsistency of perspectives.

But Greece is not only philosophy. It is also tragedy, the moment when the games of reason cannot work. Between tragedy and philosophy there is a continuity and a discontinuity: Both pit themselves against the diverging of the *lógoi*; but while the night of philosophy is mild because the conflict continuously moves within the area of friendship, the night of tragedy is unredeemable and ripped asunder by lightning flashes that illuminate conflicts that cannot be recomposed in the univocity of the logos.

This observation is crucial: The difference is not always the domesticated one of the logos, sometimes it does not know how to sit at the discussion table; a dialogue takes place between the Athenian envoys and the rulers of Melos that has in common with the Platonic dialogues only its name, because whereas in Plato the thread of discussion, of peace, and of friendship never breaks, the Athenian envoys return home with a speech that is not consistent with the one of their Melian interlocutors. Each of the two speeches remains closed in itself but one must not fall into today's very common trap of reading the autarchy of the two *lógoi* as a form of prerational and prephilosophic barbarity. Both the Athenians and the Melians have their reasons, and neither can seriously protect them without damaging the other. Peace could be achieved only if one of the two *lógoi* renounced its integrity, stooping to compromises and accepting to negotiate: if the Athenians, choosing magnanimity, accepted to provide a bad example for their allies; or if the Melians accepted to lose their freedom just to survive. As much as it was unpopular, the speech of the Athenians, like Creon's in *Antigone*,[19] has its good reasons: the impossibility of bridging the two perspectives does not depend on the obtuse resistance of one (or both) to reason and justice, but on the fact that often the world becomes too narrow to contain both. The relationship (the dialogue) between *lógoi* is not always available to the logos: one of its sides is war, *pólemos*; the *agon* is not always able to restrict itself to the enclosure of common rules.

What is extraordinary is that this discussion about the Athenians comes from an Athenian, that the circle of Greek knowledge is larger than philosophy, that it possesses the capacity to see even that which resists discursive reconstruction, though it contributed in a decisive way to its invention. When one asserts "the rhetorical exit from tragic dilemma"; when "Eschylus' dilemmas" transform themselves in "the antinomies of Protagoras and Gorgias,"[20] and the distance between "opposite and unbridgeable positions"[21] is filled by the victory of those who possess greater dialectic ability; when one opens the field to the centrality of the discussion—that is when one finds an extraordinary instrument for the "practical" domestication of the conflict, but also a procedure to hide truth; that is when one has begun hiding the nonbeing of truth itself. Philosophy will continue to perfect this concealment even though it condemns itself to start anew each time. The Greek gaze, from which philosophy itself was born, is given the opportunity, through its contiguity with tragedy, to exceed the limits of that knowledge. For this gaze the two never become one, even when the logos invents wondrous games to make one forget about it. No knowledge, not even the most sophisticated knowledge, can be under the illusion of recomposing in its nets the diversity of voices safeguarded by the contiguity of tragedy and philosophy. But nothing guarantees the permanency of this fragile and exceptional equilibrium.

When freedom needs to be protected by a thalassocracy, when the need for empire begins, all the wealth contained in that knowledge begins to vanish and the only part that can save itself is the one that can be capitalized in a universal (and universalistic) domain.

Europe and Greece

"The concept of Europe," noticed Federico Chabod, "must be created by opposition, inasmuch as there is something that is not Europe."[22] The first emergence of this difference, the first opposition, the one between Europe and Asia was born in the Mediterranean and "is the work of Greek thought."[23] That "illustrious sea" on whose shores so many races have mingled was "a kind of pre-Europe."[24] The opposition upon which Greece announces Europe, an opposition that was already clear in Herodotus, Aristotle, and Aeschylus, is the one between "the spirit of freedom," which breathes within the Greek poleis, and "Asian despotism."[25] This difference emerged already in the urban planning of the poleis. In their center one finds not the royal Palace or the temple, but the agorà, the place where men meet on equal footing, where there is not one truth, but many in conflict. The commercial center within the agorà is much more than a simple place of commodity exchange; instead, as Cyrus had already noticed polemically,[26] it is the place where the conventional rather than the natural meaning of the *nomos* surfaces: The many-voiced cities of the Greek archipelago rise against the univocity of the religious or imperial word.[27]

Europe ran its initial tests in Greece, and it is clear that there exists a continuity between the Greek and European spirit. The marker of this continuity is the sea. As Hegel says:

> In Asia, the sea is without significance, and the Asiatic nations have in fact shut themselves off from it. In India, going to sea is positively forbidden by religion. In Europe, however, this maritime relationship is of vital importance, and it creates an enduring difference between the two continents. The European state is truly European only in so far as it has links with the sea. The sea provides that wholly peculiar outlet which Asiatic life lacks, the outlet which enables life to step beyond itself. It is this which has invested European political life with the principle of individual freedom.[28]

A geographic difference between internal and coastal zones transforms itself in the difference between despotism and freedom. This continuity between Greeks and Europeans has also been reasserted by Alberto Savinio: "Those who say Europe, say Greece."[29] Before others—Savinio recalls—Greece "lost infinity," and began to talk about two instead of one; it broke away from Asia where the One and seriousness still rule, and where play, the legitimacy of the agon, can never begin. But what is the constitutive characteristic of the Greek people? They are

> a marine, more than a seafaring people. What better comparison for the special intelligence of these people than the flickering of the seashore? Pay attention: the Greeks are colonizers, they have always been. But they colonize the beaches: in Asia Minor, in Italy, in Marseille. They do not travel inland. They know that in losing sight of the sea, one loses the flickering of the seashore: one loses intelligence.[30]

Intelligence has a direct relationship with the sea, because the latter trains intelligence toward mobility and plurality; it forces it to "pass from shore to shore and from people to people." Savinio adds: "Monsters come to life in the center of Europe, not at its peripheries. It's the healing effect of iodine, the natural blood 'thinner'; but most of all, it's the effect of a full open horizon, of the distant gaze, of departures offered in perpetuity."[31]

For Savinio, as for Hegel, Europe is an expanded Greece because, even in its interior, the sea is always nearby and there is no place from which it is difficult to reach it. Michel Mollat asks himself, "Where does Asia end and Europe begin?" He answers by citing Claudel: "The West looks to the sea and the East to the mountains." In other words, "For geography, the contrast between Asia and Europe goes beyond continentality (*L'oiseau noir dans le Soleil Levant*)." Mollat remembers soon thereafter, as he retraces Helmut Berve's discussion about Greece, that: "To go swimming in the sea no Western European travels more than 350 kilometres; the distance is doubled for an inhabitant of central Europe." No Englishman "lived more than 150 kilometres from the coast, whereas among the Germans or even the French there were those who, even in modern times, had never seen the sea." It is for this reason that *Europe and the Sea* can conclude with a citation from Jacques Pirenne: "Throughout history the maritime countries have proven to be individualists and liberals, whereas the continental countries, social and authoritarian, have a taste for hierarchical organizations."[32]

Even Paul Valéry believes that the sea marks the continuity between Greece and Europe. Europe is "a kind of cape of the old continent, a western appendix to Asia"[33] (but also Derrida[34] and Savinio[35]) that turns this off-centeredness into a strength, transforms its jagged falling into the sea in a restlessness of the spirit that begins with Greece.

But even the crisis of thought dips its origins in the relationship between Greece, Mediterraneity, and Europe. This crisis is born from the self-same greatness and wealth of European civilization.

> Mediterranean nature, the resources it offered, the relationship it has created or imposed, are at the origin of the stunning psychological and technical transformation that, in a short span of centuries, has so deeply distinguished Europeans from the rest of humanity, and modern times from the preceding epochs.[36]

The difference consists for Valéry in the "precisions of methods and in the search for the necessity of phenomena through the calculated use of the mind's faculties," but especially "in the ever increasing distancing from the initial or natural conditions of life."[37] The peculiar conditions of the Mediterranean (reduced distances, temperate climate, ease of navigation) have made it a locus of crossings and competitive exchanges between peoples. The natural environment stimulates the spirit in a Hegelian way that becomes, in an extraordinary counterpoint, more and more independent from the natural environment.

Thus, it is on the Mediterranean ("a real civilization making machine")[38] that the restlessness began ("Something is still missing from our make-up"),[39] the obstinacy in overcoming obstacles that Valéry sees as the characteristic of European civilization. But in this civilization, human beings live now surrounded by the unbounded growth of the ever more sophisticated prostheses they bring into existence; they lose their balance and are constantly busied and obsessed with their own productive imagination. The Spirit is a sorcerer's apprentice; it has set sail and lives eternally on the sea, having now forgotten the idea itself of limits and homecoming. On the contrary, any concept about a limit or homecoming arouses its suspicions: Nothing "is harder for us to understand than the limit placed on intellectual fancies or than moderation in using material power."[40] The same rhetoric of acceleration and speed, the ever more suffocating law of our age, is in the end an automatic tendency, "a form of minimal action, simple comfort."[41] This form of thought-*comodité* (which reminds us, probably not by chance, of the English commodity, or "merchandise") is mistaken for thought. This is where the origins of the crisis of thought can be found, in its surrender to the predominance of technology: The sea has won, and land disappears forever in the horizon: From now on, the only thought that counts is the one that lives on the high seas, which has eliminated the idea itself of limits, of homecoming and of the land as superstitions, regressions, or self-consciousness. Having substituted the old infinity with the new technological one means only having changed the substance of the lack of moderation.

The theme of the loss of limits returns in Carl Schmitt's great little book *Land and Sea*. Schmitt formulates the most radical critique of the sea as the shore and the coast no longer exist; sea and land are opposite. "Man is a terrestrial, a groundling. He lives, moves and walks on the firmly-grounded Earth."[42] Thus, the sea is only a principle of eradication: it represents diabolic temptation, the seducer that pushes us toward the fiercest bewilderment and toward the idolatry of technology. Through the sea, Prometheus loses his chains and drags human beings toward bewilderment. The spirits of the coast and of the border, the Mediterranean, are simple transitional moments toward the lack of moderation that the sea carries within itself. The sea cannot be but Ocean, just as every woman cannot but be a sinner. Thus, it is not by chance that the industrial revolution would occur on the island of England, plunged in the immensity of the oceans:

> The organization of the mainland, at whose center is the house, has perforce a fundamentally different relationship with technology than a mode of existence at whose center moves a ship. An absolutization of technology and technological progress, the equalization between technological progress and absolute development, in short, all that allows itself to be summarized in the expression "unbridled technology," occurs only on the fertile land and in the climate of a maritime existence.[43]

After the whole sea has been conquered, humanity will assault air and space, dreaming of setting off on a cosmic trip by spaceship. Faced with this scenario, Schmitt pulls back horrified and wishes for humankind's return to the womb of the earth after an era of perdition and confusion: "I believe that humanity, after the difficult night of atomic bombs and similar horrors, one day will wake up and thankfully recognize itself as the child of a firmly grounded earth."[44] Schmitt does not say who must lead humanity back to its original bedrock, but it is indisputable that such a mission is the charge of land powers that are in closer proximity to that faithfulness and at a further distance from the perdition of the sea. His convergence on this point with Heidegger is significant, as the latter believed that one must oppose the rooted strength of contemplative thought to the calculating thought of technology (thought born on the high seas). Heidegger points to the suggestive path of abandonment, and we will return later to those deliberations. For now, we just want to point out that the inability to grasp abandonment is the result of thinking about the earth that did not want to abandon things, but wished to hold, take, and conquer, and which had bent the technology of tanks and V2[45] bombs to earthly imperialism, the same thinking that, in the concentration camps, had tried to cancel forever the restlessness of a "displaced" people.[46]

Heidegger, Nietzsche, and the Sea

When the sea overflows the measure it was given by the coast, by the latter's double nature; when it becomes ocean and uses technology as the only source of reliability; when the ship, the Hegelian "sea swan," transforms itself into a spaceship; when restlessness loses not only the ability but the desire to come back; that's when one feels, with a violent and schematic recoil, the passion for rooted-ness, when one embraces the temptation to reassemble into a whole the fragments dispersed in every direction. This phobia toward the sea is an allergic reaction to its perversity, a reaction against the universal coercion to set sail, against the eternal travel westward, against chasing the moving point where the sun sets, against the ambiguity that transforms travel around the spherical Earth into the straight line of unlimited development.

Heidegger builds a relationship of extraneous hostility with the sea, and a great part of his extraordinary meditation plunges its roots in the return of beings from the moving sea to Being, to the home-land: It is not by chance, nor suddenly, that this turning point (*Kehre*) leads theoretically to his Messkirch,[47] to the woods, to the clearings and the paths that surround it; it seeks, in this original faithfulness, the possibility of getting past the nihilistic outcomes of the age of metaphysics.

In geopolitical terms, in the *Introduction to Metaphysics*, Heidegger says something important about Germans, a deeply spiritual people inasmuch as it is deeply threatened: "We are caught in a pincers. Situated in a center, our nation incurs the severest pressure. It is the nation with the most neighbors and hence the most endangered. With all this, it is the most metaphysical of nations."[48] This placement at the center of Europe (the essay is from 1935) calls for a great destiny: "If the great decision regarding Europe is not to bring annihilation, that decision must be made in terms of new spiritual energies unfolding historically from out of the center."[49] One must fight, "if the peril of world darkening is to be forestalled and if our nation in the center of the Western world is to take on its historical mission."[50]

This metaphysical role is a nightmare that Savinio describes with extraordinary lucidity in *Alcesti di Samuele*, where Goerz states:

> This city we live in is suffocated by the land. Look at a map. We are in the heart of Europe. Land on every side. Land, land. And the land suffocates man, numbs him, leads him into despair. These crises that periodically wrack Germany, aren't they but the spasmodic movements of someone buried alive? The land surrounds this country, chokes it, renders it hysterical and crazy.[51]

This land surrounded by land, this land "to the nth degree" allows, paradoxically, for the heart of Europe to host, together with Germans, the "Asians of Europe." German civilization is a theocratic civilization, whose God "is Germany itself." "Germany"—continues Savinio—"has a European idea, but of a Europe that belongs to it, of a Germanized Europe, of a Europe built with German materials and enlivened by the Germanic spirit." Because of its extraneousness to Europe, Germany is repeatedly pushed to try to "colonize Europe—while other colonizing people colonize 'outside of Europe.' "[52]

I do not know if we can accept Savinio's conclusions in their essentialism, but they allow us to understand better the limits of the most ambitious aspect of Heidegger's philosophy. Heidegger sees, as is well known, a metaphysical, common mission between Greeks and Germans, something that ensures that there is deep communication between their two languages, an underground continuity that one needs to bring to the surface. One might hypothesize that this common, metaphysical destiny is born from the circumstance that both people are exposed to risk and at the center of manifold pressures. But this is a weak analogy since the metaphysical destiny of the two people seems quite different: What is absent in Heidegger and Germany is the pervasiveness of the sea. As soon as he meets the sea, with its fluctuating waves of beings, Heidegger grabs the anchor of Being and of presence. When for the first time he finds himself in Greece, he is deeply perturbed.

> This sea, these mountains, these islands, this sky—It surprises me more and more and it is difficult to think it through to its conclusions that here and only here could *A-lètheia* bloom, and the gods could, or rather had to, reenter in its saving light; that here Being should dominate as presence and create the conditions for human living. . . . We must bring with us to Greece many things to meditate upon, many things already poetized before, so we might receive that surplus that is incomparable: the surprise of pure presence.[53]

Greece is the place where being revealed itself, the play of maximum metaphysical presence. But, truly, the Greece described here is deeply Germanized; in it, Being has dried out the sea, and water serves only as support for the land. In Heidegger's *Geviert*, in that squaring within whose horizon we are invited to "dwell," there are only sky and land, humans and gods; there is only verticality; there are no escapes or side exits, all happens in the steadiness of the relation between above and below. Water is subordinate to land, just a part of it.[54] And here, in this water that glides away, is the difference between Greece and Germany, between a center de-centered from its origins and a center that wants to organize the world according to its own measure and, because of it, feels stifled. Germany, as the center of Europe, feels the paranoia of every center, the paranoia that comes from its ontological condition of being, by definition, surrounded, encircled. It does not know the experience of the borderland that the Greeks had internalized precisely through the fractal structure of their land and the pervasiveness of the sea. Whereas in Greece the Word separated into two (*dissoì lógoi*) or more discourses and, in their drama, entities revealed the difficulty of finding peace in being, in Heidegger the opposite is at work: One reaches a deeper and more essential dimension, a truth so strong that it chooses to base itself in a poetic-oracular language that is not exposed to the corrosive force of the logos. Heidegger reads the Greeks by letting the sea glide away, even installing his own references precisely where the sea still has not arrived. The sea is for Heidegger the logos and the metaphysics of the West. Technology and the sea begin in Greece when, through the birth of metaphysics, the logos experiences its first test trials, and begins to prepare the history of the eradicated will to power that resides in technology.

George Steiner has noticed that the Heidegger who takes technology to task is "an agrarian through and through. Field and forest are at the heart of the Heideggerian world. The woodsman and the farmer, acting in immemorial affinity with their surroundings, provide Heidegger with a touchstone of existential rightness."[55] Steiner asserts furthermore that this thought, soaked in "reactionary rurality and pastoral nostalgia," cannot but end in a polemic against mercantile society, in the exaltation of rural life, culminating in the belief "that the ancient gods, or the vital forces representing them, are innate in the land and the forest and might be resuscitated and inserted in a new dynamic. [Land—Heidegger claims—must become, once more, Spielraum, literally: "a space for play"]."[56]

This reading of the author of *Being and Time* as the "farmer philosopher" is reductive, in the same way that Adorno's is when he sees "only the more 'Rilkean' side or the folkloric aspect of Heidegger's adhesion to peasant values."[57] These interpretations in fact avoid the most important question: Why does the later Heidegger rediscover so insistently the need for rootedness? Is the formula "peasant philosophy" enough, or is there not, behind that push, also a dramatic reflection on modernity? Behind this formula, as well as the one that labels Heidegger a "Nazi philosopher," is there not a shorthand answer to the problem encountered by Heidegger, the push to avoid a critical but straight-on confrontation with the theme of the relationship between nihilism and modernity?

My conviction is that this telluric regression is an allergic reaction, endemic in modernity, to the pervasiveness of the sea, and that in it is hidden not only the past but the problem of the future. Friedrich Nietzsche represents the most violent and devastating irruption of this pervasiveness of the sea in philosophy, and it was this irruption that Heidegger had to confront for a long time.

It is not a stretch to say that it is impossible to approach the *Gay Science* and its author by displacing their push toward the sea, and that Nietzsche's "return southward" cannot be understood outside of the relationship between the South and the sea. Nietzsche constantly refers, particularly in the *Gay Science*, to the metaphor of the sea: Philosophers must jump aboard ("On to the ships, you philosophers!"),[58] get on the ships, and become familiar with the uncertainty of the sea. Nietzsche does not juxtapose by chance seafaring and the famous metaphor that men of knowledge need to build their homes on the Vesuvius (as Antimo Negri has meritoriously pointed to our general attention): "Build your cities on the slopes of Vesuvius! Send your ships into uncharted seas!"[59] The only possible home for those who have decided to go and eradicate themselves can only be on the sea: "I wouldn't build a house for myself (and it is part of my good fortune not to be a home-owner!). But if I had to, I would, like some Romans, build it right into the sea—I certainly would like to share a few secrets with this beautiful monster."[60]

There's more: Nietzsche's sea is from the beginning an ocean; it projects in the horizon of infinity, and nothing could better describe the risk that underscores the search for a "grand health" than setting sail.

> We have forsaken the land and gone to sea! We have destroyed the bridge behind us—more so, we have demolished the land behind us! Now, little ship, look out! Beside you is the ocean. . . . [T]here will be hours when you realize that it is infinite and that there is nothing more awesome than infinity. . . . Woe, when homesickness for the land overcomes you, as if there had been more freedom there—and there is no more "land"![61]

This familiarity with the sea and infinity is what allows one to leave one's dwellings without regrets and to see beyond the ruins of the past. Far from being an end, the "death of God" opens a path. It is the moment when "finally our ships may set out again."[62] This is the reason we must familiarize ourselves with the monster, and become a strong, savage, and unstoppable will, like a wave,[63] ready to harvest with the sea the gifts of the god and of the sun in the evening.[64] Regardless, how could we forget the "new open seas" Nietzsche talks about in the preface to the second edition, or the metaphor that concludes the book, "the thirst to circumnavigate all the coasts of this ideal 'Mediterranean'" that characterizes the "argonauts of the ideal"?[65] And yet again, how can we understand the same breath of the *Gay Science* without the northwest wind that thrashes the sea, without the push "toward new seas" that even in the Appendix to the *Gay Science* goes along with Nietzsche's reasoning? And isn't Zarathustra the one who confesses to "favor the sea and everything that is of the sea," to feel "that joy of searching . . . that drives sails towards the undiscovered," the pleasure when "[t]he coast disappeared—now the last chain . . . fallen from me"?[66] And isn't it precisely Zarathustra who claims that the world is "a sea of rich abysses,"[67] the promise of an infinity of worlds and prey?

Heidegger's philosophy represents, with regard to this violent irruption of the sea-ocean, the return to land, a veritable peasant restoration, a "Northern peasant revolt" against the liquefaction of every foundation. Pushed by this horror for the sea, Heidegger took Nietzsche at face value much more than some contemporary Nietzschean scholars, because he sensed, in the libertarian anxiety and in the Dionysian exaltation of the will to power, a radicalism and destructive push that the latter have often softened and rendered, in bourgeois fashion, as a safe nomadic cruising along the archipelago of postmodern consumerism.

Heidegger—who was deliberate and determined like every peasant— achieves the apex of his revenge through a perfidious and profound move: Far from being "against" Western metaphysics, Nietzsche's push toward the sea-ocean constitutes the last and most radical expression of this metaphysics. With a few deadly moves, Heidegger outflanks Nietzsche leading him back to an old story, denying him "the first privilege he claimed for his thinking, that of not being, in the rigor of Western terminology, a philosopher, but a nomad who ransacks the fallen shrines of philosophy to return to his desert."[68] According to Roberto Calasso, the most apt metaphor to describe the panorama of Nietzsche's reflection would be that of the desert, of the adventurous traveler who enters a sea without water, where the green of the vegetation, like the coast for sailors, slowly disappears on the horizon. Certainly sea-ocean and desert cross paths (see Savinio on this matter),[69] and maybe Nietzsche's sea-ocean is truly a desert, a loneliness that coherently moves toward its meeting with folly. Indeed, the feast of universal uprooting is the generalization of freedom and angst, a sea without land, a sterile stage design for the Spirit.

But the cure against a boundless sea that destroys any rootedness, against a mandatory mobility that forces humanity into estrangement, cannot be the fetishism of one's own roots, the ethnocentricity of one's own sacred, a religion that is telluric and exclusionary. In order to condemn uprooting, one cannot shut all doors; in order to give new power to the root, one cannot hide behind the bard. Heidegger should not delude himself: the risk-taking of poets that he proposes in a famous essay[70] is small change if one does not allow this risk to face the sea; and it certainly cannot hide the telluric regression of the peasant. Deep down, the ecstasy experienced when facing the sun, the sea, and the Greek mountains is just the same as the ecstasy one feels facing the perfection of the idea of fatherland. But what remains with us of this idea of Greece? Aren't we losing in this way Greek specificity, aren't we losing the meeting-clash between land and sea, its having provided that fatherland with an unbreakable bond to one's freedoms?

However, in Heidegger's retaliation against Nietzsche there is a valuable detail that we should not omit: The freeing of the will to power, far from unmasking and situating one beyond metaphysics, is instead, as Heidegger says, the last stage of Western metaphysics, its completion. There is no contradiction between Nietzsche's setting sail without return and the success and primacy of technology. In a world in which we are forced to be at sea, we have substituted the constant mobility and liquidity of "all-against-all" competition to the old faithfulness toward the gods. Uprooting is celebrated like a virtue, as man's willingness to engage in universal competitiveness. When competition exceeds moderation, it cuts off every safety and protection: The opposite of peasant idiocy is the broker's, the unhappy science that believes that life is only a race and stock exchanges, the impersonal movement of capital that no pier can hold down, and the constant readiness to set sail where more is offered. The distancing of the coasts leads us to lose our moderation: We no longer conceive the sea as an interval between lands; instead, we worship the moment when we leave all behind and decide to live forever without safety nets. That is when the superman who leaves the coasts becomes a pirate, a man who no longer belongs to any land, but only to the sea. This is Nietzsche's greatness; these are the dangers of his setting sail. After the departure invoked by Nietzsche, one cannot go back because the homecoming, any homecoming, would be a defeat and a penance. Indeed, Nietzsche did not return, as an extraordinary homage to truth: He left the coasts and lost his way. As opposed to Heidegger, he did not take a risk through someone else; and for this reason he was able to prove an outcome and a truth: like Dante's Ulysses he shows the greatness and ruin contained in the absence of a homecoming.

"Nostos" and Mediterranean: Moderation between Land and Sea

Neither Nietzsche nor Heidegger shows the path: The former's ruin confirms the latter's suspicion, his sedentary risk-taking through an interposed poet. Those who do not want either to be shipwrecked or become peasants or poets must work more modestly on a double motion, on a contradiction, on the conflicted lawfulness of departing and returning. As occurs in *The Lady from the Sea*,[71] one's roots are paradoxically something that one can choose: Ellida is further along than the two men, the husband, the being of land, and the sailor loved in her youth, the being of the sea. Both insist on their own fundamentalism, and Ellida chooses the husband only after he has granted her the full freedom of choice. This is the gift of the sea, not a metaphysics of the beyond that eventually can only shipwreck, nor an eternal search for the West, but its granting freedom to the land; not its denying fatherlands, but forcing them to be chosen, to be elective.

This back and forth, this departing-returning and this returning-departing, this leaving not to escape, but being confident in the *nostos* (return) and also its opposite, being somewhere else when one is at home, this, which was long seen as a disease, is the possible solution: This double and antinomic grammar of the crossed borderland, this finding a home not in equilibrium but in the oxymoron, this is what leads us far away not only from Heidegger but also from Nietzsche's followers, Deleuze and Guattari. The first turns the German into the shepherd of Being; the latter elect nomads as the only spiritual people, the people without land-based income. On the one hand, there are those who root themselves ever more firmly in the home, who react to the uprooting with the exaltation of the domestic and the familiar. On the other, there are those who liberate themselves of all homelands, who elevate uprooting to a spiritual principle.[72] Both are meager in comparison to the knowledge born in Greece because they know only one movement: for Heidegger, re-centering; for Deleuze and Guattari, de-centering, exodus, exile, and exit. Heidegger, in complete agreement with Carl Schmitt, thinks of Germany as the land of the center (Hearthland), of Germans as the people destined to a privileged relation with "presence." Greece is also, in its own way, a center, but it is a particular center, one that is crossed by borders. Certainly, even Greece identified itself through contrast (with barbarians and Persians), but this contrast is federal; it is the union of many poleis characterized, in turn, by a pluralistic internal structure. This ethnocentrism is destined to be paradoxical; it is condemned to experience it own antinomy as a nightmare.

Jacob Burckhardt says about the Greeks that they originally were pirates,[73] exactly the same thing that Schmitt will later say about the English. The "art of seamanship" that, according to Burckhardt, kept the Greeks far away from the Asians,[74] keeps them also away from the Germans, and destroys the bridge between Delphi and the Black Forest that Heidegger was trying to build. But the Greeks were also pirates among themselves. This difficult unity is the other face of Greek liberty, not something external to it. This ability to measure oneself with dis-cord, this constant belonging to more circles, this impossible integrity is precisely what turns the Greeks into the people of tragedy and philosophy!

Heidegger's, therefore, is not *the* philosophy, but the complete reterritorializing of philosophy, a metaphysical hand that tried to hold within itself
all of philosophy, while wishing to elide the sea, and the relationship with
tragedy and the nonbeing of truth. This is the fundamental limit of Heidegger's philosophy, its being sucked into the Hearthland, far away from
the corruption of any sea, of any border. Even in the years of abandonment (*Gelassenheit*), when Heidegger's land expands and is no longer the
narrow one in the heart of Europe, but becomes the planet Earth, the
latter seems to have lost the azure color of its seas that make it unusual in
the great chain of Being. Jacques Derrida has studied some symptomatic
omissions in Heidegger's philosophy (sex and sexual difference):[75] to that
string of omissions (and maybe in connection with them) we can add the
omission of the sea. It is precisely this fear of wandering, this obsession-
possession of one's roots to orient the last Heidegger. Yet, the sea does not
mean necessarily the rise of "unbridled technology" (Schmitt's expression,
which might echo the one Heidegger uses in the *Einführung*),[76] an ever
more titanic challenge that condemns us to the primacy of technology.
Man can mold the sea even by swimming, molding his own body to the
mobility of the water, becoming amphibious, importing and discovering
within himself the extraneousness of the sea without exporting his earthi-
ness. Unbridled technology does not signify the abandonment of earthy
grittiness, but its perfecting it through the will to power.

Mediterranean man, instead, lives always between land and sea; he
restrains one through the other; and, in his technological delay, in his
vices, there is also a moderation that others have lost. The unbridled
development of technology is not tied to the crossing of land and sea, but
to the oceanic lack of moderation, the chasing of the sunset by the sun, the
absolutization of the West. In Hegel, the West was still maturity, ability to
contain experience. Now, the infinite line of research and progress condemns people to live always on the sea, despising at all times the knowledge they already have.

Ulysses' Conflict

It is true, as Valéry says, that Europe began on the Mediterranean, but the
lack of moderation began precisely when the oceanic placement succeeded. The tension between land and sea has always converged on the
beloved and hated, but always crucial, figure of Ulysses. Carlo Diano, for
example, contrasts Ulysses—man of smarts, *metis*, full of *téchne* and ability
to swindle—to the figure of Achilles—man of passion and courage, hero
of forms.[77] Achilles breaks but does not bend; he does not learn from the

events, because he has a destiny that awaits him, as opposed to Ulysses who learns and bends in order to surpass, to reach his goals, his profit, his survival, and his home.

A different polemic from Diano's is the one raised by Emmanuel Lévinas who contrasts Ulysses to Abraham, symbol of "the movement without return": "To the myth of Ulysses who returns to Ithaca we wish to oppose the story of Abraham who leaves his fatherland forever for a yet unknown land, and forbids his servant to even bring back his son to the point of departure."[78] Here, one replaces the fatherland with the Promised Land; and to the personal, to the usefulness of egoism, one opposes the eschatology that unbalances toward the future. Whereas the return represents the narrow and repetitive force of the past, the exodus that initiates the march toward the promised land is the supremacy of the future. Against Ulysses stands, in the first case, the Greek hero; in the second, the prophet. But the differences between them, even if noticeable, almost disappear in their common opposition to the protagonist of the *Odyssey*: Whereas the latter is all bound by an earthy, almost too human goal, Achilles and Abraham are both sequestered away by a duty that transcends them. Whereas Achilles and Abraham endure and exemplify something that is greater than them, Ulysses avoids these powers and bends them even when they tower above him in grandeur. He does not recognize any good above his own.

But Ulysses is much more than this timid schemer, and, not surprisingly, some have attempted to reverse this image: Dante's Ulysses, the one who crosses Hercules' Pillars, shows the beginnings of a lack of moderation, whereby he risks even his survival to chase the desire to explore and discover. Even Ulysses "seeks" and fulfills a mission. The promised land can be that toward which we push to seek "virtue and knowledge."[79] Here the sea has become ocean, and the distances between Ulysses and Ahab have decreased. After all, it is Carl Schmitt who says of Melville that "he is to the world of oceans what Homer was to the Eastern Mediterranean": he "poeticized the great epos of the ocean inasmuch as element."[80]

Beyond every oversimplification, there's something right in this forcing Ulysses beyond the limits of the stereotype of local navigation and of Levantine cunning, and rendering visible his contradictions. By locking him into action that is purely calculating, as Horkheimer and Adorno do,[81] and making him a precursor of the Enlightenment's *ratio*, we minimize the intersection of cunning and courage, the tension between the desire for glory and adventure, and the desire for domestic peace. If it is true, as Finley notices, that "the *Iliad* is oriented Eastward, from the vantage point of Greece; the *Odyssey* to the West,"[82] it is also true that the *Odyssey* is not a shy and imperfect Moby-Dick. The difference between the man without *nostos*, Ahab and Nietzsche, and the man who instead wants to return, is a precious difference that we should learn to protect.

Gabriel Audisio sees in Ulysses, not without reason, the ambivalence of Mediterranean man, because he is contemporaneously "knight of the sea" and "peasant king."[83] This is how he conjoins "Falsehood and Truth, Love and Betrayal, Adventure with the Hearth, the Sea with the Territory, Daring and Fear, sweet Death and hated Death."[84] This "great" ambivalence belongs to the "Mediterranean . . . both angelic and diabolical, of theological as well as geographical importance," a sea that "in spite of the violence of its storms, . . . made possible Paul's missionary travels, thereby facilitating the spread of the divine Word and the establishment of the Christian diaspora."[85]

Odysseus represents, even for Roberto Calasso, the end of the age of the heroes, but his analysis is somewhat the opposite of Diano's: "Odysseus keeps his eyes downcast. But not out of fear. . . . The frontal approach of the hero holds no attraction for him. Odysseus takes one step back . . . to get the run-up he needs to leap beyond the heroes."[86] Far from bumping into a retreat we find in Ulysses a more complex dimension that allows

> mediation [to] triumph over the immediate, postponement over presence, the twisted mind over straightforwardness. All the character traits that would be assigned over the centuries to the merchant, the foreigner, the Jew, the traveling player were coined by Odysseus in himself. . . . Many centuries later, that condition seems normal, but in Odysseus's time it was a foresight granted only to one who had traveled a great deal between earth and heaven.[87]

This is true, as long as it is clear that what makes Ulysses great, what maybe leads him back to the simplicity of Ithaca, after the long Odyssey of the interpretations,[88] is the ability to house within himself this wandering and, at the same time, the desire to return. This is not a case of contrasting the value of the Exodus to that of the fatherland. Who is it that has traveled much without returning, without a story, without the transmission of his experience, without the other pole, without fathers and without sons? And what is a story without adventure, risk, and the every day desire to regain the sea?

Topicality of the Mediterranean

The sea, like every freedom, holds within itself the risk of nihilism; and the ocean is the moment when the sea loses its moderation, just as nihilism is the moment when pluralism becomes an incurable relativism, whereby the coexistence between those who are different becomes universal extraneousness and uprooting. But the cure for the scattering caused by the ocean cannot be the rejection of the sea, the apology of land, its withdrawal into its own roots.

In Greek thought, to protect the sea means therefore to preserve its having been born on a coast, within opposite drives that at times can be balanced and reassembled, at times are destined for a terrible distancing. We always belong to one coast instead of another, but a coast is also always a border. And the border is the place where two differences come into contact and they each discover, through the other, their narrowness. Far from being a location of minor theoretical density, the peripheries that meet-clash are the place where, as the nonbeing of truth reveals itself, a space is created for real thought. In a situation where the reciprocal allergy of sea and land and of financial uprooting and fundamentalist re-rooting seem to dominate, the intersection of land and sea can be found again in all those spiritual attitudes that have thematized the plurality of divine names, and have experienced the conflict that comes from knowing how to hold together one's faith and the respect for someone else's. Therefore land and sea: one against the other and one and the other united.

Yet, one must guard against the predominant versions of this ethos, against the degraded version of this Mediterranean difference. Raffaele La Capria has observed polemically: "Virtue and knowledge are somewhat devalued among us. In truth, we Mediterranean people, descendants of Ulysses, are, like him, smalltime seafarers: it took him ten years to reach Ithaca!!"[89] One could argue with La Capria that, if the distance between two places were only bridged by a straight line, no one would ever have started to narrate. But the harshness of the observation is perfectly justified, because it signals the degradation and current asphyxia of the Mediterranean, its buckling into small dodges, in the duplicities that render it a defeated slave. These limits have always followed those who live on the borders; they are the dark side of their identity. What today must be rebuilt with determination is the other side, the one on which one can stumble in that unruly wisdom and in that moderation that humanity seems to have lost. The objection according to which the Mediterranean would now be a precious fossil of the past, surpassed by the development of means of communication and transportation that annul distances, is the umpteenth example of a laughable yet resistant technological superstition, the one that reduces every distance to its kilometric measure. Far from bridging (through time and development) distances, technology multiplies them, and, in its one-dimensional vocabulary, there do not exist words to name them. The distances between the shores with which we must confront ourselves today are quite different from those of techno-industrial small-time navigation; the duties we face are extraordinarily more challenging than to remain an inefficient and corrupted periphery of the West that sells the most precious knowledge, like a postcard, on the corner of some anonymous boardwalk. Captain Ulysses cannot withdraw, tired of his role, as Savinio would have it,[90] but must continue to leave. At the other end of the sea is not only the "not yet" of development, but roads that go toward deserts and plateaus, other prayers, churches, and languages that resist translation. Hence, an ancient and great challenge faces Mediterranean man: to build connections and contacts, to build bridges, to make those high and difficult seas "pontos." This knowledge is not born of technological development, but from the intersection of land and sea. As long as we continue to believe that the inevitable running toward the West is the only possible motion of the day, and that the Mediterranean is a sea of the past, we will be focusing our eyes in the wrong direction, and the decay that surrounds us will never cease to grow.

PART II

Homo currens

CHAPTER 3

Thinking the Frontier

The Restlessness of the Frontier

"A small county is a country that was once great and remembers it," said Georges Simenon in a short and wonderful story titled *Frontiers*.[1] It is on the frontier that one measures the full and terrible restlessness that runs through human history.

The word "frontier" derives from the Latin *frons, frontis*, 'front/fore-head.' Frontiers are the places where countries and the human beings who inhabit them meet and *stay in front of each other*.[2] This *being in front of each other* can mean many things: first of all, looking at the other, learning about him, confronting and understanding what we might expect from him. But the existence of the other can be insidious. As in Hegel's dialectic of "self-consciousness in self-opposition,"[3] what is up for grabs in this *staying in front* is *recognition*. The most restless frontiers are those that are not recognized.

It is not by chance that the word *front* is also used to represent the greatest hostility, as in *war-front*: It is also at the origin of *fronting each other* (which is a verb that is used for battles), *confront, affront,* and *frontal*, an adjective that in Italy refers almost exclusively to automobile accidents ("frontal," or "head-on," collisions). Two can be "fronting" each other, like young Americans playing chicken (meaning "coward"): Two cars face each other going at top speed; the winner is the one who does not swerve and move out of the other car's path. One front excludes another.

Frontiers have been and are primarily this: places of division and opposition, places where men confront each other, each keeping an eye on the other. Fronting one another means looking, watching, not turning one's back. We can only turn our backs on those we trust and whom we do not need to control. The uncertainty of the frontier does not pertain only to borderlands, but it reaches the capital. The doors to the temple of Janus (derived from *ianua*, door, the frontier between inside and outside the house) were opened in times of war, when one needed to control all the borders: Only a bi-*frontal* god can look in all directions without running the risk of being assaulted from behind. The true god of borders though was Terminus, the only god who refused to cede his place to Jupiter when a temple was built in the latter's honor. The statue of Terminus was the only one that remained in the temple of Jupiter: no majesty without the safety of borders.

Janus, for his part, oversaw the beginning and end of all things. On *the frontier*, on the *limit*, each of us *ends* and is *defined*, acquires one's shape, accepts to be limited by something else that is obviously also limited by us. The end de-limits and the con-fines de-fine. This *reciprocity of the ending*, this *ending into something* is inevitable and incurable. The suspicion that the limit is unfair or that it is reputed as such by the other is inseparable from this reciprocal de-limiting, from our ending where the other begins. Its highest and most organized form is the paranoia found in every border, as it is seen on the faces of frontier guards, in their fear armed with machine guns. From every blockhouse one espies a desert of the Tatars,[4] and anguish becomes a daily thing. It is as if hypochondria were the only way we might become healthy. When we continuously inspect the borders (even our own, our internal ones) we are like Kafka's moles: We no longer can distinguish external noises from those produced by our brain and nerves. For this reason many ghosts wander on the borders, and enemy maneuvers blend in the fog with the maneuvers of the mind and of fear.

Recently geopolitics has come back into fashion, a subject that pertains to the interests that countries have in foreign policy, their territorial rivalries, and the contrast between existing borders and those some countries wish to have. It pretends to oversee the perennial and terrible restlessness that men have about the *limes*,[5] and it offers itself as a rational remedy to their incurable diffidence. But, maybe, all it does is augment it. There are disciplines that are as inevitable as nightmares.

The Ambivalence of the Frontier

Yet, frontiers unify just as they divide. In the first place, they unite all those who are gathered together within them, in a single unit. Each perimeter has enormous power: by dividing the space in two, it sets the fundamental rule, it brings together points in space precisely because it divides them. Every foundational act is, at its origin, an act of division: A city that comes into existence separates itself from all others; at its origin are a homicidal act and pact, a *sacrifice*.[6] Romulus kills Remus because he confused-offended the furrow delimiting the border. The border is sacred because it safeguards the relationship between identity and difference, inasmuch as it builds-identifies a community precisely through its opposition to others, to all others. Every community, even the most peaceful one, if it is a true community, is also true hostility. Nothing unites a group more than the celebration of its fallen, and no community is more connected to its pain than to the one caused by a common enemy. We are unified by our known martyrs and unknown soldiers.

Thus, the frontier does not unify *and* divide, but it unifies *because* it divides. Even where communities seem to nonchalantly overcome borders, the latter are at work: Nomadic identity, precisely because it owns a spatial instability, is safeguarded by a much stronger bond, by an austerity and reciprocal control that widen the border with sedentary people. We do not belong to the countries we cross, but to the one land that traverses them while allowing us to preserve the strength of our bonds.[7] The borderline does not necessitate barbed wire to hold human beings together. Even fraternal and universalistic communities separate and battle: Whether one wants to evangelize the world or fight in the name of Communism, everything passes through the construction of *new* subjectivities, hence *new* borders. It is hard to free oneself from borders. But more about this later.

There is another place where the frontier unites. As I have already said, *frontiers, confines, limits, edges, margins* are also the set of points one *shares*. We have the same borders with another country because the line of separation is also the tract we have in common with it, the location where our points come into contact with each other. Absolute enmity does not allow this contact: Between armies, there exists a *no-man's-land*, a separation and an interval, because the contact would coincide with conflict and aggression. It is no coincidence that those who keep rivals apart allow them to be free only when they are sure that they will not take advantage of their freedom to go back to hitting each other: Mediation is positioning in between, introducing bodies in the no-man's-land to show that hostilities can be reduced and controlled. Peace begins when people can go back to *touching each other* at the borders, when *con-tiguity* and *con-tact* are possible.

Con-fine in fact also means contact, points in common; and the frontier guardsmen share the scenery even if they keep it separate. In other words, it is possible for a *weak* sign of the border to exist, a confine that unifies and does not set in opposition, a confine where the first part of the word (*con*) wins over the second (*fine*), a separation that contradicts itself, because to manage the separation one uses men; and these, as we well know, can also betray us and talk with the enemy. In all the borderlands, when the tension is not explosive, complicity and connivance can ensue, a consensual weakening of the confine. There exists an illicit economy that often ties borderland populations and weakens the holiness of borders, making them permeable.

Where separation exists, it is also inevitable to find a crowd of verbs and nouns that use *trans* as a suffix: One transits, traverses, transports, transfers, transmits, or transplants; and it is possible to meet traffickers, translators, and traitors, transporters of transients and transgressors in disguise.[8]

In short, the tendency to separate asserts itself. Yet, the opposite force, the one that connects, doesn't just idly watch, but uses even illegal means to assert itself: The weakness of human beings in itself spares them the fundamentalism of nations. At night, when the oversight of nations is weaker, one can cross the border; and there exist expert *passeurs* who know which passes and crossings to take. Every frontier carries within it, like a shadow, its transgression, something that goes against the prohibitions of nations.

The Frontier as Wound

When a country suffers through a war, refugees who live in train cars and out of need crowd its borders, as they do in a beautiful film by Angelopoulos.[9] They are clearly provisional beings, who can be sent back or can dream of going somewhere else, even if their destiny is to remain border-land refugees for the rest of their lives. Countries build and guard lookouts or bar means of communication with the other side while multiplying those with their own military headquarters. Entire garrisons voice their loyalty with every hoisting of the flag, while the river-border separates wedded couples. It is near the borders that, like spontaneous vegetation, the proletariat of history and politics grows, a humbled and offended humanity, victim of the police and of ethnic cleansings,[10] divided by language, religion, and politics, and unified only by its being the waste and residue of power: something that remains on the margins of triumphant rhetoric and which has not yet discovered words capable of reconstructing its thousand, contradictory dreams.

Angelopoulos seems to suggest that it is not by going toward the center of identity and country capitals that we will find the future. In the capitals, where one would think it is possible to find the core of these communities of human beings, there exists instead only its separation from other communities, from those on the other side of the border. This unity, which at times their people praise chorally and with pride, contemporaneously affirms the dis-unity of humanity: It is a unity that, to safely preserve itself, needs frontiers and exclusionary practices. This restricted solidarity, established and at the same time throttled by the *limes* (crossroad), is a sign of the penury in which we live. The triumphant arches and the boulevards to victory, the seemingly innocent celebration of one's "sacred space," silently dig impassable chasms. The barbarians, Constantine Cavafy reminds us,[11] were a solution.

The opposite direction is the one that goes toward the border, a long route along which all becomes less stable and secure, and the univocal meaning of words and signs weakens. There, where even road signs give directions in two languages, all becomes uncertain inasmuch as it redoubles itself. But the debris accumulates near the frontier: Among the harsh diaspora of all the refugees, one finds humanity unified by suffering and by the shipwreck of its dreams. Along the borders shared humanity is divided and torn apart. Angelopoulos contemplates these festering sores and seems to indicate the need for a *promising time*. Not a feeble aesthetic of the Other, but the creation of a strongly rooted belief, in which fraternity acknowledges its daily failures, a wait that could last for eternity or end tomorrow, when a word will come into existence that is unimaginable today. The *wait* makes sense where the laceration is deepest. The title of Angelopoulos's movie, *The Suspended Step of the Stork*, reminds us that storks do not know borders: a metapolitical hint that comes to us from birds.

Universalism Divides Us

But many things oppose this politics of storks. Those who build their own national State force others to wish for and fight to build it: it is a true process of dissemination of frontiers. After having exterminated or driven out the others, everyone will have his/her own "state," the small house whose door is shut on one's neighbor. The dream of the abolition of borders is far from being fulfilled: The young Kurds who are persecuted by three States do not dream of surpassing the limits of borders but to add those of their own national State to the existing ones. Angelopoulos's proletariat is built the same way as Marx's: One becomes a proletarian by misfortune, not by choice; and, as soon as one can, one abandons one's role as a proletarian to save oneself. One does not seek to unify people but to organize one's own domain.

The most effective strategy to weaken the division created by borders is certainly not their abolition by decree. Universalism dreams of a world without borders, but often its faith in its own good reasons leads it to build new confines, different and stronger than the ones it has abolished. The communist dream believed in a world without borders; but in Berlin this world had to be shielded by a twenty-foot wall and, internally, by the barbed wire of the gulags.

This unifying strategy was defeated by the same dividing lines it claimed to surpass, despite the great means it deployed. Marxism toyed with nationalism, thinking it could shrewdly use it, but we all know who ended up toying with whom. Long before the fall of the Berlin Wall, the dream had vanished that morning of 1979 when the armies of two "internationalist" revolutions (China and Vietnam) found themselves armed at the borders, facing each other. That day an entire vocabulary became powerless to name what was happening.

It then becomes natural to ask: Does the possibility to weaken borders even exist outside of dreams and poetry?

The Market, the Media, and the Attack on Protectionist Policies

At first glance, a better answer seems to come from a set of diverse associative forces, quieter and stronger than political ideology: the development of world markets and the growing planetary integration in the global village of the media. The associative capacity of these two processes would seem, at first glance, to weaken and take down borders, uniting the planet. Indeed, one would be tempted to streamline the process the way that postmodern philosophy does, the one great narrative that talks about the end of great narratives. Instead of a missionary universalism (whose idea is always and only to convert), a lay one, mobile and agile, based on trade, mobility and tourism; instead of the autarchic closure of national reporting, the great emporium of *the news*.[12] After all, the first true, nonviolent desecrator of borders was the merchant with his cargo of merchandise and stories: The rule of money and relativism share an intense and ancient relationship. Trade requires more flexible and less violent strategies than conquest. As opposed to evangelizing fundamentalism, trade does not believe there are noble reasons for what it does: It does not propose to convert others, but wants only their agreement on the convenience of its exchanges. The first foreigner we do not fear but only mistrust is the merchant. The spread of exchanges coincides with the mercantile coexistence of bodies: Markets are throngs of unarmed people, the intersection and contamination of individuals ruled by personal interest. The private vices of single sellers-buyers produce the public virtue of free-trade ports, market cities, and life forms based on intersection. This commingling of people has continued to grow first in the tent camps outside city walls, then in the hospitality of homes, and finally in the promiscuous and mysterious humanity of taverns, boardinghouses, and hotels.

Contrary to what Jacques Le Goff believes,[13] the difference between the time of the Church and of the merchant does not lie solely in the success of universal calculability, but especially in its premise: universal fungibility.[14] Whereas the time and space of the Church are based on discontinuity and on the qualitative singularity of times and places, money only differentiates in prices. It links us because it relativizes; it makes everything venial and venal. Merchandise becomes a fetish,[15] only by abolishing ties (and borders) with all other sacred spaces. Money is the *Deus absconditus*[16] of disillusionment.

Conversely, the media bypasses frontiers. This is why the main targets of Islamic fundamentalists in Algeria are satellite dishes. At night, on the roofs of the kasbah, followers of the prophet lurk, destroying those stations that compete with Allah's message. But to what effect? After all, any one among us can figure out from the early shots of a movie whether it is set in New York or San Francisco, Los Angeles or Chicago.

The media's universe performs an operation to a certain extent analogous to the one performed by money: Nothing is out of reach, and all of us become, inevitably, members of a world community built on communicative relations that go through the media. They uproot us from localism, just as money and commerce have uprooted us from the community based on localized personal consumption. At the same time, we become close to very distant people and events, and distant from people and events that are very close to us. Here too, then, the ancient bonds of membership are loosened in favor of a membership without place.[17] The Bosnian horrors reach every home, just as the streets of Algiers and of Central African cities empty out when *Dallas* is on.

It is here, from this pervasive intrusiveness that the new game of frontier multiplication comes into existence. Very often, frontiers are seen as a residual and archaic phenomenon, the unleashing of primordial identifications we are still unable to control or surpass. It is instead a much more contemporaneous one. The open and borderless universe is also a permanently open frontier: The infinite expansion of the mercantile universe exposes us to a contingency that is also theoretically infinite.

The market uproots and tosses us into the unsure universe of competition.[18] We are all thrown into the great, universal religion of the rat race: Uprooted from our cultures, habits, and vices, we are called to the starting line. Economists are the theoreticians of *homo currens*, the knowledgeable doctors who are never tired of repeating that, to stay healthy, we must run at all times of the day and of our lives. Our health depends on how much we run; and our cities are full of pathetic figures that are happy to run even during their free time. This breathless and red-faced religion, this morning or evening prayer recited as we sweat in the shadow of skyscrapers, serves to fill every corner of our mind and to block the idea of an equally legitimate way to live from appearing at our doorsteps.

Why should everybody like this universe? Do we truly think that those who lose every time they play enjoy the game as much as those who always come out the winners? Even inside the mobile universe of the rat race and of competition, there are centers and peripheries, capitals and frontiers, the chosen and the damned. Not all borders are as visible as the ones separating countries: But how many borders are there in a world that opens you to every desire and does not give you the means to satisfy any? Isn't the right of property itself (*ius excludendi omnes*)[19] full of borders, so much better protected the greater the riches to which they prevent access? Around a property are there not, just as clearly as along the borders between states, obstructions, checkpoint guards, German shepherds, walls, alarm systems, and barbed wire? What happens when everything is presented as if it were at your beck and call, but you then realize that the most you can do is to watch others celebrate? What happens when, after hiding for nights on end in the hold of a ship and having debarked as clandestine pilgrim in the new holy lands of consumerism, you end up in one of the world's many Bronxes?

Uprooting or the fear of it, the collapse of all the old *protections* or safety nets, and the ruinous transformation into loneliness of the freedom *homo currens* once had prepare us to ask for protection, be it simply to protect financial interests or our identity. Nationalist and fundamentalist leaders offer an answer to this question, a simple and cutthroat answer to an obvious problem: The Western model is neither universal nor universalizing, and pretending to make it so dooms the overall majority of humanity to become extras in a production controlled by others. Fatherland and religion *tie together* human beings (setting them in opposition, as may be, with other fatherlands and religions), and remove them from unlimited contingency, from an insecurity that is directly proportional to the dimensions of the marketplace. The menace of universal uprooting leads to the search for roots and to the (not disinterested) offer of roots by those intellectuals and politicians who belong to the areas most exposed to this uprooting. Tradition does not arrive from the past through inertia, but rather is an invention of the present to control and reduce unlimited contingency.[20]

Uprooting and the West

The word *uprooting* (which we borrow from Simone Weil)[21] examines from a harsher perspective a phenomenon that, if observed from a different angle, constitutes one of the great prides of Europe and of the West: *freedom*. This is where the immanent tension with the border that cuts across our culture comes into existence: Every limit ties us down; every root holds us, suffocating our freedom to be human. The right to intellectual and territorial mobility, the ability to enter and leave any relationship that might restrain us as if we belonged to it, this giving hospitality and respect to everyone as long as they belong most generally to the human race, this holiness-transcendence of the individual—these beliefs are so big and important that the West that created them struggles to see their other side.

Indeed, freedom, like every other God, possesses fields where, at night, it empties out the trash, where those pathologies that are its birth-children (but which it refuses to see as her own) pile on top of each other. This should not surprise us. Every culture thinks that those aspects that are recognized as its strengths correspond to its true essence, while those for which it is constantly reproached are contingent and accidental. The latter are either considered irrelevant or are treated as provisional phenomena that, with some attention and some patience, will be eliminated sooner or later.

Freedom and uprooting discover they are siblings, born from the one thrust that has severed humanity from its ties. However, this double game has two very different endings. There are those who handle contingency and insecurity very well, those who are sure they will perform every duty well, because they are "the best," *born to win*[22]—for them, it is easy not to have roots, because they will always receive the welcome that is given to those who excel; they will be marketable in any market. They are those whom Robert K. Merton, in a famous essay, calls the *cosmopolitans*, those who are less tied to a community because they are "conscious that they can succeed in other communities."[23] But there are also those who, on the contrary, will never succeed or will succeed only in American movies from the forties, or in Sunday homilies: those who are *born to lose*. For these, uprooting prevails over freedom, inasmuch as the latter translates in a merciless and fierce exposure to the contingencies of the world. Every so often those who sing the praise of freedom awake from their dogmatic slumber:[24] They then discover that humanity allows itself to be seduced by dangerous Sirens, by the nostalgia for strong ties, by a desire for community that curtails freedom and tolerance and enters into conflict with the Other, the extraneous, whether it be Muslim, Hebrew, African, or Turk.

Europe had found in the "social" State the instrument to render compatible freedom and security: It was a secularized and materialistic instrument that subtracted some resources from the market and from production to allocate them for the protection of its weakest members. Now it seems (probably because the weakest were not always the ones who took advantage of them) that this road can no longer be traveled: So one begins to see a return to the old protectionisms, those that are founded on ethnic or religious affiliations. Freedom produces uprooting, which in turn creates the request for protection. The latter, however, changes shapes: instead of *development* and *money*, what comes back into fashion is the sacrificial toughness of *the solidarities of belonging* (religion or nationhood), if and where a *criminal economy* has not already established itself.

The Universal of Translation

The West should stop looking with facile and haughty horror to the *barbarism* of fundamentalism, nationalism, and criminal economies, and try instead to fight them by controlling its own fundamentalism, the one tied to the economy. Only by restraining *homo currens* can we stop the uprooting and the reactionary uses of tradition, its violent and smothering return. To be aware of the dark and aggressive side of one's culture means to finally abandon ethnocentrism. There are many ways to reach God, a plurality of tongues to name him. If every culture took stock of its own dark side and of the poisoned fruits it produces (which it likes to disown, ascribing them to others), we could begin to talk. As long as the *homines* produced by other cultures will be considered only intermediate steps on the way to attain *homo currens*'s status, it will be perfectly fair for the losers not to want to shake hands with those who have chosen to play the game they always win.

From reciprocal translation and a level playing field for different cultures, we might instead manage to broaden the cultural heritage of humanity and create the premises for a planetary conscience in tune with our "community of terrestrial destiny,"[25] an *elevated crossroad of freedoms and protections.* The West must face the extremely difficult (but not new) task of mistrusting its noble and universalistic desire to come to the rescue; and it must not think that its institutions are a neutral field on which cultures engage and challenge each other on equal terms.

I would like to conclude with a personal reflection that is the result of spending my summer vacations in Greece: It is probably a tangle of beliefs more than an organic and careful reflection. I have always noted that wherever tourists arrive, religious people disappear: Wonderful and no longer remote monasteries, inhabited by a few surviving monks, are consumed daily by thousands of tourists (including myself). There is always something bitter each time we return from these tours: the feeling that, regardless of our tasting everything, an earnest and important flavor is missing from our palate and from our knowledge. The premise for every overture lies in the awareness that we cannot know a place, and that it will evade us and our experience, if we cannot understand that our being-there, in itself, could constitute an outrage. Indeed, traveling is at the same time an incredible way to know the Other and an unconscious series of desecrations. Our free and light mobility is *also* an intrusion, a transgression, and a fault. It should never be considered the best way to see, a winning epistemological move; instead, it should move within its own contradiction, being faithful to it to the end. We should embrace relativism to the nth degree: it should be capable of making itself relative, of discovering itself stuck in a root at the precise moment when it feels free and in the open, beyond all confines. There is no single solution, just the desire to keep the problem alive.

CHAPTER 4

The Fundamentalism of the Rat Race

"Well, in our country," said Alice, still panting a little,
"you'd generally get to somewhere else—if you ran very fast
for a long time, as we've been doing."
"A slow sort of country!" said the Queen. "Now, here, you see,
it takes all the running you can do, to keep in the same place.
If you want to get somewhere else, you must run at least
twice as fast as that!"

LEWIS CARROLL, *Through the Looking Glass*

Beyond Cultural Truisms

The question is inevitable: When we talk about relationships "between" cultures, do we in fact place ourselves outside them, like an unconnected and impartial judge (as the word "between" would suggest), or do we play the old game where one of the sides disguises itself as the third? If I start off with this typically spiteful argument (used so often against relativism), I am not doing it to blackmail those who are trying to build bridges by accusing them of double-crossing; instead, I am attempting to unmoor the discussion about the relationship between different cultures from an understanding so banal that, in most cases, it keeps the discussion floating in the midst of a preachy and impotent methodology. For example, those who have at heart tolerance and understanding between cultures must condemn the terrorism that seems to have become the privileged fighting method of Islamic fundamentalists. The first duty of any intellectual who is confronted by the harshness of a fanaticism that kills the most open-minded and creative human beings, and by the "resentment" that conceives their works only as betrayal and sin, is to publicly condemn them and show solidarity with the victims. However, this is just our first duty. Instead, today it seems to have become the only one, as it exhausts almost everything that one might do at the level of conceptual elaboration in deference to neoliberal ideas that seem to constitute the most evolved frontier of thought.

Indeed, today we proclaim the superiority of liberal principles as a cultural truism that resembles another equally and similarly boring cultural truism, the one that, about twenty years ago, allowed people to believe that, by shifting "more to the left," they could gain the best perspective on the world. I do not wish to question here the value of a liberal understanding of politics and of the State, nor do I want to ignore the harsh rebukes that history has bestowed on the many glib theories that claimed to have "surpassed" liberalism. I do, however, want to avoid thought from stopping even before it has begun to walk toward a face-to-face that ignores the dramatic complexity of the conflicts that is being played out. Using (ironically and without nostalgia) a metaphor that old cultural platitudes employed repeatedly against the one that dominates today, we want to descend from the plane of circulation, where all subjects seem the same, to the plane of production, where differences are instead evident.

In other words, I would like to discuss thematically the relationship between cultures without avoiding the areas of greatest conflict. More specifically, I would like to emphasize a cluster of questions that are closely connected with each other. Can one reflect on the relationship between cultures while neglecting the negative conditioning that the stronger culture exercises on the weaker one? Is the cultural model of the West, with its power and with its constant tendency toward expansion, capable of tolerating societies governed by different organizational principles and by cultural models not founded on constant dynamics and on unlimited production? Conversely, can a cultural model founded on parameters that differ from production and consumerist models resist nowadays the cultural (but also economic and political) attacks of the West?

These are not disinterested questions, nor do we wish to organize a World Wildlife Fund refuge for survivors of noncapitalist cultures that is financed by guided tours from developed countries (even if it could be a splendid trick devised by market laws). The problem is not archeological but political. If in fact, as many claim, the Western cultural model and way of life are not reproducible, and the idea of extending its income and consumption levels to the rest of the planet is a dangerous utopia, we must ask: Is the protection of nonproductive cultural models an unrealistic nostalgia, or is it instead the fundamental problem that humanity must face for decades to come?

Deculturation

A discussion of the relationship between cultures must therefore take its point of departure from the analysis of an unbalanced relationship, from what Serge Latouche, in a superb book, has defined the "Westernization of the World." In that book, Latouche reintroduced the concept of deculturation to describe all those situations in which the encounter between two cultures "does not lead to a balanced exchange but to a massive flow in one direction, the receiving culture is invaded, threatened in its very being, and can be seen as the victim of actual aggression."[1]

Nowadays, the dominant pattern of deculturation coincides with the imposition of "economic development" values even on countries that are different from the West, as they are forced to internalize the "bookkeeping terrorism" that corresponds to the essence of business logic. When nonindustrialized countries choose to call themselves such (or "developing," "underdeveloped," "backward"), they have basically lost their cultural identity and have begun judging themselves from the outside: They have started down a path that will lead them, in the most favorable of circumstances, to become a poor copy of the model they are chasing.

Reflecting on the "alternate answers" that a society can give to the pressures or challenges of a "superior, external force," Arnold J. Toynbee believed they could be reduced to two basic models, antithetical to each other: Herodianism and Zealotism.[2] The Herodian takes the Other as model and proposes to imitate him; the Zealot, confronted with an unfavorable relationship and fearing that defeat and humiliation will follow an attempt to imitate the Other, turns back upon an "archaic" and closed defense of his identity. Toynbee who, between the two, obviously prefers the first, does not nevertheless hide its limits.

> It is at this point that the two inherent weaknesses of "Herodianism" reveal themselves. The first of them is that "Herodianism" is, ex hypothesi, mimetic and not creative, so that, even if it succeeds, it is apt simply to enlarge the quantity of the machine-made products of the imitated society instead of releasing new creative energies in human souls. The second weakness is that this uninspiring success, which is the best that "Herodianism" has to offer, can bring salvation—even mere salvation in this world— only to a small minority of any community which takes the "Herodian" path. The majority cannot look forward even to becoming passive members of the imitated civilization's ruling class. Their destiny is to swell the ranks of the imitated civilization's proletariat.[3]

The Herodian is destined to chase forever. He has located outside of himself every evaluative criterion and will become, more and more so, a caricature of what he is chasing. In fact, in the best of hypotheses, he will be able to imitate satisfactorily his model, running the risk of isolating himself from the masses of those "left out," those who, being unable to "imitate," are open to all resentments and thus to the radical and simplifying appeal of Zealotism. Even though these thoughts are over half a century old (1947), they continue to have incredible currency. To these, we should add a further clarification: Herodianism represents, even in its feebleness, a somewhat successful example of imitation of the West (indeed, Toynbee is referring to the revolution of the "young Turks"). Thus, it describes cases of successful modernization, even if limited and unstable. It works, then, only for a very limited segment of non-European and non-Western countries, while the great majority of other countries faces a much more dramatic situation.

I would like to examine two other ways in which countries respond to the process of deculturation. The first accelerates the process of decomposition of the subaltern culture by optimizing everything that allows it to survive under the new conditions. The result of this optimization is a response that we might label as the prostitution of the subaltern culture. Clearly, not every entry by a culture into the world markets, and not all attempts to transform one's natural resources into merchandise, are examples of prostitution. The latter only occurs when the merchandizing of life radically transforms every parameter of a society and sweeps away old cultural and moral bonds without building new ones: In doing so, it spreads on a massive scale social pathologies (absolute poverty, deviance, willingness to take any job just to have an income) that modify the equilibrium between legal and illegal economies. The exponential growth of the latter is the most successful way that some of these countries have to function on the world markets, in order to offer an income to whole segments of their population. The growth of widespread and capillary criminal economies represents the surest and fastest way for many of the world's Souths to establish a foothold in the international economy, since they cannot do so otherwise. The world Mafias, this strange hybrid of modernity and tradition, constitute the natural ruling class for this type of entrance into the world markets. The poisoning of tradition and its recovery through corrupt and predatory models are the price that the frailest societies pay to survive under the new conditions. As Hubert Prolongeau recognizes, the manifold activities related to drug trafficking allowed Colombia, in the eighties, "to stay afloat while others sank."[4] Conversely, the phenomenon gains ground anywhere a State, as it falls apart, is no longer able to fight criminal powers (one need only think of the European countries in the former Communist East, from Russia to Albania): On the international markets, where one expects the arrival of the new bourgeoisies, arrive instead, early and with more power, the new, emerging mafias.

The reaction of the opposite sign is what Toynbee calls Zealotism, but which we, with less imagination, would call fundamentalism. This reaction is bent on safeguarding the identity of the subaltern culture by reasserting its value, and by rescuing it from its condition of inferiority through a sectarian reaffirmation of the present-day validity of tradition, as well as by demonizing the dominant culture. This answer, widespread especially in Islamic countries, represents a powerful element of unification and solidarity, one that fuels the belief that it can provide a global alternative to the West. This polemical resistance, obviously, does not only oppose the colonizing foreigner, but also, and more clearly, those segments of the population that have opened up to a relationship with the culture of the dominant country: primarily the ruling classes, the politicians, the entrepreneurs, and the "Westernized" intellectuals. In Arab countries, terrorist activities against "betraying" intellectuals are nothing more than the latest evidence of this reaction, which proposes to rebuild the integrity of one's cultural identity by cutting off those parts that have been "infected" by the Western Satan.

It is necessary to note, however, that fundamentalism is not the first answer to the challenge raised by the West. Until the mid-sixties, Arab and near-Eastern elites (one need only think of Egypt, Algeria, Syria, or Iran) had all laid their bets, even if with a different level of commitment, on forced modernization (Herodianism); but they were all defeated. Fundamentalism is thus a makeshift solution that occurred only following the failures and ruinous uprooting induced by modernization. Where a culture can only produce an often-corrupt caricature of the model it seeks to imitate, it is easy to retreat to the defense of one's identity. Having tried to imitate and to tag along unsuccessfully, it is to be expected that, to regain our self-confidence, we might demonize those who, for a long time, had subjugated and dispossessed us of our identity.

Competition Breeds Losers

One might object that this description is too pessimistic. This dilemma is not unavoidable, because one can leave a dependent relationship! Deculturation is not a destiny: We can react to it with an original creative effort that grafts our country's history onto the flow of modernity and discovers a new use for ancient traditions in their relationship with world markets. In other words, one might suggest that, on the one hand, Herodianism holds sway over a greater expanse; and, on the other hand, Herodianism itself might be a tormented and difficult, but at times surmountable, stage of development. It is a reasonable objection based on the evidence provided both by countries that have gradually risen in the international hierarchy (like Japan and, trailing it at the proper distance, Korea, Singapore,

Hong Kong, and Taiwan), and by the recent dynamism of great countries like China. But the objection must face three of its own.

First, we should be more cautious in projecting into the future growth trends of non-Western countries (like China or even India), and remember that in the past decades they have been overrated and based on ephemeral and even one-time events (one can remember Brazil in the seventies, but also Khrushchev's dream of "overhauling" the West as presented in the Soviet Union and other socialist countries in the early sixties).

Second, it is not redundant to remind ourselves that the view of international competition as a race capable of creating shifting and mobile hierarchies is idyllic: If these growth trends were confirmed and truly started to challenge the dominant economies (but as one grows, one must compete in more advanced sectors of the economy and the climb becomes steeper), the latter would not just sit back and watch. Do we truly believe that their improper responses would be limited to elbowing the competition as happens in Olympic races? In truth, more frequently, these situations have resulted in harsh conflicts or even wars. World competition is a sum-zero relationship, in which one cannot increase the number of winners. Not only is it difficult to climb up; but those already ahead try to do everything possible to keep the others trailing behind them. Every competition, as such, results in few winners and many losers.

Third, theoretical objections, by focusing on whether this assimilation works or not, deflect attention from the main problem, which is the imposition on everyone to modernize. The relationship between cultures happens on a tilted slope, because one assumes that there exist universal imperatives. In reality, the relationship is based on the imposition of the cultural model of the few on everyone else: It is a relationship in which one culture dictates to all others how they must be. So if it is reasonable to think that, in some cases, it might be possible to escape the choice between prostitution and fundamentalism by joining capitalist modernity without disastrous imbalances, it is equally reasonable to believe that the imposition of a single cultural imperative ("You WILL modernize!") might cause a planet-wide uprooting, where the instances of creative and winning responses are rare. This leaves us with one very profound difference between the poverty that preceded the uprooting and the current one: The latter has learned to compare itself to others and can never forget the despair and anger of those who have earned the label of "loser" only from this emphasis on competition.

We might thus sum up the situation: Few countries have joined the leaders, while those that cannot close the gap wrestle with ever-increasing difficulties, because those who cannot keep up with the leaders not only are left behind but see the distance between them increase. Among those who are the most uprooted and defeated, some react by prostituting themselves, others by choosing the fundamentalist struggle against the lifestyle and culture of the richest countries. In the former we see an increase in the overall clout of criminal powers, illegal economies as an entryway into world markets, and the rise of socially disruptive phenomena (witness the conditions of children in Brazil). In the latter, the defense of one's identity is tied to capillary repression, to the closure of cultural frontiers and to the grotesque demonizing of the Other. Where previously it had been the norm to meet and unite beyond religious or ethnic affiliations, the violent hygiene of separation and "cleansing" now returns.

The Fundamentalism of the Rat Race

If we can at least accept in its main outlines the picture I have painted, then any discussion about the relationships between cultures that avoids the extremely rigid nature of their power structure runs the risk of pointing the analysis in the wrong direction. Let me try to explain myself.

In general, discussions about the relationship between cultures follow a well-worn and familiar script that revolves around the (great) theme of tolerance and the relationship with the Other. It thus happens that people divide between those who believe that one should respect in toto cultures that are "Other," and those who believe that the acceptance of intolerant practices—or practices that are damaging to the autonomy and physical safety of individuals (such as infibulation, polygamy, the stoning of adulterers, physical punishment, and death penalty)—runs counter to the principles of tolerance.

I do not wish to underestimate these discussions, but I believe that they should be understood in the context of the power relationship between Western culture and other cultures, between a culture founded on the primacy of unlimited production and cultures whose core and balance are to be found elsewhere. The pathologies of deculturation I have discussed are not brought about by the intrinsic limits of certain cultures but by the forced insertion of a dominant model that commands them to change or perish. Prostitution and fundamentalist drift are two opposite and complementary responses (adaptive and repulsive) to an unbearable imbalance. As a consequence, before we can address the contentious issue we alluded to earlier (and certainly not because we wish to forget it), we need to add to the topics of discussion the intolerance of a model that forces all others to change in order to survive. This not only because, in discussing the relationship between cultures, it is fair to foreground the intolerance of the strongest, the one that has made itself the "structure" of the world in the belief that it can camouflage its motives, but also because the imbalance that this relationship creates forces weaker cultures into deformed and grotesque parodies of themselves. As we have already shown, fundamentalism is not just a form of traditionalism. Instead, it is also a reactive and charged reaffirmation of ancient customs that expunges from within patterns of tolerance originally present in the tradition; patterns that fundamentalism—caught as it is in its own warrior logic—sees only as subaltern deference to the enemy.

We should, therefore, first question the aseptic fundamentalism of development. Without its wane, it will be very difficult to encourage the wane of others. But in order for this waning to occur a lengthy process of cultural transformation needs to take place: We need to stop the process by which Western cultural identity has been gradually reduced to the imperative of unbridled expansion; and we must believe that the resistance to commodification and the technical pervasiveness of all aspects of life will not be seen as an archaism, the resentment of intellectuals who are behind the times, or the testimonial request of a pope. In other words, we must find not only beyond the West, but also inside it a hard and unyielding core of principles that will allow us to fight effectively against the steady advance of commodification. Here we must address delicate and unpopular issues that sooner or later we will have to face: Nothing seems to resist universal commodification anymore, as everything is for sale, from bodies to organs, from arms all the way to one's image and to the news. Science itself does not seem to acknowledge fetters to its development: More than once we have heard talk about the impossibility of limiting "scientific progress" and experimentation. Trying to set limits to development is like the embarrassing point on the day's agenda that everybody wants to avoid by postponing its discussion to the next meeting. Indeed, facing the issue of limits would open us up to a new and difficult cultural phase that, despite its urgency, does not seem anywhere imminent. Paul Valéry explained the reason why in a very simple and effective manner: "Nothing . . . is more difficult for us to conceive than limits set to intellectual fancies, and moderation in the use of material power."[5]

If it is true that our favorite activity is to "make the universe too small for our movements," controlling the absolutism of development means going to the heart of our identity to question its rhetoric of infinity. Then, as in a trauma of youth, we might inadvertently discover the intimate relationship between the absolutism of development and certain values that, in public, feign not to recognize it by looking in a different direction. This is where we discover ancient and painful repressions, questions that we would gladly avoid: Can a society confederate the unlimited growth of freedoms without an equally unlimited increase in its production and in the "enormous collection of commodities"? Is commodification an alien monster, or is it rather the inevitable condition and consequence of increasing freedoms? Do noble and strict ideas of freedom exist that might avoid residual costs and dumping grounds in a different world? And, finally, could such a working hypothesis be popular?

Going back to our initial problem, we might conclude: The duty of every intellectual is to condemn the homicidal terrorism of fundamentalists and to save all the voices that, within other cultures, have tried to dialogue with ours. Yet, by itself this stance is insufficient. The West can take a decisive step against the fundamentalisms of others only by starting to deconstruct its own, the straitjacket it has foisted on itself and on the whole world by establishing the law of the competitive rat race. Repression adapts its guises to different cultures: We might want to ask which guise it assumes in our society and who today is in a position analogous to the one occupied by the treacherous intellectuals against whom the fundamentalists direct their rage. Maybe all the talk about markets, their ties to production cycles, the unending checks on the productivity of work and knowledge, or even the smiling glorification of a purchasable world that leaps at us from the walls of our cities, will provide us with the clues to the internal characteristics of our fundamentalism, to its "organic intellectuals" and its victims. The straitjacket I am talking about resides in the pervasiveness of the business metaphor, in the dogmas of international competition dispensed by the priests of the GDP, in the systemic hedonism of consumerism, in the apology of mass rudeness. Fighting against this soundproof and beguiling imprisonment becomes more difficult by the day, and those who stand against it are accused of being irresponsible or men of letters (thus acknowledging that literature is free to tell the most difficult truths). Our fundamentalism does not kill: It outmodes, dismisses, and banishes from the market. It has other temples, breviaries, punishments, and hells. Who are you if you do not privatize, if you do not have something exclusively yours that you can lean on and which provides your freedom with a concrete hold?

Only by unmasking the repression camouflaged in the cold fundamentalism of competition and in the restless religion of ownership and consumption can the dialogue be again on equal terms, thus preventing one culture from having to choose between surrendering its dignity and demonizing the Other. Any strategy against other people's fundamentalism that avoids this issue will face increasing difficulties and the inability to help those it wishes to defend. This effort does not run counter to our identity, and the person making this point does not place himself between cultures, but inside one of them. The most universal and coherent act of our universalism should consist in recognizing our own pathologies and our own biases.

PART III

The Friction of Thought

CHAPTER 5

Albert Camus: The Need
for Southern Thought

History and Nihilism

God is not center stage, but it is not true that everything is allowed; on the contrary, the exact opposite is true: "If God does not exist, nothing is permitted."[1] God is not present, but there is the sun ("At the center of my work there is an invincible sun"),[2] and nihilism does not win in any of its incarnations, whether it is the debilitated and tired one, or the cynical and imperious one. At the center of Camus's thought, and even earlier at the center of his life, there exists a proud and responsible behavior where eclipsing God does not mark the beginning of nihilist celebrations but of greater responsibilities, precisely because it is without tutors or masters. The light that illuminates the field is neither the light of religious revelation nor that of enlightened reason, but the ancient and natural light of the sun, a light that owes nothing to progress and is free of every theology or philosophy of history. Maturity means not having to rely any longer on a providential concept of history, nor having to accept any longer its justifications. It means becoming aware that we have no guarantees that the wind that fills our sails is pushing us in the right direction. There are men whose course is always and only given by the direction of the wind and, therefore, always navigate rapidly, downwind, even if this leads to awful places. Instead, we must hold the course even when the wind blows in the opposite direction, when we can only sail under the wind or by rowing, and we despair of being able to reach the shore. Camus's philosophy is antiopportunistic but does not have the haughty tone of those who hate opportunism because they cannot stand the pungent smell of the common men.

The absence of God and the freedom from every theology or philosophy of history does not condemn men to an eternal state of mourning: The sun does not abandon them, and the earth is not a fallback option vis-à-vis the sky, but rather the true stage of man. Turning upside down the canon that Christianity and Marxism have in common (both optimistic with regard to the final end of history but pessimistic toward humanity), on a number of occasions Camus declares himself pessimistic toward history and optimistic toward humankind:[3] If history is not the history of salvation, revolution, or progress, and nothing can be expected from it, then the only option lies in humanity and its dignity.

For Camus, the aversion to the religion of history is not a secondary theme, the opportunity for a brilliant polemic; rather, it is a decisive juncture. Camus's reflection on history and historicism is certainly full of gross simplifications, but it is precisely its summary character, its disregard for distinctions and nuances, its keeping the distance from a subtle respect for the "Spirit of the times" that makes it interesting.

Commenting on Hegel's statement that "only the modern city offers the terrain in which [the spirit] can be conscious of itself," Camus affirms with indignation: "Significant. This is the time of big cities. The world has been amputated of a part of its truth, of what makes its permanence and its equilibrium: nature, the sea, etc. There is consciousness only in city streets!"[4]

This spirit that scours the streets of the city celebrates as a conquest the loss of every root on earth, the removal of origins. The primacy of history implies forgetting about nature (for Hegel "nature is abstract. What is concrete is the mind"),[5] dismissing it and the constraints that it imposes on the power of man. The passion for history and the exaltation of technology are undistinguishable and belong to the same lack of moderation: "As human works have gradually come to cover the vast spaces where the world was asleep, . . . peopling the deserts, subdividing the beaches, and even erasing the sky with flights of planes, . . . simultaneously (and for the same reason) the feeling for history has gradually covered the feeling for nature in the hearts of men."[6]

This unbridled protagonism of humankind coincides with the substitution of the "silent natural creation" with the "human creation, hideous and flashing, resounding with revolutionary and warlike clamors, humming with factories and trains."[7] To have torn creation from the hands of the creator, to have lost the sense of moderation and beauty and, with it, the realization that all the clamoring is not worth "the fleeting scent of the wild rose, the olive grove, the beloved dog,"[8] is a step full of consequences. In polemic with Sartre, Camus states:

> It seems that to write a poem about spring today would be to serve capitalism. I am not a poet, but I should delight in such a work without mental reservation, if it were beautiful. One serves mankind all together or not at all. And if man needs bread and justice, and if we must do the necessary to satisfy that need, he also needs pure beauty, which is the bread of his heart. The rest is not serious.[9]

A liberation founded on this exclusion is so obsessed with itself that it is destined to lose it way. The outcomes of idealism are necessarily totalitarian because humankind's separation from nature situates it exclusively in the sphere of history, in the solipsistic kingdom of that which it itself has produced, where every limit becomes crossable, provisional, and surmountable. Totalitarianism, then, is not an incidental outcome of idealism because the latter, by pulling nature into its activities, sets the premises for the abolition of every limit to the will to power and plunges humanity in the dream of a world where the absolute and triumphant protagonism of the Spirit is celebrated.

Thus, even for Camus there exists a *German ideology* to unmask and fight. However, this ideology is no longer the frail target of Marx's arrows but, on the contrary, it implicates Marx himself because his heart lies in the absolute triumph of immanence that finds its highest expression in Hegel's philosophy. The polemic against *formal virtues* and *beautiful souls*[10] is the point through which history absorbs, annulling it, every transcendence, the passage point through which Hegel's *panlogism* and *pantragism* affirm themselves.[11] History hands itself over to power: It is no longer judged according to a criterion that transcends it, but becomes the judge itself. The belief according to which "only the absence of activity is innocent, the existence of a stone and not even the existence of a child"[12] (a thought that Camus could also share) leads Hegel to exalt effectiveness, to place reason on the bandwagon of force, the greatest force, the force that prevails. *German ideology* has invented, through the constitution of historic thought, "its negation of all principles":[13] Which historicism will ever be able to judge the victors?

The contempt for *formal morality* culminates in the Empire: Humanism grants itself the right to Terror just as Prometheus substitutes his own statues for those of the gods. The liquefaction (in its literal sense of rendering liquid, taking away solidity and capacity to resist) of every form of transcendence leads to the worship of the transcendence of power.

Historic thought was to deliver man from subjection to a divinity; but this liberation demanded of him the most absolute subjection to historical evolution. Then man takes refuge in the concept of the permanence of the party in the same way that he formerly prostrated himself before the altar. That is why the era which dares to claim that it is the most rebellious that has ever existed only offers a choice of various types of conformity. The real passion of the twentieth century is servitude.[14]

The idea of the unlimited feasibility of the world (of nature and man) that celebrates itself as liberation from the prison of natural bonds discovers with terror that it has de-legitimized every limit, that it is a racing car with broken brakes. It no longer has the tools to stop the practice of the will to power: "The empire supposes a negation and a certainty: the certainty of the infinite malleability of man and the negation of human nature. . . . If there is no human nature, then the malleability of man is, in fact, infinite."[15]

Rescuing humanity from natural fixity, which had seemed the way to free it from ancient subjections while extending its freedoms, instead delivers people defenseless in the hands of the *elites*, and turns them into wax to mould according to the shapes of dream. The critique of *German ideology* is, first of all, a critique of the idea of the infinite malleability of man, the quest for materials resistant to the will to power and for a measuring stick that is not the one of effectiveness and success. And the only point of resistance capable of slowing down the ever more irresistible pace of history is faithfulness in the idea of human nature: "life itself in preference to what is forgotten in the world of reality, in other words the purely mechanical and blind aspects of the world."[16] Therefore, there exists a solid base, though it has been discredited by idealism, on which to anchor the resistance to all the attempts to subject mankind. It is this point of resistance, this out-and-out foundation that differentiates between *revolt* and *revolution*, and allows the first to contain the totalizing and totalitarian celebration of historicity. Mind you: The idea of a human nature is necessary to the revolt but does not force human beings in the cast of an unjust order. The man in revolt is, first of all, "a man who says no," but "this no affirms the existence of a frontier." Camus's polemic against history and his appeal to the common nature of mankind never aim at a reconciliation with the given. The freedom of revolt is born out of a dissonance with the quiet self-reproduction of the world, out of fracture and attrition with it, since this freedom does not feel any nostalgia for the ancient transcendence. On the contrary: Between the old transcendence of God and history's "modern" one, it is possible to see more than opposition, continuity and complicity.

Revolt and Moderation

If God is not center stage, it is also because Camus's revolt is a *metaphysical revolt*, having come up against something that is always there for humankind to see: the suffering of the innocent. The existence of such suffering is radically irreconcilable with the existence of God and especially with the idea of a just and omnipotent God. The book of Job, the first grandiose document of the *metaphysical revolt* within religion itself, is there to show that the rift in the universe of meaning is an ancient one, and that God and his defenders have had to measure themselves with it for centuries, often with awkwardness and through third-rate arguments. But if we can allow that, in that book, Job deceives himself or is guilty of presumption regarding his own innocence, how can we accept the suffering of children? What history of salvation or of emancipation, what historical mission can justify the suffering of even a single innocent? Doesn't the wait for a time when justice will be restored imply a passive acceptance and even a multiplication of the horrors of the present? This is precisely the argument that Ivan Karamazov chooses to explain his rejection of God to his brother Alyosha who is incurably locked into his faith: nothing can justify that suffering and no one has the power to forgive its maker.

> And if the sufferings of children go to swell the sum of sufferings which was necessary to pay for truth, then I protest that the truth is not worth such a price [. . .]. Besides, too high a price is asked for harmony; it's beyond our means to pay so much to enter on it. And so I hasten to give back my entrance ticket and if I am a honest man I am bound to give it back as soon as possible.[17]

"Camus était Ivan Karamazov,"[18] wrote Jean Grenier.[19] Indeed Ivan Karamazov's rebellion against the suffering of the innocent and the justification he gives are themes that Albert Camus addresses on many occasions, a constant motive in his work that becomes central in *The Plague*.[20] The agony and death of a child constitute a crucial episode in the novel, the moment when a priest, Father Paneloux, must measure himself against the absolute absence of justification for the death of an innocent. The clergyman, who is devastated when faced with a pain without guilt, shortly thereafter falls ill to the disease and dies, a victim of his engagement in the fight against the plague, engagement that is rendered even more radical and reckless by the desire not to survive the child, by the incapacity to handle the contradiction between the faith in the existence of a just and omnipotent God and the unanswerable death rattles of a child.

Doctor Rieux, the lay counterpart to Paneloux, knows all along, just as Camus does, that "creation is imperfect" because it is traversed by *divine arbitrariness*, by events whose cruelty is so evident to eliminate from the beginning the illusion that humanity can count on someone beyond and above itself. Humanity certainly cannot modify creation, but it can do something more than what Ivan Karamazov does, something more than return the ticket to wander without light and direction. Indeed, desperation vis-à-vis the silence and absence of God, and the anguish of metaphysical revolt, open the way for a humanism that too easily can turn into Terror and transform rebellion into murder. Camus's concept of revolt is contiguous with but also very different from Ivan's rebellion: The latter is desperate and without remedy because it lives walled up inside the triumph of the "no," and the multiplication of these "nos" does not lead toward a single "yes." The same obscure limit is perceived by Paul Nizan who in *Aden Arabie*, immediately after having recalled with Alain that "to think is to say no," feels the need to clarify: "But only the spirit of Evil says no eternally. The time will come when the mind will no longer fear the things it believes in; then man will be ashamed to have remained on the defensive so long."[21]

Conversely, revolt "says yes and no at once," a "no that leans upon a yes," inasmuch as "it only refused one aspect of reality while simultaneously affirming another."[22] The "yes" of revolt lies in the recovery of that which unites human beings and, by uniting them, reduces their fragility. Human nature acquires here a precise physiognomy that is far from any humanistic rhetoric. Nothing allows human beings to escape from a fragile and insecure condition; but it is possible for them, on the one hand, to avoid adding the victims of *human arbitrariness* to those of *divine arbitrariness*,[23] and, on the other, to rescue from *divine arbitrariness* the greatest possible number of innocent victims. The doctor is the symbol of "the only indisputable human community there is, the community in the face of death."[24] This is not an exaltation of technology, a fall into the superstitious belief that every limit is provisional, changeable, surmountable; or even being in awe of the new divinity of progress. It is rather the opposite: It is precisely the desire to confront the truth of the plague, a desire to confront disease and death that allows human beings to rediscover themselves as brothers, to form a community. Doctor Rieux is not an optimist and knows that he is destined to "never ending defeat,"[25] just like Sisyphus. But the experience of one's limits, far from being a defeat, is the privileged antidote against any intoxication of omnipotence.

Fraternity in Guilt

The human nature Camus speaks about, the nature in whose name revolt is legitimate, possesses another level of solidarity that is contiguous with and related to the one that comes from facing death together. No human being is so innocent to think it can judge others, and dispose of their life and destiny: Those who proclaim themselves innocent are asking to become judges of others and are working to build a gradation of order, a power structure. Albert Camus, whose "Greek heart" feels removed from the prophetic aspects of Christianity,[26] nevertheless gives it credit for a painful wisdom.

> In short, the Gospel is realistic, whereas people think it impossible to put into practice. It knows that man cannot be pure. But he can make the effort of recognizing his impurity; in other words, of pardoning. . . . Criminals are always judges. . . . The only ones who can condemn absolutely innocent. . . . This is why God must be absolutely innocent.[27]

But the God that lightheartedly allows us to practice the butchering of meaning cannot be innocent. The idea of *mediation* that Christianity introduces by breaking the harsh transcendence of the Hebrew God seems to Camus like an admission of guilt on the part of that God. Not even the Christ of the *Fall*[28] can avoid this guilt since He is tormented by the memory of a massacre of children caused by his entrance into history.

But the impossibility of innocence affirmed by Camus is very different from the one enunciated by Hegel: Whereas Hegel's call for complicity flattens his assessment about force, Camus's leads to the discovery of the brotherhood of men. In the opening page of *Reflections on the Guillotine*, Camus describes an execution that his father had witnessed in Algiers a few years before his death and the birth of Albert. The trial was followed with great interest because it pertained to a crime that had greatly shaken public opinion, a multiple homicide where even children had been murdered. The accused (whose guilt was not in doubt) had been sentenced to beheading. Camus's father had gotten up in the middle of the night to witness the execution but, having returned home distraught,

> [he] refused to speak, threw himself on the bed and, suddenly, began to vomit. He had just discovered the reality concealed beneath the great formulas that ordinarily serve to mask it. Instead of thinking of the murdered children, he could recall only the trembling body he had seen thrown on a board to have its head chopped off.[29]

After all, a very similar experience happens to Camus himself when, immediately after the Liberation, having witnessed the trial of a collaborationist, he runs away, having realized that he feels close to him even though convinced of his guilt.[30]

Brotherhood in frailty and guilt prevents not only any purity but negates, at its root, the right to homicide that any purity and innocence usually claims for itself. No State can legitimately suppress a life because the expression "legitimate assassination" is a contradiction in terms: A society that authorizes capital punishment believes it can protect itself more effectively, but in truth it is destroying itself because it has begun to strike the foundation upon which every society is based: *solidarity against death*.

But the idea of a communal guilt is not an absolution, a conspiracy of silence between accomplices, or the premise for confusing victims and perpetrators. Instead, it carries the awareness that justice contains within itself an imperfection and a dimension that only Greek tragedy has been able to fully render. The *just* ones are neither those who abstain from action nor those who think that they can act and be exempt from guilt. The just one is Kaliayev who, when he murders the tyrant, does not absolve himself but is ready to pay the consequences for his action, which he nevertheless does not repudiate: "For him," Camus underscores, "murder coincides with suicide."[31] The just one is he who understands the imperfection of justice and can handle the costs that are necessary to limit that imperfection.

Southern Thought

But the nature upon which it is possible to base one's resistance is not only characterized by finitude and brotherhood in guilt; it does not revolve, all distressed, around this sense of imperfection. Human nature is part of a greater nature: It shares solidarity with the land that hosts it, in acknowledgment of a communal and silent mother. This primordial and deep relationship with the earth can be found only by recuperating the Greek heart of our civilization, that "classical love for the cosmos" that has been shattered by the Judeo-Christian tradition.

The latter, in fact, dramatizes the opposition between man and world and between man and nature. The desert is its privileged space, and waiting is the authentic dimension of faith: Only where life is extremely harsh, if not impossible, where the present does not exist and one waits for the end of time, as was the case for the early Christians, only there can the spirit rise. Nature must be dominated because it always pulls in a direction opposite to the one that the spirit must take to be closer to God. But for Camus, Christianity does not remain (as we have already mentioned) completely closed within the "unhappy conscience" of Hebraism: "Christianity was obliged, in order to penetrate the mediterranean world, to hellenize itself, which caused its doctrine to become simultaneously more flexible. . . . In its concept of mediation, Christianity is Greek. In its idea of history, Christianity is Judaic and will be found again in German ideology."[32]

Already in 1937, in a memorable conference at the Maison de la Culture of Algiers, Camus had tied the success of Christianity to Hellenization and the softening of a "harsh, exclusive, and admirable" original Judaic nucleus.[33] The Mediterranean, by introducing the idea of mediation and a less exacerbated and harsh relationship with nature, allows Christianity to produce admirable fruits, such as the flowering of the Albigensians and Saint Francis (one can recall among other things, the *Canticle of All Creatures*). But these are wonderful though temporary fruits because "with the Inquisition and the destruction of the Albigensian heresy, the Church again parts company with the world and with beauty, and gives back to history its pre-eminence over nature."[34]

The place where it is (and has been) possible to say in the purest way "yes" to the world is the Mediterranean. Here is where one preserves the secret of Moderation, that harmony between man and nature that is collected in the Greek myths and Greek gods, in the architecture of classical tragedy. Thought is not independent from the world in which it is born, from the light and shadows it finds; and Southern thought is one that has known the sun that meshes with the sea, the love of beauty, the strength and suffering of heroes, their being at once challenge to the cosmos and a part of it. In contrast with that "yes," with that tradition of solar harmony, stands Northern thought, pushed by its darkness toward an incurable desire for revenge. The protagonism of the spirit, its becoming autonomous and in opposition to nature, is a process that is born from the dramatic needs of a world in which the environment presents itself immediately as hostile. It is not by chance that the oppositional relationship between spirit and nature came to life in the burning heat and the mirages of the desert; nor that it was reborn in the North where nature becomes again hostile. The entrance into history of Northern people, "who have no tradition of friendship with the world,"[35] carries with it this lack of moderation.

As a matter of fact, Hegel, in a famous passage from *Lectures on the Philosophy of History*, positively acknowledged the Mediterranean as the axis of world history, where Greece, "the shining beacon," lies. The Mediterranean, not being an ocean "which stretches out indefinitely and to which man has a purely negative relationships . . . positively invites him to venture upon it." It is undoubtedly the axis of world history, at least of the Old World, as "the great states of ancient history lie around it, and it is the navel of the earth."[36]

But this extraordinary center is destined to be surpassed by a course of history that is projected toward the West, the West that is called Europe.

The Mediterranean, though it has left in the words East and West the footprint of its own ethnocentrism, cannot stop a world history "that goes from East to West," and condemns it to being a simple prelude to the sunset. The task of the Mediterranean was only to lead the spirit to an initial and imperfect consciousness of itself, removing it from the identification with nature that characterized it when the East was still dominant. Without any hesitation, Hegel states: "Europe is the absolute end of history, just as Asia is the beginning."[37] And "world history imposes a discipline on the unrestrained natural will, guiding it towards universality and subjective freedom."[38] All of history must proceed North, toward the West, to finally flow into the highest spiritual density concentrated in the ethical power of the State.

We can almost hear Camus: Here is the lack of moderation! The Spirit as absolute protagonist of history, here is a world that is ashamed and avenges itself on nature! "The whole effort of German thought has been to substitute for the notion of human nature that of human situation and hence to substitute history for God and modern tragedy for ancient equilibrium. . . . But like the Greeks I believe in nature."[39]

Camus's thought proceeds in the opposite direction: The *Midi* rebels against the *Abend-land*, against the idea that suggests that everything culminates in the land of the evening that is the West. In truth, that West is the crossing and fusion between the northern cold and the western ocean that train and harden the spirit, preparing it to the grand endeavors of the lack of moderation. The interval of sea and land that characterizes the Mediterranean, the balance through which the memory of the common origin that constitutes the foundation of *Moderation* never disappears, here fails, overcome by the *hubris* of the spirit. Thus what goes missing is the counterweight that would have helped the revolutionary spirit avoid the nihilistic drift.

> This counterpoise, this spirit which takes the measure of life, is the same which animates the long tradition that can be called solitary thought and in which, since the time of the Greeks, nature has always been weighed against evolution. The history of the first International when German socialism ceaselessly fought against the libertarian thought of the French, the Spanish, and the Italian, is the history of the struggle of the German ideology against the Mediterranean mind.[40]

The conflict between moderation and its lack that animates European history hinges on precise oppositions: "The masses against the State, concrete society against absolutistic society, deliberate freedom against rational tyranny, finally, altruistic individualism against the colonization of the masses."[41] In this century the fundamental conflict is not so much between historicist ideologies and Christian politics (which are, to a certain extent, accomplices), but "between German dreams and the Mediterranean traditions, between the violence of eternal adolescence and virile strength, between nostalgia, rendered more acute by knowledge and by books and courage reinforced and enlightened by the experience of life—in other words, between history and nature."[42]

Even though history seems to turn against the tradition of equilibrium and moderation, the Mediterranean seems capable of resisting and preserving the secret of human nature "where intelligence is intimately related to the blinding light of the sun."[43] It carries with it the primacy of beauty that the West, whose name is even trapped in nostalgia[44] and in the pain that is born of distance, no longer knows how to recognize. It is not a question of contrasting the Mediterranean and Europe, because Europe has never been other than this clash between midday and midnight, but of fighting to affirm within Europe itself the rights of the day.

The fatality with which the West succeeded the Mediterranean, the serene superseding toward maturity that Hegel seems to project in the overarching structure of his work, is only a clever metaphor through which the lack of moderation presents its own supremacy as inevitable (as happens for the course of the day). But there is nothing inevitable in this dynamic, and to counter it with the force and topicality of Southern thought does not mean to chase a literary myth, but to give an answer to the problems of the future: "Naturally, of course, it is not a question of despising anything, or of exalting one civilization at the expense of another, but of simply saying that it *is a process of thought which the world today cannot do without for very much longer*" (italics mine).[45]

Moderation: The Right and the Wrong Side

The idea of a Southern thought is an area where Camus is clearly and deeply indebted to Nietzsche (a constant reference for Camus, as he is cited many times in the *Notebooks*). And it is difficult to think that Camus did not find the fascination and depth of thought of the *great meridian* in Nietzsche's rediscovery of the South as a cure "for the horrible Northern chiaroscuro, for the spectral muddle of concepts and poverty of blood that exists where the sun is absent." Those who love the South can find in it "a great school of convalescence, for all the diseases of senses and spirit, as a tremendous abundance of sun and transfiguration by sun, spreading itself over an autonomous existence which believes in itself."[46]

But on this particular point, on the necessity of a Southern thought, a more direct and concrete role was certainly played by Jean Grenier. Grenier, a professor of philosophy at the Lycée of Algiers going back to October 1930 and a teacher that Camus never disowned, arrived in Algiers after spending his youth in Saint-Brieuc, in Brittany, and began to write what will become his most famous books (*Inspirations méditerranéennes, Les Iles, Voir Naples*, etc.); books that reveal his love for Mediterranean life. Grenier too, then, becomes like Nietzsche "a southerner, not by descent but by *faith*."[47] This is the faith that the young Camus encounters, and he will recall this meeting and the debt to *Les Iles* in the preface to a new edition of the volume in 1959 ("I was twenty in Algeria when I read this book for the first time").[48] Although Gide, who in the *Nourritures terrestres* had sung of a happiness that came from a blessed land,[49] could not inspire young men who were already living in the sun "among the colors, the waves, the good smell of the earth" ("we practice with insolence the profession of happiness"), Jean Grenier, writes Camus in the preface, had been able to mould and enrich that "joyful barbarism": "We required more subtle teachers, a man, for example, born on other shores, yet also in love with light and the body's splendor, who came to tell us in an inimitable language that these appearances are beautiful, but that they must perish and that it is necessary, therefore, to love them without hope."[50]

This beginning of the disenchantment allows one not to substitute, but to put on the same level of the spontaneous "yes," and of the immediate embracing of beauty, the feeling of its impermanence. And maybe we should ask if such deep understanding of the impermanence of life had not already hit young Camus when the discovery of the disease had hurled him, one day to the next, from the soccer fields onto a hospital bed in one of the city's poor neighborhoods. Maybe the harsh discovery of the obscure limits of life within one's body came to him, prior to his readings and intellectual encounters, from the loneliness of being an adolescent forced to let go of his dreams in the space of a few days, through a maturity learned before its time and without room for objections.

Only from the encounter with death, does the "yes" achieve its perfection: Only when one discovers, even on one's own skin, the universal destiny of death, when the *right* side is accompanied by the *wrong* side, does the "yes" become culture and lose the simple and barbarous unconditional nature of the origins. Death and the end are not overcome in Hegelian fashion through a superior awareness, but become like a thorn that adds the pining of despair to a love that had been until then uncomplicated. We are dealing quite simply with two sides that the Greeks had already explained: "What is more complex than the birth of thought? The right explanation is always double, at least. Greece teaches us this, Greece to which we must always return. Greece is both shadow and light. We are well aware, aren't we, if we come from the South, that the sun has its black side?"[51] The dark face of the sun, shadow and light: When Camus, twenty years later, will return to present in a preface the collection of his early writings titled *The Wrong Side and the Right Side*,[52] he will identify precisely in the weaving of love and despair the constant nucleus of truth in those compositions: "'There is no love of life without despair of life,' I wrote, rather pompously, in these pages. I didn't know at the time how right I was."[53]

The right and the wrong side, and therefore the discovery of the limit as a bonus, as an experience that makes life at once more real and more desperate. The desert that Camus writes about is not the Judeo-Christian space of fasts, temptations, and spiritual perfection, but one where we gain awareness that to say "yes" to the world also means to say "yes" to the limits of our life. In the desert, "coagulated memory of the world," life is visible only in its memories, in its "fossil footprints."[54] The silences of the desert stand guard over ancient ruins, like in Djemila, almost as if to remind us that "the world always conquers history in the end."[55]

Camus discovers his thinking about the desert at the end of a journey to Italy, almost as a reaction to the seductions of beauty. To those who tell him, "Italy, the Mediterranean, ancient lands where everything is within the measure of man," Camus's first temptation is to reply, "The human scale? Silence and dead stones. All the rest belongs to history." This because even "Italy, like other privileged places, offers me the spectacle of a beauty in which, nonetheless, men die."[56] Beauty and death chase and call each other. Camus rediscovers this relationship in Melville, capable of mixing "the Bible with the sea, the music of the waves with that of the spheres, the poetry of the days with the grandeur of the Atlantic."[57] The scene of the execution of Billy Budd, where at dawn the perfect body of the topman hangs above the silent crew, and nature, splendid and unmoved, reabsorbs tragedy in its grand scenery, appears to illustrate impeccably the human condition for Camus. But one can also remember Mersault, in *A Happy Death*, who closes his eyes after having inhaled with all his senses the beauty of the sea, of the sun, and of the fragrance of plants.[58] In its most ferocious tears beauty shows itself with all of its striking force.

Moderation, then, is not wisdom or balance, but something deeply set in passion and contradiction: "Moderation. They consider it the resolution of contradiction. It cannot be anything other than the affirmation of contradiction and the heroic decision to stay with it and to survive it."[59] The contradiction pertains to the entwining of "yes" and "no" that is at the origin of the revolt: "Moderation is not the opposite of rebellion. Rebellion in itself is moderation. . . . The very origin of this value guarantees us that it can only be partially destroyed. . . . It is a perpetual conflict, continually created and mastered by intelligence." And the thrust of this conflict, the guarantee of its authenticity, resides in an expression that we must constantly keep in mind: "One cannot build anything conclusive if not on a 'despite it all.' "[60]

This *despite it all* is what protects the oxymoron of contradiction, the pivot on which two opposite forces discharge themselves: on the one hand, the knowledge of our frailty, the awareness that "We belong to the world that does not last. And all that does not last—and nothing but what does not last—is ours";[61] on the other, our passion that does not allow itself to be blackmailed by the thought of the end. In this case the revolt is nothing but "the relative—but the *relative with passion*. Ex.: Torn between the world that does not suffice and God who is lacking, the absurd mind passionately chooses the world. *Id.*: Divided between the relative and the absolute, it leaps *eagerly into the relative*."[62]

This passion, far from being mortified by the feeling of our frailty, is born precisely from it, pours all of life in that "despite it all," and for this reason makes it extraordinary. Confronting Kafka, Camus sees, in contradiction with the suffering and condemnation of Kafka's heroes, the culmination of the absurd and the tragic in the description of a happy man's life: "The more exciting life is, the more absurd is the idea of losing it."[63] Moderation looks at the absurd from the other side; it reads the oxymoron the opposite way. Faced with the rebounding in one's consciousness of the transitory nature of everything, passion not only survives but is rekindled. The pain that we feel in the soul is precisely what allows us to give back "to every being, to every object, its value as miracle."[64]

Poverty and the South

More than once, looking back on his own childhood and youth, Albert Camus made a point to underscore that they had been happy despite poverty: "I was born poor under a happy sun, in a nature with which one feels harmony, not hostility. Therefore, I did not start with laceration, but with fullness."[65] The mature and by then famous writer confesses to have always continued to draw his essential strength from that childhood lived among the voices of the poor neighborhood of Algiers. Indeed, poverty on the streets of Algiers was not alone but always accompanied by light and its capillary pervasiveness. It was an existence halfway between utter poverty and the sun, in which one finds the roots of both revolt and moderation: "Poverty kept me from thinking all was well under the sun and history; the sun taught me that history was not everything. I wanted to change lives, yes, but not the world which I worshipped as divine."[66]

The presence of sun and light gave Camus a "happy immunity" from resentment and envy; the generous beauty of nature freed him forever from the pathologies of mimesis. There where the most important goods are still capable of being the public goods, the goods accessible to all, it is possible to control envy.

> The lovely warmth that reigned over my childhood freed me from all resentment. I lived on almost nothing, but also in a kind of rapture. I felt infinite strengths within me: all I had to do was find a way to use them. It was not poverty that got in my way: in Africa, the sun and the sea cost nothing. The obstacle lay rather in prejudices or stupidity.[67]

If a young boy has known a wealth that does not require money to be enjoyed, if beauty has waited for him on every corner without asking for compensation, then he has freed himself forever from the claustrophobic universe of the accumulation of private wealth: "A long time ago, I once lived a whole week luxuriating in all the goods of this world: we slept without a roof, on a beach, I lived on fruit, and spent half my days alone in the water. I learned something then that has always made me react to the signs of comfort or of a well-appointed house with irony, impatience, and sometimes anger."[68]

Camus knows full well that he is privileged and that his position of superiority vis-à-vis possession could seem a simple accessory of wealth and success, an insult to those who experience poverty concretely rather than from the twice-removed distance of affluence and memory. But can we just end the discussion here? Can his meditation on poverty be dismissed by assigning it to the crowd of easy thoughts that are not worthy of serious consideration, but are a luxury permitted to writers? Is it not better to follow Camus's line of thought, trying to determine if it does not contain instead some useful reflection for today's world?

The South that Camus writes about has changed profoundly and appears to have completely hidden poverty, as if it were a shame. It almost seems as if it is running from poverty to find a space, at whatever cost, in the commodity circuit, where wealth knows only its private form, the one that makes it accessible only to those who have money. Perhaps "happy poverty" is only an idyll or something that could be experienced in those privileged areas of the South where land meets sea; we can definitely say that, from a certain point of view, regardless of the extraordinary increase in income, today the South is poorer. Undoubtedly, it was once traversed by terrible injustices, by prevarications that masked their daring with neutrality and sacredness. Toward them and the misery imposed on men (or women) by other men we cannot feel nostalgia. Nevertheless, today many injustices, exclusions, and poverties have not disappeared but have only transformed themselves; and the desperate escape from that misery loses "the freedom that disappears as soon as there is an excess of things."[69]

This is not a defense of pauperism, but the awareness that the new expression of freedom requires increasing amounts of money and that the sun and the sea, which once upon a time were open to all, now give themselves, like prostitutes, only to those who can pay. By selling the sea and the sun in small apportionments, money has increased; but what has vanished is freedom, the communal mother that was at its origin, the happy wandering in places illuminated by a communal light that rests within the memories of Southern childhoods. More money, more enclosures, more rage due to new exclusions: The South sold but lost itself. And the problem surfaces: Faced with a discourse that speaks of "happy poverty" will the South respond with a condescending laughter or will it stop for a moment to think about it? Can the South do something other than follow? Or has it gone down the path of no return with pockets full (often of dirty money) and without a soul? And if the South does not want to be a poor copy of the North, is there a different path than pride? A path that, by de-commodifying at least in part the sun and sea, makes them become again shared public properties and the center of Southern identity; a path that removes the negative sign from all statistics on the South, because it stops comparing it with that which is other than itself?

Thus, there exists in Camus's constant mentioning of happy poverty something more than nostalgia, something more than the absolving indulgence of the man who has achieved fame and success. In order to avoid turning the South into a failed North, should we not be capable of conceptualizing an idea of wealth that is different from the one that encourages the masses' desire for private hoarding. One of the most dramatic aspects of the lack of moderation produced by the hegemony of Northern culture resides in the impossibility of generalizing it to the planetary level. But if this is the case, is there anything more timely than a thought capable of imagining a different form of wealth and of giving theoretical autonomy to the South? What more than this thought can distance the world from the suicidal mirage of an infinite and impossible replica of the North?

In June of 1949, while presenting approvingly and with involvement Simone Weil's *The Need for Roots*[70] ("one of the most lucid, lofty and beautiful books that have been written in a long time on our civilization"), Camus finds the key and the secret of the book in its proposal for a *return to tradition*: "Not tradition as it is meant in some political circles or in our nostalgic history books, but the one that consists of thinking right, of seeing right."[71]

The South has reneged its own tradition and has taken it on as a sin, but now finds it deformed and prostituted vis-à-vis huge gatherings of commodities. Today, it looks in the mirror of these masks, discovering itself only as vice, but sooner or later it will have to rediscover a higher and more austere image of itself; it will have to find roots that are *new but not external* to its own history. And here tradition does not mean restoration, nostalgic dreams of unquestionable hierarchies (and therefore doubly obscene), but democracy of moderation, a freedom that goes hand in hand with dignity. In order to prepare for that moment and make sure it does not come at incredible costs, we must, starting today, speak of Southern thought. Camus's libertarian revolt cannot be understood without being rooted in this faith in the future.

Style and Honor

In November of 1953, Camus writes on a piece of paper the ten most important words for him: "world, pain, mother, human beings, desert, honor, poverty, summer, sea."[72] In the course of our discussion we have encountered all of them except for "honor," a word that merits special consideration.

Remembering the coldness with which the pupil, by then already ill with tuberculosis, had greeted his home visit, Jean Grenier remembers he carried for a long time the memory of that rejection: "For reasons that I could not understand back then, the man I was dealing with refused my outstretched hand: in my imagination I saw him putting his hand behind his back; and that image remained with me for a long time."[73]

With time, Grenier understood that the rejection contained already all of Camus: his pride, his dignity, his high sense of self, "the desire for greatness, the nostalgia for nobility." This is the point that is most important to emphasize at a time of hasty re-discoveries of Camus: Revolt is not only aspiring to freedom and liberation from ties, but also the desire for a higher loyalty.

The first, decisive aspect of this loyalty resided in Camus's capacity for admiration. Camus maintained this capacity, which ended up embarrassing even his professor ("I felt troubled by the admiration that he showed me"), into the latter years of his life, when he repeatedly confessed, even as he dealt with the praise of thousands of interviewers for the Nobel Prize, his own awe and humility "in front of the poorest of lives or the greatest adventures of the spirit." Only the magnitude of suffering and of the spirit deserve respect, not that grey zone that extends between them, "a society that makes one laugh."[74]

But this admiration is not simply the mimesis of an old pedagogical model: "Great souls interest me—and they alone. But I am not a great soul."[75] Here Camus is not belittling himself: His strength resides precisely in the distance that he perceives between himself and the great souls. Very few have been able, as he has, to perceive this distance, this being at once unequal (to the task) and eager to fill the gap, this need not to be sucked in by the underground in which we live. This admiration for great spirits is respectable because it results from a journey in which we meet characters such as Mersault and Meursault (the protagonists of A *Happy Death* and *The Stranger*);[76] it is not born out of conformist adaptation, but from dissociation with the existing moral order, from a refusal wherein everything seems to go astray except perhaps a sensual tenderness toward nature. What is *The Fall* if not the practice of suspicion toward oneself, against the facile nobility and great no-cost battles of the intellectuals, against the private and unmentionable uses of success? It is from this contradictory web that the originality of Camus is born: The underground man looks upward, knows all his weaknesses, but deals unrelentingly with what one should do. Admiration has known suspicion and criticism but has not been poisoned by them.

Camus always admired radical personalities that expressed their ideas without protecting themselves, but putting themselves completely to the test (from Nietzsche to Simone Weil). He was, and certainly we can believe Grenier, one of those people who "translate into action their ideas," not one of those who "profess beliefs that have no consequences on their life."[77] After all, the only superiority that Camus gladly recognized in Christianity was the decisive one of the power of example, of searching in Christ and the saints for "a style of life."[78] In the *Notebooks* he records with admiration how Nietzsche had successfully ended a discussion with a group of his contemporaries who were skeptical about the authenticity of Mucius Scaevola's sacrifice:[79] "Nietzsche . . . takes a burning coal from the stove without saying a word and shows it to his friends. He carries the scar from this his entire life."[80]

Honor counters an *omertà*[81] that is masked as skepticism with the exemplary simplicity of greatness. Camus will return to the topic of honor many times, to reclaim its value in polemic with a world that thinks it can deliver it to the museums as an old and ridiculous word that has fallen out of favor. In an interview given in 1957 to *Demain* he articulates comprehensively a recurrent thought.

> In the fights of this century, I always felt solidarity with those who are obstinate, especially with those who never abandoned some degree of honor. I agreed and continue to agree with many of today's crazy ideas. But I could never bring myself to spit upon the word honor, as many have done. This is because, without a doubt, I was and am aware of my human weaknesses and of my own injustices, because I knew and know that honor is

like compassion, this unreasonable virtue that stands in for justice and reason when they have become powerless. He who is given to the most common weaknesses by his blood, follies and unsteady heart, should look for something that might enable him to think highly of himself and therefore of others. This is why I abhor a certain self-satisfied virtue and the horrible morality of the world. I abhor it because it leads, exactly like absolute cynicism, to despair of human beings and to prevent them from taking charge of their own lives with all the weight of their errors and greatness.[82]

Honor and the sense of honor train us to look upward, to constrain and to demand that we give the very best of ourselves. The need for honor in contemporary society is reaffirmed in the preface to the reprint of *The Wrong Side and the Right Side*.

> If only we could live according to honor—that virtue of the unjust! But our society finds the word obscene; "aristocrat" is a literary and philosophical insult. I am not an aristocrat, my reply is in this book: here are my people, my teachers, my ancestry; here is what, through them, links me with everyone. And yet I do need honor, because I am not big enough to do without it![83]

And from the mouth of Diego, the protagonist of *State of Siege*[84] who sacrifices himself to save the city from the plague, the word that recurs most often is always the one: honor.[85] If Diego represents Camus's conviction that it is necessary to "live according to what is honorable in oneself and only that,"[86] dying can also belong to this kind of living. The maximum of honor lies in overturning the relationship with death, in the discovery that it can shape and sign off on our life: "Death gives its shape to love as it does to life—transforming it into fate. . . . What would the world be without death—a succession of forms evaporating and returning, an anguished flight, an unfinishable world. But fortunately, here is death, the stable one."[87]

In a world where we cannot hope in any future salvation (heavenly or mundane), honor represents the feeling of belonging to the community of human beings, the admission that there is value in upholding a high opinion of them: It is that very earthly force that gives us "assurance that one has something to say and especially that something can be said—assurance that what one feels and what one is, has value as an example—assurance that one is irreplaceable and not a coward."[88] One can arrive at this empowerment from the most different paths: from desperation, from an elementary sense of human solidarity, or from the need to find an answer to some question one carries within. The discussions among the protagonists of *The Plague* are the result of meetings between men who are very different but united in having chosen to fight on the front lines against the epidemic. However, they meet not to separate from all the others, but through health organizations, in the concrete practice of solidarity where one fights for "the honor of mankind."

Aristocracy and Freedom

Not all human beings are capable of taking such risks, and every admiration presupposes an aristocracy. Even though Camus points out on a number of occasions that he is not an aristocrat (wasn't he born poor even if happy?), in the *Notebooks* the conviction that *today* one needs an aristocracy recurs often, and it elucidates a constant theme: We cannot let freedom close upon itself. Without the feeling of honor, in fact, freedom drifts along because it risks turning into its opposite, either the opportunism that is prone to every form of power or a destructive and suicidal refusal. Honor, then, not only completes freedom but watches over it: It is the mythical nourishment of every revolt. This is why Camus always ties together freedom and honor: "Without true freedom and without a certain honor, I cannot live."[89]

The admiration for "people greater and more genuine than others"[90] does not mask nostalgia for a hierarchical society but aims to give criticism the courage and foundations it needs. Without the vitality of the contradiction between the desire to meet "the greatest possible number of human beings" and the attraction for the examples of great (historical) figures, freedom risks turning into a blind gathering of many wills to power that have no other criteria aside from their own unlimited growth. Greatness is not a gift or an ascribed status, but a tension, a quest, a friction: "Greatness consists in trying to be great."[91]

One encounters here the Hispanic-Castilian side of Camus, the side that Grenier has recognized as early as the visit to his sick student, the side that leads Camus's journey to intersect that of Ortega y Gasset ("perhaps, after Nietzsche, the greatest of the European writers").[92] Ortega's and Unamuno's reflections on the need for an aristocracy and on the meaning of Donquixotesque action in the epoch of "the rebellion of the masses" inspires a brief but illuminating piece by Camus published in 1955 in an anarchic paper (*Le Monde libertaire*), where he indicates what Europe could learn from Spain. The "paradoxical genius" of the latter is personified by King Alphonse VI (who, having discovered that he had defeated the Arabs in Toledo thanks to deceit, returned the mosque to them, only to re-conquer it with his army); and by Miguel de Unamuno, who, reclaiming as honor the lack of productivity of Spanish culture in an age of techno-scientific thought, chooses the outdated as destiny. Of this *paradoxical genius*, *Don Quixote* is the highest representation, "the Gospel of Spain," the message that the latter still sends today to a "Europe intoxicated by its rationalism."[93]

The ability not to follow the flow of the river, to remain standing while everyone else reasonably takes a seat in the armchair of the present, being outdated not as a sign of affectation but of friction that accompanies another way of being of the mind and of the heart are themes that bring Camus near to another austere Southern dignity, Ignazio Silone. Tarrou in *The Plague* is tormented by the question, "Can one be a saint without God?"[94] Pietro Spina and Severina (in whom it is not difficult to recognize Simone Weil) are nagged by the same question: "Never abandon the search for truth, not even in the middle of a dark night"; "to create new forms of heroism, of sainthood, of devotion, of consecration to the universal human truths."[95] And is Pietro Spina not a typical Camusian hero when he asks: "Saved? . . . Is there a past participle of saving oneself?"[96]

But the stern mountains of Abruzzo are far from Camus's Algeria. They have never allowed the body to relax in thrills of happiness between sun and sea, and are more reminiscent of the asceticism of the deserts: They are the mountains of resisting hermits. Camus comes from a world that is warmer and more sensual, from an underground where passions and drives crowd together, from a solitude that needs others, from a more extroverted body language, from the knowledge of the dynamics of desire. The call to honor keeps vertical aspirations grounded and, through the admiration for the great figures of mankind, keeps human beings rooted to a loyalty toward their fellow men. Its force does not derive from solitary ascents, from a sixth-degree level climb of the spirit, but from the encounter with the solidarity of the enterprise, from the community that is born out of the shared task.

More than once Camus fondly remembered how sports played a great role in his moral education ("sport, from which I learned the only true lessons of morality").[97] This because in sport one learns "loyal obedience to rules of the game agreed to together and freely accepted."[98] The sport that Camus loved was a collective sport, soccer (even when lived through an individualistic role, that of the goalkeeper). What was fascinating about the sport, something that Camus confesses to have rediscovered later only in theater and in journalism, was a shared feeling of being engaged in an assignment, the solidarity of the task. Speaking of the collective exaltation that is born from this coming together of the many in a single objective (as in the construction of monuments, works of art, performances), Camus recalls:

As far as I am concerned, I have only known in the team sports of my youth that powerful sensation of hope and solidarity that accompanies the long days of training up to the day of the victorious or losing match. Truly, the little morality that I know, I learned on the soccer field and on the theatrical stages that will remain my true universities.[99]

Here men come together just as the protagonists of *The Plague* do. In order for each of them to give their very best, they need to come together, to confront one another, to cooperate with each other, and settle their differences in a collective movement: "What balances the absurd is the community of men fighting against it. And if we choose to serve that community, we choose to serve the dialogue carried to the absurd against any policy or falsehood or of silence. That's the way one is free with others."[100] This community (which recalls very closely the one in Leopardi's *La ginestra*)[101] does not fight with other communities or recognize the legitimacy of homicide. Its final aim is to "join forces."[102]

Someone has observed how, with a few exceptions, the world of Camus is populated by lonely men, while women are almost always in the background and only "virile qualities" are discussed. I hope to have shown that the central theme of a nature capable of making us rich and happy allows us to see Camus's work in another light. With regard to those qualities, only an extraordinary optimism and a great superficiality could allow one to think that those encounters, those solitudes that for a moment (as they do in *The Plague*) dissolve with a swim in the sea are masks of power from which we must break free. If no providence is looking after us from above, we cannot afford this mistake.

CHAPTER 6

Pier Paolo Pasolini: Life as Oxymoron

Impatience toward "Collective Destinies"

There is still a large crowd milling around Pasolini, different people with different questions. My question is very simple: What allowed Pasolini's prophetic vision? How is it possible that a poet ("I sense the problems of the moment; I am not a scientist who does research . . . I am a writer")[1] could see much further than the politicians or the scholars trained in the analysis of society? I do not believe that there exists a privileged language to gain access to the world (such as science, the revolutionary point of view, or, as is fashionable today, poetry or mystic experience); and I think that the belief of those who think they have found one only increases intellectual laziness and conformism. Instead, I believe that the paths that allow an access to the world that is fulfilling and worthy of being known are many, but all marked by the experience of a strong yet not arrogant friction with dominant truism. This is why I am interested in Pasolini and why I wish to verify if the secret of his prophetic ability does not reside precisely in the centrality of the experience of contradiction.

I must say right away that this discovery is neither mine nor recent but was pointed out already twenty-five years ago by Franco Fortini. Yet, Fortini's conclusion, in the admirable pages that in 1959 he dedicated to *The Ashes of Gramsci*,[2] is still valid today only if it is totally reversed. Fortini admitted having had to overcome a first reaction of rejection toward *The Ashes*, and of annoyance and nausea for "the vulgarity of the psychological and ideological conflicts" proposed by Pasolini; for the "melodramatic insincerity" of addressing Gramsci with the colloquial "you,"[3] for "its complacency towards resignation and defeat"; for "the double-crossing attitude of tears wept over a red flag but shared with a circle of literati"; and for resorting, at the stylistic level, to "the old stock clichés of the *prosa d'arte*."[4]

Here, as elsewhere, Fortini's suspicion toward Pasolini emerges: the suspicion of a fundamental duplicity, the almost obsessive fear that behind Pasolini's display of pain and rage could hide a cynical adaptation to present conditions, a consorting with the soft underbelly of Italy that consigns to the attic the hopes of the Resistance through some public display of suffering capable of masking opportunism: "Beautiful soul flagellating itself!" At times, Fortini's reproach is even harsher because it denounces the ties between the complacency of self-flagellation and the search for an easy popularity: a weakness for spectacle.

The "Jewish" Fortini[5] looks suspiciously at Pasolini's "Catholic" psychology and at the "nexus populism-aristocratism," the softness and the sweetness, the willingness to absolve oneself that lies in waiting behind every uncontrolled and public exhibition of his pain and guilt. Nevertheless, while sliding toward such harsh tones, Fortini retroactively reduces the importance of all that was profound in his reflection of *The Ashes*. He trivializes the strong points of his argument, which lay in the conviction that "the inspiration, the thrust of all that Pasolini writes is based on the antithesis, on a contradiction . . . that can be detected at every level of his writing."[6] This interpretative key will become the dominant one, and many critics will take it up again, expanding and developing its meaning.[7] In truth, subsequent critics are more generous than Fortini, who, only belatedly, will free himself of the suspicion that in Pasolini, "behind contradiction and antithesis," is hidden "simply the modern posture towards expression," that attitude which, in laying claim to its own "stylistic freedom," in the end arrogates for itself other greater liberties and exemptions from "normal" constraints, issuing itself a convenient moral pass.

> I have never hidden a certain objective suspicion . . . towards you; that is, aside from self-awareness and good faith, I do not think you feel compelled to observe, in your practical, and therefore in your ideological and political behavior, the current norms of coherency and responsibility that are demanded of me and others. . . . [I]t is too obvious from what you write and are, that you lay claim, at all times, to the right of contradiction, to the road to Damascus, to betrayal, to gestures or, more simply, to the verbal solution to problems.[8]

In short, one side of Pasolini's personality, his exhibitionism, self-com-
placency, and an authentic and confessed passion for display, is here ampli-
fied to the point of allowing his interest for performance to prevail over
rigor and coherency. Fortini's sober and demanding demeanor is baffled
by a vitality that does not allow itself to be contained, and this leads him
to reply to Pasolini's recriminations with a vein of regret: "Do not allow
even yourself to believe that my 'character,' rather than my 'soul,' is true."[9]
In other words, he reclaims precisely the freedom and the right not to be
misunderstood that he is refusing Pasolini, as if we could protect ourselves
from the risk that our soul is nothing else than the nobler and dearer
version of our character.

I would like to revisit Fortini's precious suggestion (liberating it from
the suffocating urgency of ethical-political concerns) and start anew from
the statement that locates in the experience of antithesis the juncture
between Pasolini's life and work. However, it is my intention to move in
a direction that is completely opposite to Fortini's, based on the conviction
that the fire of contradiction not only functions in Pasolini as a rigorous
and necessary relationship with the world, but that this nondialectical
experience of contradiction is precisely the reason that led Pasolini to say
things that still interest us today.

Oxymoron and Guilt

As many have observed, one of the essential points of this constant contradictory tension resides in the crucial oxymoron that was Pasolini's homosexuality, the "diversity that made me wonderful."[10] Thus, diversity as
suffering and choice, as cause at once of exclusion and raised status; diversity that is, in turn, discovery of that oxymoron in one's own flesh, when
one feels "that virgin joy/as sacrilege."[11] Sexual pleasure, the moment
when we give ourselves to the world and, trembling, we feel life running
through us, discovering that we are part of it; the moment when we feel
the shuddering of the Other touch our own body; the moment when we
can know life, enjoying it "with such infantile/and feminine abandon":[12]
All this, through a Catholic upbringing, becomes a sin even though it is
simply a normal pleasure. One meets the lacerating contradiction immediately by discovering that one's body, a body that is at the origin of everything, must suddenly be banned. Here is the paradox!: "[T]he body, the
body, is the source of everything and it has to be made to disappear."[13]
Thus, the oxymoron is already contained in the simple sin, in the innocent
pleasure that one finds forbidden and remains marked by this necessary
intersection with guilt. But this experience becomes a terrible burden

when prohibition and guilt are multiplied by diversity, when searching for others becomes a shame, something secretive and nocturnal that one hides even from one's dearest of friends, and this desire clashes with everything, even with the party that you have enthusiastically joined and loved.[14]

Herein lies the trauma and acute cross of contradiction: to discover love as guilt and to do so on the thrust of a life initially thought to be immune from division; a life in which one's naïveté and the approval of others had happily intersected: "for many years," he writes in a letter to Silvana Mauri, "I apparently did not have a religious or moralistic education or past but for long years I was what is called the consolation of my parents, a model son, an ideal scholar";[15] and, one might also add, having gained a precise idea of the separation between good and evil, with the conviction of being solidly on the side of good. The immense pain lies in the discovery that the same "frighteningly honest and good youth" who continues to act so and pours into the world this same capacity for love, suddenly and imperceptibly has crossed to the other side, the side of evil. The same person, so eager for contact with others, for friendship and affection, still "virginal and boyish," suddenly finds himself indicted: The innocent discovers his guilt. But mind you, this is not a simple dissonance, but an antithesis: good where there is evil, and vice versa. This experience—this knowledge through pain of one's erroneousness, which Fortini, whose gaze is fixed on "collective destinies," often deals with quickly and impatiently (except to recover it heavily at times)—is, on the contrary, the epistemological secret of Pasolini's entire work.

The oxymoron, then, is present from the beginning in Pasolini's life as a crucial form of his experience and, since then, as a genetic code replicated and represented an infinite number of times. The homosexual condition is certainly decisive in the construction of such a heightened sensibility, but I must repeat that homosexuality simply magnifies the sharpness of a contradiction that is already verified in sin, one's being torn apart by "hated purity and imagined sins." Pound's *Amo ergo sum*[16] is transformed into a Christian identification of sin with being in the world: The intense and passionate experience of life coincides with a fierce collision with the norm. Pasolini lives this experience, which all of us remember from our sentimental education as Catholics, through homosexuality, but in an infinitely expanded manner: What reaches us as sound reaches him as an excruciating and a deafening scream. Herein, in the discovery of the culpability of the loved body, lie both discontinuity and the relationship with common sense, the bridge that has always allowed Pasolini to speak to the many, and his perennial inability to feel satisfied communicating with the educated and the privileged. All of this is obviously ambiguous and can lead to the confusion dreaded by Fortini, to the indistinctness between good and evil that convicts and absolves all. The painful and sensual intimacy with sin leads to a baroque contamination between desire and the sacred, between incense and death, between empathy and guilt in a game of crossings and blasphemous surprises that finds its expression in the atmosphere that dominates the poem *The Nightingale of the Catholic Church*.

> I love my madness of water and absinthe
> I love my yellow boy's face
> the innocence I feign and the hysteria
> I hide in heresy or in the schism
> of my jargon, I love my sin
> which, when I entered the museums of adults,
> was the crease of the pants, the pangs
> of my timid heart.[17]

To love sin. Everything gets complicated, but everything also de-composes: There is no longer a clear border, but many are created, each of them ambiguous and uncertain. Once this confusion-contamination occurs, no one can cast the first stone, and one embarks toward an infinite and labyrinthine dissemination of one's sorrows and pleasures. Not only does one love sin, but sin is loved as such, prohibition is eroticized, and one becomes attracted to prohibition and not to that which is prohibited. Pasolini has crossed this land of Catholic and ambiguous flavors creating his own original figure of decadent narcissism, and he has done it with a nonchalance and ease that can raise reservations and suspicions: We all know that self-pity can hide and, at times, has hidden connivances, because those who keep their eyes fixed on their own drama have good reasons not to look around.

The Diversity of Pasolini's Diversity

Nevertheless, the oxymoron is much more than a trite authorization to equivocate and behave nonchalantly: It reveals the construction of a very strong relationship between love and despair, between the passion-desire for the Other and exclusion. From this perspective, the unique trait of Pasolini's creativity resides exactly in its fundamental extraneousness from a gay culture that aims at the dissolution of the oxymoron, at a critique and reform of the idea of normality, and at the return to a normality that is "enriched" and open to "differences."[18] Conversely, Pasolini's oxymoron is strongly based on the conviction that diversity owes precisely to its weight as scandal, suffering, and contradiction, the possibility of having a say about the world that is capable of touching everyone's humanity; and that it owes to its extraordinary and "pathological" dependency on the Other an ability to speak that is not destined only to the homosexual universe.

In the already cited letter to Silvana Mauri, Pasolini writes "with extreme sincerity and I am not sure how little shame" words that still move us today.

> Those who like me have been fated not to love according to the rules end up by overvaluing the question of love. A normal man can resign himself— that terrible word—to chastity, to lost opportunities; but in me the difficulty in loving has made the need for love obsessive: The function made the organ hypertrophic when, as an adolescent, love seemed to me an unattainable chimera: Then when with experience the function had resumed its proper proportions and the chimera had been deconsecrated to the point of being the most miserable daily matter, the evil was already inoculated, chronic and incurable. I found myself with an enormous mental organ for a function which by now is so negligible.[19]

Diversity, then, is a deforming lens that leads to an exasperated need for love and passion, to a despairing exaltation of vitality, to a piercing desire, perhaps at the single glance, from a moving streetcar, of "a boy sitting on a wall."[20] The world fills itself with lost loves and opportunities which, if they are not taken at once, are missed "for ever and in every place." It is exactly from this point of departure that Pasolini will derive his being perpetually on the road, a "brother of dogs."[21]

It is clear, however, that here we are not only facing the traits of a general diversity but the way in which it intersects Pasolini's particular sensibility, with his formidable drive and sense of guilt, with his desperate passion to be in the world. In other words, it is precisely the "Pasolinian" way of living diversity that makes it interesting to us. Pasolini's "hefty" sensibility derives from the fact that, for example, unlike Sandro Penna who lived all his life "at the margins,"[22] he also loved history, institutions, and normality, and did not accept the alternative between reticence and separation. Sandro Penna knew full well the pangs of yearning for a boy and the experience of wandering around, asking people for "daring alms"; but Penna's sentiment is not crossed by the heartache and contradiction that occurs in Pasolini. Penna is like "one who feels punished and tortured unjustly: He twists under the pain of punishment and believes he is innocent. If even the suspicion of guilt presents itself to him, he removes it."[23] In Penna there is only one conscience. In Pasolini, conversely, conscience is double. In addition to Penna and his truth, "mad but marvelous," there is a sense of guilt for the continuous temptation to reduce "the world to the theatre of the events and the past happenings of the self,"[24] there is the tension toward conscience and history.

In Penna's verses the light that strikes is this estrangement from the large river of history and its lateral and minor geography: a geography made of roads and railway stations, of tender awakenings and silent good-byes, of mornings caught by surprise and stolen from the tyranny of time and planning. In Pasolini all of this is present, but flayed and disfigured by its clash with the unfolding of collective events, by his relationship with the virile world of politics and ideology, of history and responsibility. He knows full well "how no society contains the world,"[25] and how sin is born from rules, but he has always been attracted to the necessary breaking of the excess of life against the solid need of institutions. Even if he loves, and he cannot but love, the transgressive and revolutionary transcendence of charity, Pasolini knows that the institutions are "moving" and that "humanity—this poor humanity—cannot do without them."[26] In the institutions (be they the Church or the Communist Party), there is something mysterious that bonds, makes us kneel and moves us, something that Dostoevsky's Great Inquisitor knew full well. To love charity, therefore, does not mean to remove oneself, to escape the many, but rather to try to transform it into the norm and then toss it to a world where it cannot but be disfigured, persecuted, and betrayed.

To choose these territories as spheres of one's action means not to appease contradiction, nor to cushion it by reducing the tension and to aim finally at solving it: It means to multiply it. For Pasolini, to remain in the oxymoron means much more than to be tied to his diversity, condemning himself to its simple and infinite repetition. It means instead to exalt and superimpose the many forms of antithesis and contradiction, to look for and be open to those forms with feverish and inexhaustible eagerness, to live a life far from those who find a home in it and judge the world from that vintage point, even when this home is the uncomfortable and painful one of "diversity."

Pasolini never even turned his life on the streets into a new home, the home of a mobile and light nomadism that is so fashionable today. To him, life on the streets did not extinguish the nostalgia and the strong desire for roots. What allowed him to speak was the feeling of exclusion, the suffering it produced. And all of this was not (or at least not only) the effect of a banal and decadent attraction to pain, the effect of a morbid and Catholic familiarity with a not so secret wound. Rather, it was the effect of the lay belief that the crossed-eyes of contradiction allow one to see much more than the perfect sight of conformism; and that guilt and contradiction are the mechanisms through which we remember each time the other side of the moon, the one that remains hidden at that moment.

So, each time he felt on his own body the gravitational force of the obvious, he had to rush in the other direction to show others the zone that was disappearing. Friction, burning, and abrasion produced knowledge precisely because they were not (only) the projection of a mix of self-punishment and exhibition, but the insertion of his own body at the point of greatest conflict with what Barthes called *doxa* (that is, "Public Opinion, the mind of the majority, petit bourgeois Consensus, the Voice of Nature, the Violence of Prejudice").[27] Nevertheless, what in Barthes takes place by way of a delicate swerve, with a whisper and subtle and diffused eroticism, in Pasolini always occurs aloud, seeking confrontation, clashes and conflict, with a manly and Italian theatricality.

As we have already observed, and to conclude on this point, it is precisely Pasolini's "backward" way of living his own diversity that engenders his extraordinary productivity, this attempt at looking for points of contact and communication between two ways of "loving men," never reduced *ad unum*, never recomposed around one of the two poles, but always lived in conflict and opposition. One finds neither the simple metaphysics of overcoming the scission nor the easy and relativistic dissemination of differences: Paradoxically the unity of the opposites manifests its more authentic meaning only within the hell of scission itself. "Passion is not always grace," but grace arrives always and only from the side of passion.

The Friction of Passion and the Distance of Humor

Passion: Few words recur with such frequency and constancy in Pasolini's works and are so important to approach his vision. Passion is what one throws violently against things, what allows life to become feeling; it is the violent and unsheltered relationship with life, the opposite of maturity, control, and wisdom. Passion is being immersed in a current that is stronger than us, becoming exposed to the suffering that occurs when feelings have neither protective walls nor mediation. In *The Ashes*, but not only there, passion announces itself where to live is to tremble. Life arrives through tremors, and being in the world means to be present, first of all, with the body, to communicate with others through it, to listen and make oneself heard through tremors that transmit with physical nobility, to say it with Hegel, "the soul of the bodies." Even where this trembling is somewhat vile and repugnant, one should not escape it; and it is necessary to listen to life even where it arrives through the deformed configuration shown in the poem "The Tears of the Excavator."[28] On the other side of passion stand—like a sin—detachment, contemplation, resignation ("the terrible word"), and apathy. One moves away from passion with age and reason: aging reduces our capacity to react trembling to the world, and reason transforms the burning of passion into the will to gain detachment and control. To grow is learning "to defend myself, to offend, to have/the world in front of my eyes and not/only in my heart."[29] "Experience/is ironic toughness,"[30] the transformation of yesterday's pain into a lesson, a lessening of the ability to feel. And this distance comes at a price: "Only love, only knowledge/counts, not to have loved,/nor to have known. The extended life/of an exhausted love causes/agony. The soul no longer grows."[31]

To love and to know are not each other's opposite; on the contrary, they coincide. It is not possible to know without loving, without feeling attraction: the most radical opposition, instead, is between love-as-knowledge and a newly developed coldness; the most terrible sin, but also the most terrible ignorance, is using the verb "to love" only in the past tenses, the mediation of distance that seduces by presenting itself as wisdom, irony, and humor. And Pasolini always mistrusted humor, symptom of a distance between bodies, of a cold and resigned proxemics.

> Since I lack humor, it would be logical that I would love humorists very much. But if I really have to confess, I would say that I feel for them only a dark admiration: the usual respect for what others have. Truthfully, I do not love them for two reasons: The first is that they are champions of objectivity, if one employs this word in its common, practical, and non ideological sense, as it anticipates an anti-lyrical, non-subjective and non-autobiographical behavior: the complete lack of the "I," removed from the text as a troublesome element, indiscreet, uneducated, and totally deprived of humor. The second reason is that humorists are always conservative, if not reactionary. In order to laugh about the world, it seems, one must not believe in it: that is, not believe in its evolutionary destinies. In short, I feel more uneasiness than sympathy for these people of generally excellent upbringing who are the classical humorists, people who detachedly laugh of things that cause me despair.[32]

This passage was written in 1961, but well represents the estrangement, even more than the hostility, that Pasolini felt toward humor, an estrangement and hostility that will remain constant throughout his life, even though, obviously, Pasolini himself will practice different kinds of humor. To Jean Duflot, who pointed out the presence of humor in *Theorem*, *Oedipus King*, and *Pigsty*[33] as a corrective to bitterness and cruelty, Pasolini answered repeatedly: "Yes, but it is a typically bourgeois defensive reaction, a way of being bourgeois. Unlike influential people, heroes never have a sense of humor"; or, "the populace is not humorist . . . it is comic, facetious." And finally, "Humor is detachment from reality, a contemplative posture in front of reality, and therefore a dissociation between the self and this reality."[34]

The polemical target is the cold and controlled relationship between bodies delivered by Anglo-Saxon humor, humor, that is, "belonging to the most bourgeois society in the world." What hurts and pains Pasolini the most is having to discover within all of us, day after day, the "alien" presence of humor, a "biological degradation" that is present "in all of its inertia," an "unfruitful ill" that has now installed itself permanently inside us and that does not "even help us to live." Humor is the inseparable companion of defeat, both ideological (the "decline of the hope of class-warfare") and biological as the loss of vigor ("because I have grown old, because I have grown 'wise' . . . because I have accepted things too much"). Humor is the attempt to transform into virtue the terrible disease of apathy and indifference: "bitterness, detachment, contemplation, rather than active participation and real solidarity; the smiling over things that, in the past, would have thrown me into the purest state of seriousness, passion, even rage."[35]

Passion versus humor, then, with age facilitating the passage from the first into the second: Humor is directly proportional to aging and to the loss of vitality. With regard to "desperate vitality," it represents the moment when the only thing that remains is despair. Humor, with its contemplative posture, is resignation: It is that side of despair that leads to adaptation and conciliation, while Pasolini prefers the other side, the side of rage, the only way in which vitality can survive in the age of despair, retaining its oppositional strength.

Pasolini movingly entrusted Giorgio Bocca with the anguished discovery of signs of aging in his own body, which had been the mainstay of his life: "Some mornings, when I awake, the thought of aging is like a lightning bolt. Ulcers, a month in bed, weakness, taking care of myself. I have felt old, for the first time."[36] And to the same Bocca, who invites him to tone down his rage in exchange for irony and resignation, and for the wisdom and rest (and also bodily care) that he had consigned to boredom, he replies sharply: "No, an angry man does not become wise, bored or learn his lessons. He is like litmus paper: He reacts. Except that, while he is young, he has hopes for his future life, but as time goes by, doubts and discouragement assail him. Then, rage grows, and becomes obsession."[37]

In *The Religion of My Time*, and especially in *Uncivil Poems*,[38] this transition and the feeling of having lost one's burning vitality (in parallel with the feeling of a collective decay) is explicitly thematized. Here the protagonist is senile avarice whose temptation emerges when "the world flies/ towards its new youths." Faced with this transition and simultaneously with it, the awareness emerges that "every road ends, even mine." And here old age, as the inability to tremble in delight, takes the stage: "As every old man, I deny it: denial being the only/consolation of those who, if they tremble, die."[39]

This association between reaction, passion, vitality, and shaking also returns in *The Rage*: "Why don't I react, why don't I tremble/with happiness, or enjoy some pure anguish?/Why can't I recognize/This old knot of my existence?"[40] This old knot returns at the end: Rage is what allows one to preserve a semblance of youth even if one is forty and "wrecked by passion." The opportunity to continue to talk with young people is completely handed over to the loyalty he feels toward his old inability to experience peace: "And, like a youth, without pity/or modesty, I do not hide/this state of mine: I will never find peace, never."[41] Trembling, living, not knowing that pause called peace: Even when "the boundless percussion instrument/of sex and light" no longer happily buzzes (as in *The Ashes*), one can continue to listen to its dull and ever more distant thuds.

Paternity and Institutions

In Pasolini's diversity there is also, on many levels, the rejection of the father, a frontal collision with conventions, traditions, and the authorities. But, as Gian Carlo Ferretti has noted with great acumen, a decisive moment in Pasolini's biography can be situated exactly in the progressive evolution from a first, "maternal" season to a successive "paternal" one, a season in which the figure of the father no longer generates just negative responses but also positive ones. As always, this moment is situated at the crossroads between biography and history, at a juncture where probably nothing would happen were it not for this intersection of collective and personal destinies. The biographical moment is to be found in the already cited passage where Pasolini discovers the signs of aging in his illness (in March, 1966, he faints in a pool of blood at a restaurant, as the result of a perforated ulcer); the body upon which the oxymoron was fastened registers the beginnings of decline, the definite loss of any possibility to identify with young people and children. More and more his destiny is to become a father, even if this is in contradiction with "an overall desire not to be a father"[42] and to identify with one's own father and with fathers in general.

Historically, the evolution toward fatherhood becomes visible in the light of another dramatic date: "Exactly in 1968, the year in which without much sorrow he died experimentally, he had the first true crisis of his life. Why? Because for the first time he realized that he was a father."[43] An absolutely unique father, a nonbiological and contradictory father, at times reticent and long-winded, at times authoritarian; a father unable to understand with serenity the reasons of the sons and obstinately tied to the repetition of his own rules; an apocalyptic father, fiercely critical of the new times as all fathers are.

If Pasolini stopped at the crossroads between his own biology and history, his becoming a father would be of no interest, just as the entire "corsair" season would be uninteresting:[44] It would be difficult to tell it apart from the sensational display of the most terrible avarice, that senile avarice that clothes itself under the mantle of experience and is unable to accept decline. But—and here lies the great intuition of Pasolini—the claim to his role as father is tied to an analysis of Italian society and its transformations that redefines all roles. The revolt against one's fathers that seems to be the dominant and common trait of the culture of protest of 1968 is not in contradiction with the long-term logic of Western societies; on the contrary, it is in many ways the most effective instrument of their transformation, in keeping with the imperatives of consumerism. This process of "homologation," of "restoration or real reaction" no longer finds shelter behind old authorities but "literally tends towards erasing the past, with its 'fathers,' religions, ideologies and ways of life." Obviously this transformation does not assume the traditional forms of reaction, but rather the opposite ones of revolution; it does not want to preserve but change, destroying "revolutionarily (with regards to itself) all the old social institutions—family, culture, language, church."[45] In a nutshell, all seems to move in the direction of what Alexander Mitscherlich has defined as a *vaterlose Gesellschaft*, a society without fathers, where fraternal envy is taking the place of the old oedipal rivalry. The crisis of the father figure has a long period of incubation, but the critical ferments already delivered by psychoanalysis and Marxism are nothing compared to the homologizing and captivating power of the market: "Mass society . . . creates a gigantic army of rival, envious siblings. Their chief conflict is characterized, not by oedipal rivalry, struggling with the father for the privileges of liberty and power, but by sibling envy directed at neighbors and competitors who have more than they."[46] So writes Mitscherlich, in a crucial passage of his analysis to which Pasolini's is very close: "fathers expect to castrate us,/ but brothers expect us to castrate ourselves./This, then, is Terror."[47] Or again: "it really is the true new power that wants to get rid of such fathers. It is precisely this power that no longer wants the sons to enter in possession of such ideal inheritances."[48]

It is not a matter of revaluing those fathers and those ideal inheritances but of understanding that the revolt against the father, a revolt that once was the action of the few—risky and sacrilegious but also authentically and painfully liberating—in the new society becomes a mass exercise, a gymnastics with neither tragedy nor pain because carried out with impunity, in the shadows, and under the directives of a new power that is more widespread and inescapable than the old one. The fathers also participate in this mass parricide, as they too are inclined to follow the ideology of a society without fathers.

It is exactly the by-now-obsolete figure of the father that leads Pasolini to recognize it as a value, as a point of observation removed from dominant conformism. Mind you, it is never a question of a total or definitive identification. More than once Pasolini will turn the roles upside down and propose himself as the son or even grandfather of the movement's youth.[49] Yet, to identify with the role of the father does not mean to place oneself at a radical and unbridgeable distance from the movement, but to position oneself as its critical but privileged interlocutor. That argument, which many did not understand, allowed him both great proximity and distance from the topic. The point of greatest distance resides precisely in mistrusting the shared meaning that seems to ensure that one does not have to commit much to be on the right side. Pasolini's misgivings about the cultural clichés of his own time are always very much watchful and present, almost to the point of a paranoia that is as subtle as it is pervasive. In a letter from 1970 to Walter Siti (who had sent and dedicated his doctoral dissertation to him), Pasolini reproaches the subtle yet categorical conformism of a generation that takes for granted judgments that are but the expression of one group: "Reproaching my wicked use of these notions ["populace," "sub-proletarian," "history," "reason"—F.C.], you appear to address yourself to a small circle, where everybody understands each other immediately without having to waste time to speak about them." In this, "resides all your immaturity as a youth who imitates the optimism of his contemporaries. . . . With your thesis you have flattered your 'strong' contemporaries or the 'professor who was allied to your contemporaries.'"[50]

Even in a letter of the following year, his criticism to Guido Santato is that he takes for granted the reasons of "proletarians in uniform" who, instead, "have their own faults which are too easily blamed on power. . . . Power that is not only outside those young men that are humiliated by it, but also within them."[51] Certainly, fathers have their own serious and tragic responsibilities, but too often pointing out these sins has produced the simplistic and unfortunate result of hiding the responsibilities of the sons. Any sound argument must start from acknowledging everyone's responsibilities, before all else the ones of those who arrogantly proclaim their complete innocence. To be sure, often the sons must answer for sins that are not theirs, but their fathers'; yet, "the negative paternal legacy may half explain them but for the other half they are themselves responsible. These are no innocent children."[52]

The Hidden God of Desacralization

The "paternal" season is thus not only the defensive reaction of a dated
and resentful anticonformism vis-à-vis the more progressive critique of
mass political praxis held by the generation of 1968. Ultimately, this is the
criticism that many of those who identified with (or influenced theoretically) that movement direct to Pasolini: They reproach him for having
misunderstood and lost his way when confronted with events whose fundamental fault was to have completely changed the traditional relationship
between politics and culture, and, above all, surpassed and minimized the
antagonistic nature of his work. This criticism has its good reasons, but
too often it has just been happy to wrap itself within them, looking down
on Pasolini's position and pointing a finger at him. Pasolini, in his perception of some events from that period, and perhaps due to a desperation
that had its roots in his generational and personal history (but who could
ever avoid the suspicion of speaking, in the end, for personal reasons?),
went farther than his critics who were part of the "movement." The
farthest point was the affirmation of the relationship between the new
culture's hedonism and the consolidation of a new power, between a desecration already trapped in purely negative methodology and the omnipotence of the market's bonds.

In the interview with Duflot, Pasolini states: "I am more and more
scandalized by the absence of the sense of the sacred in my contemporaries."[53] Secularization sweeps away all forms of resistance opposed to a freedom that wants to be infinite, but is evermore dependent on the market.
The progressive demolition of the sacred establishes the sacredness of
commodities (Marx's "fetishism"), and lets loose a dynamic of desire that
internalizes the negative infinity of a desire that is characterized by "a
permanent dissatisfaction, which seeks to placate itself through the obsessive quest for material goods."[54] If, in the past, desecration enabled one to
fight the conservative and hypocritical structures of society, the transformation of the latter toward hedonism and consumerism renders desolately
obsolete old intellectual figures and their certainties.

> Now one of the commonplaces most typical of the left-wing intellectual is
> the desire to deconsecrate and (to invent a word) to desentimentalize life.
> In the case of the old progressive intellectuals, that is explained by the fact
> that they were brought up in a clerico-fascist society which preached false
> sanctity and false sentiments. And so the reaction was correct. But today
> the new power does not impose the false sanctity and those false senti-
> ments. Indeed it itself is the first, I repeat, to wish to be liberated from
> them altogether along with all their institutions: the army and the church,

for instance. So the polemic against sanctity and against sentiment on the part of the progressive intellectuals who continue to grind out the old values of the Enlightenment as if it had mechanically become part of the human sciences is useless. Or else it is useful to the existing power.[55]

These are self-critical considerations that Pasolini discusses in the famous *Abjure* from *The Trilogy of Life* (on June 15, 1975, a few months before his death and coinciding with great electoral gains by the PCI).[56] The films in the trilogy (*The Decameron, The Canterbury Tales*, and *Arabian Nights*)[57] were devoted to a celebration of free expressions of sexuality that fit well "in the struggle to democratize the 'rights of expression' and to liberalize sex, two fundamental moments in the progressive drives of the Fifties and Sixties."[58] At a time when power still appeared bigoted, hypocritical, and obscurantist, it was plausible that one could locate a point of resistance, "the last bulwark of reality," in "'innocent' bodies and the archaic, dark, vital violence of their sexual organs."[59] But now that the situation had radically altered, a general reorientation became necessary: The classical goals of the progressive struggle failed and "expressive democratization and sexual liberalization have been brutally surpassed and neutralized by the decision of consumerist power to allow for a tolerance that is as far-reaching as it is false."[60]

Even the factual reality of bodies that seemed to hold the last line of resistance has been "violated, manipulated and tampered with by the power of consumerism." The new power threatens in new and sweeping ways what seemed to be the last, impregnable domain: In this area, to de-sacralize and de-sentimentalize coincides with inscribing the bodies within a new disciplinary code that is omnipresent and invisible at the same time. As Foucault has pointed out with masterly lucidity that borders on paranoia in *The Will to Knowledge*,[61] sexual liberalization organizes a field of visibility and knowledge of sexuality that removes it from the power of agency and resistance of the individual. Sexual freedom possesses within itself a new normative code that is not experienced as such but as its opposite, that is, as a liberation from old ties and rules for the more complete fulfillment of one's freedom.

This is where Pasolini's belief that the sacred might change its function and become a space of resistance against the new normative codes of consumerism originates, and, following this path, the sacred might approach the "authentic" transgression that makes a stand against the mass transgression presently guaranteed from above. Here another of Pasolini's oxymorons asserts itself: the assertion of a sacred that inspires criticism and becomes heretical; the use of tradition against power, a revolutionary use of tradition. In this new framework, it is possible to defend the sacred: "I defend the sacred because it is the side of man that offers less resistance to the profanation of power, and is the most threatened by the institutions of the Churches."[62] Faced with the establishment of the "sainthood" of the majority,[63] and of the "new, never mentioned, sacredness of commodities and their consumption,"[64] Pasolini polemically reaffirms the value of another sacred, finding its example in the life of the unborn child; hence, his position against abortion. One can find many reasons for this polemic and not all are equal in value (Pasolini himself did not shun at times debatable arguments); but the most significant one resides in the ability to show the other side of the moon to all those who live walled in the ideology of infinite emancipation, without ever asking any "ecological" question about the effects produced by this way of life.

Faced with a power that has radically changed its nature, to be true to itself the Left must be capable of recovering some of the reasons of the Right. But not of any Right: only of the "sublime" Right that can teach those who have remained prisoners of the Critique how to resist the dissolution of the world. And this in full coherence with the "rationalistic and humanistic spiritual tradition": The old progressive spirit of critique can survive only if it understands that "we must no longer fear—as we once did correctly—having a heart and not discrediting the sacred enough."[65] The logic that makes everything possible as long as consensus is achieved and which thinks it can rewrite everything according to the simple grammar of (human) rights, produces, on the other side of the world, illegal dumping grounds and mass graves it does not want to hear about. This is the resisting function that pertains to the sacred: to resist making the entire world available solely to the religion of commodities. This is something more sophisticated and complex than a reactionary nostalgia: If it is true that development does not coincide with Progress, the latter will mean something only if it regulates (and limits) development from a perspective that is external to it. The ideology of endless emancipation is not external to development but constitutes its mythological soul; and the affirmation of a sacred that is in conflict with it is the attempt to experiment with the concrete possibility of thinking of a world that grows out of development, but with the memory of other meanings and other forms of the sacred.

How can it be denied that all the cultures of the limit, which are so widespread today, were not anticipated in Italy by Pasolini's reflection on the sacred? Certainly, there is in his polemic a provocative dimension, personal issues that at times are annoying. But without those flaws it is unlikely that we would have had those reflections, without that fierce courage nobody would have dared challenge the doxa. We would have had only the countless arguments of those who criticized him, with some good reasons, but also with the irresistible boorishness of cultural clichés that were stifling them.

Is it possible to maintain a leftist identity by recovering the values of the right and using the sacred heretically? Is a revolutionary use of tradition possible? To what extent is this not an attempt to shape a mass of contradictions, the illusion of piling together values that constitute an algebraic sum and therefore annul each other? Is this political ambiguity or, rather, in line with Fortini's old criticism, the narcissistic display of one's personal conflicts expanded to worldwide contradictions? Everything would be easier if it were so: All the accounts would be settled. But then it would be difficult to compare these accounts with what has happened in the twenty years that now separate us from Pasolini's death. Water has not stopped flowing under the bridges just to please yesteryear's accountants, and those contradictions, far from being obsolete and the expression of a private oxymoron, were shown to have anticipated future events. When just a breeze was moving in the air, this exasperated sensibility anticipated future whirlwinds, those that normal people, even when professionally trained, perceive only when there is a full wind that blows us away.

Mine are metapolitical reflections and do not presume to be anyone else's recipes. Besides, Pasolini himself was well aware that his ability to anticipate the future, his healthy crossed-eye vision, had no easy political solution. His profound awareness about the ambivalence of the sacred is witness to this: "Conversely, I realize that in my nostalgia for an idealized sacred that might have never existed there is something wrong, irrational and traditionalist—considering that the sacred has always been institutionalized, first, to give an example, by shamans; then, by priests."[66]

Pasolini certainly does not lose the ability to see both sides of an issue, as is demonstrated by his interest in Saint Paul to whom he wanted to dedicate a movie and to whom, it has been said, he felt very close in the last years of his life. In the screenplay to the never realized film, the double nature of the sacred, this ambivalence of religion, finds its fulfillment in the figure of a rebel who is also a builder, a man who breaks the law while affirming a higher and more compelling one. In Saint Paul are present two inseparable and contradictory dimensions: the prophetic one that clashes violently against the insufficient wisdom of the world by proclaiming *stultitia* as the higher form of knowledge ("Do not delude yourselves: If someone among you thinks to be knowledgeable in this world, may you turn ignorant to become wise!"),[67] and the organizational one, which wishes to make preaching less volatile in order to turn it into an institution. On the one side is he who, talking to the world about something that does not belong to him, deeply confounds human beings and succeeds in shaking and silencing even the skepticism of the intellectuals; on the other, he who (with faithfulness and coherency, and without contradicting what he says!) is inevitably tempted to regulate, keep under surveillance and punish. Here, the world is made prodigiously relativistic; there, the Church engages its organizational-repressive tentacles. On the one side, absolute impotence, also symbolized by the beginning crisis of a disease that prostrates Paul; on the other, the astute smiles of those (like Satan and Luke), who know that the fascination with impotence prepares new power, the moments when Paul gains strength, confident, productive, and eager to trap life in the thick web of norms. On the one hand, the revolutionary force of charity, its extraordinary ability to subvert; on the other, the institutions and their reassuring concept of time, their readiness and support; tangible, not volatile.

Institutionalization is a trap, but a trap into which human beings gladly fall: It would be "too easy if the institutions were only negative."[68] Instead, "they are touching,/human beings identify themselves in them, and life/humble life, yes, it cannot be distinguished from them/like the brood from its nest—as long as it stays there."[69] An institution, with its "divine vulgarity," is the kingdom of ceremonial, rhetoric, and simplifications, the locus of that repetition in whose shadow the humble live (even workers in the shadow of their party!). And for those whose only siblings are dogs and who are "forced to live, like bandits, at their margins," institutions exert a formidable attraction.

> Because institutions are touching: and human beings
> Can only identify themselves in nothing else but them.
> It is they that humbly turn men into brothers.
> There is something mysterious about institutions—
> only form of life and simple model for humanity—
> compared to which the mystery of an individual is nothing.[70]

> We are brothers in the institution, in the anxiety of the norm:
> This is paltry and vile; but moving.[71]

But this touching brotherhood is not something that Pasolini can experience. It implies a submission that he has always found impossible, a conciliation that he is denied.

> But I? Mary, I am not a brother;
> I fulfill other roles of which I am not aware;
> not the one of brotherhood,
> but at least that of accomplice
> so close to the obedience and the heroic unawareness
> of human beings, your brothers despite it all, but not mine.[72]

It is to the secretly homosexual Paul, who suffers from his same disease, that Pasolini feels close; to a man who becomes extraordinary only in the abyss of his solitude and diversity, the times when he is a saint, but not a priest. But, just as the institutions are not only negative, even the extraordinary hides within itself something that is insidious. A "pure" heresy does not exist, because it always is orthodoxy *in nuce* ("the struggle has always been between the old and the new orthodoxy"),[73] and every desire for purity gives birth to "an infinity of guilty, impure and untouchable ones."[74] Even contrasting Saint Paul's two sides is impossible: The saint prepares the priest and clears the road for him. Pasolini, strengthened by the awareness of his "impurity," an impurity that he seems to recognize (though removed and sublimated) even in Saint Paul, knows well the dangers of sainthood and is aware that the sacred experiences the irresistible tendency to become institution. His call to protect the sense of the sacred is therefore not a naive return to a candid and impossible submission; it is only the desperate desire to point out that which, by removing itself from the ideology of progress, can build the materials necessary to contain it.

Commenting on J. G. Frazer's *The Golden Bough*, Ludwig Wittgenstein notices that, in his explanations of the ritual of "savages," the famous British anthropologist reveals such coarseness as to make one think that savages are not as removed "from an understanding of spiritual matters as is a twentieth-century Englishman."[75] To a certain degree, the last Pasolini has not done anything substantially different, because he has constantly tried to render relative (therefore, to fight) the great ability that the new power has to convince and corrupt. He has done so in his own way, throwing himself on the front line and looking for every opportunity for confrontation. His proposals are all unpolitical or metapolitical: The Left should recover the ability to resist the sacred without allowing itself to be drawn in by the irresistible tendency of the latter to become power, orthodoxy, discipline and repression; it should rebuild limits that are both as powerful as if they had divine origins and freely accepted by all. Finally, it should rediscover the sublime side of the Right without falling into its intolerance toward the Other. All in all, it is a call to do impossible things. Yet, if the future holds in store for us something other than the endless repetition of development and its myths, some aspect of this impossibility will not remain such forever.

PART IV

Other Essays on the Mediterranean

CHAPTER 7

Europe and Southern Thought

Greece, the Sea, and Philosophy

It is not by chance that philosophy was born on the sea, when the word "being" came into existence, floating between being and nothingness; when "becoming" became a word charged with a cognitive sense, calling into question truths that had been so strong as to never have been doubted or discussed. Knowledge escaped its oracular and sacred form and became a matter of opinion, debatable, the opportunity for a challenge, rhetoric, the capacity to persuade and argue: It moved from the temple to the market.

As a result, humanity no longer awaits the verdict of the oracles: It becomes instead the one we find in Plato's *dia-logoi*, where Socrates' final answer is just a secondary detail, and the great protagonists are the continuous search for knowledge, the questioning, the meeting, and the discursive *agon*. In the background this society of men freed from other duties; friendship and dialectic competition; and discussions late into the night, until one is overcome by weariness. The *logoi* are challenged and questioned, and the game shuts down only temporarily, before starting all over again, incessantly, like the sea's undertow. It is difficult to imagine philosophy without these a priori geographic conditions: without the pervasiveness of the Greek sea and the sweetness of the nights, the pleasure of a prolonged discussion, the masculine friendships, and the competitions. It is easy to observe, and people have repeatedly done so, that the free exercise of the mind presupposes the slavery and exclusion of women: This is clearly an observation that needs no rebuttals. However, it is almost too easy to object that, while the history of humankind is full of male freedoms predicated on the enslavement and exclusion of women, only the Greek one gave birth to philosophy.

What is extraordinary about philosophy is not the solution given to its issues by the single philosopher, but the essence of its interplay, the cultivation of controversy and discussion, something that goes on, and lasts longer than any theoretical closure to the interplay by this or that philosophical school. The temptation and hope of any philosopher is to bring closure to this interplay; but in this pursuit, the philosopher himself is played because his answer, far from ending the interplay, reopens and revives it through the formulation of the argument for subsequent discussions.

It is surprising that today the structure and history of this interplay have been simplified and reduced to a single scheme and purpose—technology: Philosophy has been reduced to science, and the latter to technology. So the *logos* has been reduced to a single use, and the will to power has been unstitched from that complex interplay as the only and most authentic vocation of the *logos*: As a result, a determinism worthy of better origins has completely been traced back to a primordial DNA. It is as if modernity and unbridled technology were the necessary destiny of Greece, as if, in subsequent eras, leaps and intervals, external developments and grafts to that primordial root had not contributed to give modernity its contemporary shape.

I believe that, as long as the Mediterranean was the gravitational center of civilization, the sea allowed navigation between lands: Being, just like a ship, set sail but landed again in the bay of Essence. The emphasis on becoming and the tipping over of the Greek balance happens later, with the full advent of modernity and the passage to the oceanic dimension, when the sea is no longer kept in check by land, but becomes ocean, sea without limits.

To suggest that Greece exhausted its usefulness by giving birth to unbridled technology (as if the myths of Dedalus and Prometheus had never existed) is to diminish its contributions, to use up the complex weave of its possibilities to follow the journey of a single thread. Although this is not the right place to discuss this issue, I wish to say that Greece is also polytheism and tragedy, the borderland that has constantly questioned itself about the plural statute of truths, their contradictions, and the suffering caused by this plurality.

Philosophy is the peaceful and discursive ritualization of that contrast, the move that attempts to avoid its cruel statute, a sweetening of the tragic clash over the nature of truth and good. This anti-tragic ritualization of the struggle in a discursive *agon* is the great Greek epistemological move, a move that Nietzsche understood with extraordinary clarity. Without *agon* that interplay is meaningless, without Dionysus there is no Apollo.[1] But the opposite is also true: Without Apollo, Dionysus destroys with his power and his excesses. Apollo does not represent a frigid and abstract equilibrium but is the instrument that controls *hubris*, balances it out, gives it a peaceful appearance, diminishes its drive through the logic of coexistence.

The Greek miracle lies precisely in the representation of the contrast between beauty and the power of one's passions, and in the need for balance, whether the latter comes from the opposition of the gods, the blind power of an unstoppable destiny or from an eminently human discursive reconciliation. And the centrality held by conflicts and plurality is incomprehensible without understanding Greece's dramatic dive into its sea; without the scattering of its city-states and the multiplicity of its fatherlands and islands; without the length and pervasiveness of its shores, the borders of contiguity and confrontation between land and sea; and without understanding that it lies at the border and at the origin of the distinction between three continents.

Not surprisingly, this anti-tragic idea of the need to mediate is also at the origin of the Roman invention of jurisprudence and of the idea that power should be controlled through rational and discursive practices. Rome never produced great philosophical currents, and its memory has been greatly damaged by the aggressiveness of Fascism; but we must not forget that it gave Europe a discipline that, through its own existence, places conditions and limits onto power. Here too is the horizontal side of the *logos*, the one that ties discursive practices to power and, by injecting rhetoric within the state's foundations, anchors them to the soil of individual rights, and rescues them from the discretionary judgment of the powerful. *Logos*, but within its measure: Excesses are not of the *logos*, but of something that comes later and might be impossible to name. Certainly, this development, this normative and legal effectiveness of the *logos*, is ambivalent because it requires the submission to a single jurisdiction, its centering within the one power that must administer the sanctions meted out during the trial. Here the *logos* gains effectiveness and power but loses some of its mobility and restlessness. But the *mare nostrum* is not only regression vis-à-vis Greek plurality. In it we also find the valuable idea of holding things together, of the price that every freedom must pay to other freedoms to avoid rushing into war: The idea of a vast and pluralistic house, where the emperor can come from Spain, Africa, or Illyria.[2]

The End of Moderation: Europe between the Mediterranean and the Ocean

The continuity between Greece and Europe is granted precisely by the sea, as Hegel felicitously noticed: "In Asia, the sea is without significance, and the Asiatic nations have in fact shut themselves off from it. In India, going to sea is positively forbidden by religion. In Europe, however, this maritime relationship is of vital importance."[3]

It is sufficient to look at Europe, this Western appendix of Asia, as Valéry has called it,[4] to realize that what characterizes it is the energy it receives from its daring dive into the sea, from the multitude of its docks and ports. The weight of the sea even leads Hegel to say that the "European state is truly European only in so far as it links with the sea. The sea provides that wholly peculiar outlet which Asiatic life lacks, the outlet which enables life to step beyond itself. It is that which has invested European political life with the principle of individual freedom."[5]

This European love for freedom was born in Greece, "the realm of beautiful freedom."[6] And the character of the Greek spirit is incomprehensible without "the layout of the land, inasmuch as it is a coastal strip that causes individualization and singularity." The coast, through the idea of travel and departure, through the invention and building of ships (the "swan of the seas"),[7] produces the first emergence of the individual, the beginnings of singularity, courage, cunning. It announces technology. But, in the Greek universe, this technology is still prisoner of the *kosmos*; it is still the relationship between two ideas: departure and return, *agon* and *nostos*, counterpoise and retribution of any character, marked indelibly by the art of tragedy.

To see all of Europe (even the oceanic absolutism of technology with all of its excesses) fully developed in ancient Greece is to have forgotten that the will to power never was its gravitational center; and that, as Karl Löwith noted,[8] no Greek ever focused his existence on the future and on development, since no Greek ever believed he could exceed the horizon of the cosmos and exit his closed circle by chasing the straight and ascending line of progress.

Europe, instead, becomes a world power when its gravitational center shifts from the Mediterranean to the Atlantic; when, as Carl Schmitt points out,[9] the sea turns to its advantage the relationship with the land, accepting no boundaries and becoming ocean. The breach and eclipse of the Mediterranean coincide with the wane of moderation, and the rise of sea-based fundamentalism in complete opposition to land-based fundamentalism. The flowing of the sea beyond every boundary, its absolutization, marks the birth of modern economy, the unbridled freeing of technology, universal uprooting and total nomadism, and the disappearance of every return route, as man becomes a ship always at sea without moorings. It is the end of the coast, of the port, of those points where land and sea come into contact creating boundaries and thus knowing and limiting each other. Every man is completely submerged in his singularity, and reduces existence to the pure projection of this singularity, without bounds or solidarity, without any "us" or even a weak sense of fatherland. Whereas land-based fundamentalism (the East) wedges the individual in the wall of "us," preventing his departure and his beginning, sea-based fundamentalism (the West) prevents one's return to shore: It allows the individual to be free like the wind, without ties, without origins and without progeny. The individual becomes more and more individualistic, free and alone; he has the advantage of self-determination, but facing him is the rest of the world: Like William Gibson's *Neuromancer*,[10] he could sleep in a house slightly larger than his body, a casket.

Let us mention Deleuze's opinion in the matter,[11] his praise of drift and sea, "the smooth space *par excellence*," the one that escapes all organization and branding, a nomadic anarchy that moves in a region occupied "by intensities, winds and noises, by tactile and sonorous forces and qualities, like in the desert, the steppe and the glaciers." Smooth space is inhospitable and escapes inhabitation and calculability; it is available for deterritorialization more than any other space. Deleuze points out that the sea, even though it is the archetype of smooth space, "has also been the archetype of all the streaks left on smooth space." Therefore, Deleuze's nomadism is the space of individual freedom, the Dionysian motion characteristic of a world dominated, unified, and organized by economic principles. The oceanic dominion is the dominion of the universal marketplace, from the small waves of labor union disputes to the billows of the stock market, all the way to the violent storms of restructuring, where the impersonal nature of business can knock us about and drown us like a huge wave. This universe, with its animalistic vitality and impersonality, with its innate amorality and its suddenly euphoric and/or catastrophic cycles, escapes the organizational grids and branding of States, their attempts to reterritorialize a world that, just like the sea, escapes fixity, sedentary life, and sameness with itself. In the same grammar of interminable economy, even ownership and profit can never stop: They are returned, through investment, in the circuit of risk-taking and production; they can never rest on a shore, but must resume incessantly, their seafaring ways.

The West is Europe, but it also has eluded Europe. Now Europe, which once was the starting point of the ocean, finds itself coming into existence as a political entity in a world that is completely oceanic, where the primacy of business applies, and the balance between land and sea, impulse and safeguard, work and life is ever more precarious, almost impossible to attain. The bureaucratic machines that attempted to shape this drive, the national States that tried to control and direct this power all to one country, in the past century plunged for this reason in two massive and fierce conflicts. European humanity cannot just wax nostalgic about totalitarian political bureaucracies! It freed itself first of Fascism, then of Communism, but not of the need for protection and shelter.

The Necessary South

It certainly is not the desire for land that has failed, except that now it is misplaced; it has suffered a metamorphosis unthinkable until ten years ago. Places and cities have started talking again, after a lengthy period when they had become transparent, blurry and insignificant backgrounds, or scenes of dramas written and thought elsewhere. The sea has arrived everywhere and, to say it with Massimo Cacciari, has transformed the world into an archipelago.[12] The problem that remains unresolved is how to prepare these lands, now communicating with each other, for a new phase, for a new relationship between land and sea. This is not nostalgia: If the sea surrounds us, the problem of what constitutes our land rests entirely upon us: We must decide what we must keep dry, what we must save of our history and geography, of our memory and our experience. It becomes necessary to reinvent our tradition, interpret it anew, reconstruct the bond without allowing it to smother us, build new protections without becoming their hostage.

This is where we meet the South, its ancient resistance to Becoming and history, to the Spirit and to technology, and to their rule, a rule that does not tolerate borders, levees or dams. The South is perched on the most anachronistic of resistances, the one of body and nature that the *logos*, with its wordplay, thinks it can sidestep. The South is before the *logos*; it is tied to the spreading out of the sun, to its light and its Southern demons. The South is absolute presence, its perfection so strong that it terrifies. The South is the search for shade and night as relief, but also, on the Mediterranean, for that common mother that results from the intersection of olive trees and sea, for the beauty that Venus did not create, but which created her. The South anchors our desire to leave, and when the wrenching away, made inevitable by the sea, occurs, it charges it with nostalgia, with the pain of separation. As happens to Ulysses at the beginning of the *Odyssey*, all the riches and adventures find their counterpoint in the tears for Ithaca. The balance between departure and return was born on the Mediterranean, and it explains why the *logos* rather than quickly seeking power in experimentation and technology, and embracing the North from the beginning, allowed itself to be captured by the pleasure of discussion and debate. Work is wedded to pleasure and logic to friendship. Here, experience has yet to become experimentation: It is much less powerful, subtler and individualistic, richer in contrasting voices, in the back-and-forth of bodies; it resembles a game.

Just as the *logos* is departure, pleasure in separation and individuation, the South is agreement with the world, the pleasure of the pause, the perfection of presence, the part of us that remains sitting in the sun; it is the point where metaphysical musings mix with the mirage, the dream, and the flight of fancy, as if we were still children and it were a kite. In the glorious era of modernity, its Southern shores have always been under attack, pursued as if they were hardened criminals, so that the policing forces of business, reason, and permanent speed have sought them out to put them behind bars. The South is indeed a crime for thoughts based on reason, thoughts that hate (because they do not understand) all that is not technologically reproducible and believe that knowledge begins with knowledge and not with pleasure, with the quick glancing of a mirage. Yet, as much as it is banished, it keeps growing back in the most unexpected places: It toys with us and reemerges in every desire we have to be interrupted and enjoy a place in the sun, when we appreciate life beyond work, just like the sky beyond the clouds.

After a long period of being demonized, nowadays the South is sought for the opposite reason, because we have discovered that, even in the accounting obsessions of business, it is a decisive factor of production; in a world where everything seems to become liquid, the longing for the South is a longing for land, our sensual memory, the moments when we and the earth pay homage to each other; or it is the time when our work is not a divine punishment, but a happy landing for our flight.

If I insist on this "need" for the South, it is because I do not believe it to be an exclusive prerogative of Southerners, an ethnic party just for them. Instead, I think that the South's marginality is a steep price that humanity as a whole is paying. If this is the case, maybe the history of the twentieth century is more complicated than how technological determinism wishes to present it, whether in its apocalyptic or apologetic manifestations. Here I provide only brief suggestions about this other way of looking at history. Cesare Musatti loved to say that psychoanalysis "had been invented by Jews to convince Anglo-Saxon people to behave like Italians."[13] Supposedly then, from its inception, this discipline reveals the need to move mankind's gravitational center southward. Significantly, James Hillman suggested a similar movement when he claimed that "the re-vision of psychology" is nothing more than a shift "southward," the shifting of "the seat of the soul from the brain to the heart . . . , from cognitive comprehension to aesthetic sensibility."[14]

Human beings whose Southern side has been repressed are deformed and condemned to suffer, exposed forever to the aggressive and pathological return of their repressed side: Those who study human emotions and their pathologies discovered this pattern before others, early in the twentieth century; so it is not surprising that they cleared the way for analytical discourse to study the Southern paths of the Unconscious. Since then much ground has been covered and this movement southward has continued in a variety of ways. The emergence of the feminine as a dignified theme of theoretical inquiry, one of the strongest and most profound transformations of the post–World War II period, follows this path by reclaiming nurturing as a value: No longer is it an ontological curse against women, but the communal good of a demilitarized condition that is not dominated by the obsession of competition.

Southern Thought

Southern thought is tied to the idea that, for too long, the south has been thought *by* others, especially, with the full advent of modernity, more so by the North, by its artificial light, by its rational and disciplined life. From this perspective, the South is only a collection of negative qualities, inertias, resistances, regressions, immaturities and vices. The South, however, does not only inhabit the South, but resides in every human being. For the South to start thinking about itself, it must break free of the belief that the history of the world moves in a North-West direction, and that those who are without roots must coalesce in the one and only unhappy and inexhaustible root of technology. Ironically, the favorite prize for those who live the whole year within the Northern walls of work and business is a vacation to the South, something they wish for all year long. They speed up to arrive in a place where they can get out, and avoid being stuck inside their whole lives. The oceanic excess of business and technology rediscovers, once it reaches its limits, the need for restraint. If we do not want to be stuck inside our whole lives, if we are not business fundamentalists, ayatollahs of company profits, if we wish to resurface and breathe, after having held our breath for a long time, what we need is the oxygen of the South, the one that drives us not to destroy machines, but to get off them and go on foot, without the obsession of planned domination.

In a certain way, this is already happening both in high culture, when someone like Bateson rediscovers the mind as nature,[15] when Heidegger reflects on abandonment,[16] when we learn that Zen can be helpful in dealing not only with archery but also with computers, and in mass culture, when we discover that an oftentimes crude need for re-enchantment follows technology. The South we are talking about is not a fundamentalism of the South, nor the oppositional creation of extremist parties; it is not a narrow closure back on one's values, an entrenchment that bemoans an imaginary past. It is instead the South offering itself again as a vehicle for experiential modes that interest everybody. Even the North, after all, does not live of North alone: It does not practice what it preaches, when it discovers the need to find the "after" of modernity, and, in order to deal with the risks of frivolity and hyperconsumerism, it invents the postmodern, the need to relativize the empire of reason. Isn't what emerges from the colored world of advertising—the overflow of beaches, sensuality, and seduction; of domestic warmth and pristine landscapes; of direct and intense interaction with the world—a confession of sorts, albeit filled with lacunae and contradictions? Those who ransack through our dreams, even if only to sell us something, know their essence and which of our desires they need to appease with their goods. What do the world plunderers amass in their lairs, what is the bounty of the powerful if not a bit of prostituted beauty, a slice of South, enslaved and fenced away from the outside?

Southern thought is the rediscovery of this repressed South, and its link with a life that is not hostage to technology but capable of restraint. The South itself risks running into excesses, but the risk is mitigated by the sea, by the ability of the Mediterranean to mediate between lands and to be horrified by fundamentalisms, the one wearing the turban and the one in the three-piece suit. The governors of its central banks cannot continue to hold Europe captive with their asceticism. Europe must learn how to allow back into its heart even the rhythm of the South, its hopes and dreams. If one goes beyond easy stereotypes, the great strength of American mass culture, from cinema to music, is to have captured this drive through the black, African soul of its music, music like rap that reaches us through the roar and conflicts of the metropolis. The Southern revision of culture is not a dream, but something that is already happening in areas that are allowed greater freedom: in certain types of cinema; impetuously, in musical and theatrical productions; and, in a more belabored fashion, where high culture is still dominated by modern orthodoxy. The rediscovery of the South and of the Mediterranean, the transformation of its innate polytheism into a positive value, the flavor of the restraint that comes from this ancient destination at the crossroads of peoples, is possible today: It is the only thing to do. Here and not only here.

CHAPTER 8

Cardinal Knowledge

Compasses and Navigation Books

North: It rules from above. The place of cold and of the winter solstice, of industry that delays gratification because its flowers will blossom only with the heat. The place of austerity and of the ability to wait, of restraint and control over the world and oneself. It is discipline and planning; light that is scarce and precious; active and sturdy loneliness. Cold, duration, patience, industriousness, reason, rigor: a sea one can only hope to navigate, distant from sensual pleasure; revenge on the harshness of the environment; cold and everyday *epos* against rhetoric and demagoguery; the order and repetition that relieve and free us; cleanliness, distance between bodies, precious and encircling light. The North is the place of constancy, faithfulness to one's goals, emotional control and modesty, restraint and the neutrality of affections.

The extreme North, the "Great North," has its own balance and moderation, it knows the majestic force of Nature, the difficulties one encounters when trying to surpass its limits and power: Finland and Alaska, Canada and Siberia, are different among themselves, but they can never reach the point of thinking of nature just as a source and reservoir of production. The challenge heightens ingenuity, but the excess of technical power is something else. One can live in the artificially heated cities of

Siberia, but outside, Nature remains "North." There's a tipping point, though, where the North transforms its harshness in lack of moderation: when, on the borders with the temperate climate zone, it becomes technological will to power, unbridled technology. Northern people, through their protestant ethics, make this discipline sacred and methodical, and they thrust themselves toward world hegemony. The opening onto oceans, onto the infinity of space and sea, gives value to and encourages this discipline, making it the form of life most prepared to dominate distances. The North joins the great Western adventure, and technology projects itself into space without fear. We should remember the appraisal that Paul Morand, Fouquet's defender, gives of Colbert: "Marble man," paralleling the one of Mme de Sévigné, "Colbert is the North"; thus discipline, method, measurable perseverance, quantity.[1]

The North does not exhaust itself completely in its modern version, because there always lies in wait its most hidden and exoteric side, the one that speaks the higher language of gothic and magic. It is the world of mystics and of the poets of the deepest North, the one of the *sagas*, castles, and fairies; the romantic one of *Kultur* that stands in opposition to *Zivilisation*, of *Gemeinschaft* in opposition to *Gesellschaft*, the one that does not avenge itself on nature with discipline and work, but tries to dominate it through magic, with private access to the secrets of the world; the one that does not like to discuss, but poetize; the one that does not like to reason and know through experimentation, but owns other more direct, difficult, and impervious pathways to truth. It is the world of great forests and snow-covered expanses, of secluded castles, of steppes and of cold seas made of silver and ice scales, of shadows long as spires. This deep and magical North is the Northern side that seems completely antithetical to the other one: It remains savage, reserved, and hostile to every form of domestication. When its gaze rests on Greece, it chooses the Pre-Socratic philosophers because attracted to the mysterious and oracular side of that knowledge that, as it decayed, would become philosophy. It is the Northern side that does not makes itself universal, but remains tied to places; the one that has inside itself great chiaroscuro regions and suddenly reemerges even within modernity.

There exist strong ties below the surface between these two seemingly antithetic Norths, though their being hidden does not make them less significant. The connection lies in their same passion for excess through the vertigo of Faust's myth. Science would seem to be at the antipodes of magic, but is the most coherent fulfillment of the latter's dream: It is a cold shamanism that makes human beings very powerful, but incapable of escaping their own game. Humanity gains through science a knowledge that exalts its will to power; but it cannot liberate itself from this knowledge because it cannot see its lack of moderation and is quite impotent against it.

West: crossing the threshold; going toward the sunset, between and beyond the mountains; adventure, departure, and discovery; not settling, the love for the new, abandoning the comfort of home and clan; virile maturity, courage, and the belief that one can control even that which lies beyond the horizon; the chase and expansion of the sun's reach; the abolition of night and the dream of conquest. One is born and inhabits the East; one "goes" West. In the West one always asks, "Where are you from?" The West never sees the Native Americans, "savages" that it vanquishes and exterminates. Freedom, separation, breaking away, testing, new beginnings, emancipation, individuality, road, ocean, continuous conquest, progress, accomplishment, exceeding one's past, Dante's Ulysses, America, modernity, the expansion and exporting of light, constant Enlightenment. Travel as absolute control of purpose, navigation and the open sea, burning one's bridges, growth, the sense of adventure, infinite accumulation, always leaving behind what one has gained and what is solid and secure, the need to push forward. Frontier, Western, North-West passage. It is the caravan, moving onward without respite, without pausing in one place, the eternal departure, the horseman riding onward, first the horse, then the motorcycle and the car. In John Ford, the West stands in opposition to the comforts and the vices of the East: The West is the barren place where men are made who test their moral strength and measure their virility and the span of the bridge. The East is artifice; the West is raw contact with nature. The East is civilization, wealth, *comfort*; the West is one's testing ground, man coming face-to-face in the open with his destiny. One escapes West with *The Shawshank Redemption*.[2] In Darabont's movie the location where the protagonist escapes is on the ocean's shores, not simply West, but South-West: The magical place is in Mexico—Zihuatanejo, twenty miles from Plaza Azul and from Mexico's Highway 37, a hundred miles North-West of Acapulco—and faces the Pacific, an ocean that the Mexicans say "has no memory."

The West is in a hurry and makes everything a competition: It crosses finish lines, beats records, and finishes first; it succeeds and dreams of successes; it believes that losers lack virtue and do not deserve salvation. It always has stories of winners and victories: The other face of the world, the one that loses, the majority of humanity, does not exist, or, if it really means to and is not just making excuses, can redeem itself in the next race. It is from these constant dismissals that are born Stephen King's nightmares, the fierce irruptions of that part of us that lacks progress.

The West for Europe, the West of Hegel and Spengler, is sunset, late maturity, decline, and announcement of fulfillment, of something that comes after the greatness of the West, but is at the same time its destiny. There are those who believe that we must invest ourselves in this direction and that the apex of philosophy is technology and nihilism, those who are at the same time part of the system and believe in the apocalypse, the mystics of success. But the West as sunset can also be the awareness that is born when the shadows are long: awareness of the limits, the idea that there may be many truths, and that no language holds within itself the world. The West as sunset can open to a self-relativity of the West, it can help one to perceive the need for moderation, for a freer and more balanced game between the cardinal points, and to perceive the proximity of thresholds and borders.

East: the place of origins, the point where the sun rises. The place we distance ourselves from, but where we are destined to return. The motherly unity that holds us all, the language to which we all belong, the faithfulness we will honor again; but also the Spring, the Saturday of the sun's growth, hope, the blossoming of fruits, the always new return of colors, when it is still fair to expect everything. Memory, the importance of the past and of what comes before us, the awareness that we come from others and from the Other, that we are part of a world that has given us life and holds us within itself, that life is not self-generated, but is found. Places and nature, the necessary holism, our knowledge as preceded by and contained in a whole. Nature, mother, unity, land, origins, provenance, community, knowledge, circularity, belongings, roots, attribution, translation, the feeling of time, being part of a greater design, born to give birth, the legitimacy of regress and regression vis-à-vis the rhetoric of progress, the need to reconcile and care, the beauty of "trusting in" rather than "emancipating oneself from." Finally, the idea of dawning knowledge, born from a primordial illumination, from the simplicity of a beginning or an early morning.

The East is also the home that holds us back and hinders every departure and freedom as if they were betrayals of ties and faithfulness, sins against the group and the community, crimes against the others. The East is primacy of the community, of the *homo ierarchicus*,[3] belonging to an order that has been written before us and does not wait, nor accepts, to be recognized and authorized by the single individual. It is the right of way of the whole, from the natural to the social, the belief that men belong to rules, and that the space reserved for the individual lies particularly in interpreting in the best possible way one's role in the cosmos, together with one's rank, orders and duties. The name of the individual can never exceed, nor can it break ranks with, the preestablished order. The only chance one has is, as for knights and samurai, to become the highest representatives of collective symbols. This collective harmony might be pleasing or not, and it might be obtained spontaneously or achieved through the harshest and most demanding force. In our idea of the East there is always the conviction that it came before us, that it is the primordial beginning: For some it is that which we must emancipate ourselves from; for others, that to which we must return. It is interesting that the West should look out on the Pacific coast, on the extreme West, almost to confirm the roundness of the earth; that the most "advanced" world, the one that has always forced the limits of the horizon, should rediscover the great circle beyond the ascending, straight line of progress. There where the development of science and of the many specializations increases in every way its dominion over nature, the idea of a "new wisdom" appears, a knowledge of the whole or the wait for a new era, a *New Age* that places centrally, once more, what progress had discarded as useless old stuff. Certainly the East that returns is an East *prêt à porter*, which might look like the meeting of consumerism and infinity, after the affluence of material goods; the arrival of incense and green valleys, a narcotic weak and deprived of anger. But the risks and limits of an analgesic and tranquillizing faith cannot distract us from the most relevant point: This need for the East comes after development, after the extremism of the West, as recognition that the infinity of scientific progress might not be enough and could become a spiritual prison, a bad infinity.

South: Summer solstice, the disappearance of shadows; slowness, immobility, stops, pauses, waits, proximity, sensuality, torpor and suspension; but also elation and the unbearable fullness of life, the mature fruit that begins to lose itself when ripe, the sweetness that reminds us of death, the peak and the beginning of decline. At the height of life, the absence of shade; state of grace and malediction, sweetness, wisdom, sensuality and death, demon of the afternoon, stasis, dream, white light; the perfection of being in the moment, ecstasy, loss of control, light and openness, perfection and the height of presence, perfection of the here-and-now, of the present in its pure state. The absence of compasses, passion and sunning, magic and sortilege, fatalism, passivity, a space inhabited by demons, the nostalgia for what we have, the body and its senses as beginning, as strong knowledge of the world, rhythm and dance. It is not the past, the origin, the reverence of memory, the East; it is not the future, competitive projection toward it, the West; nor the frigid superiority of universal laws that aspire to be valid everywhere and for all time, the North. But it is the strength of the heart, of the present; the moment when the sun offers no shelter: It is relief, freshness, interval; rest without rules. There is no attempt to program, control, plot, and plan, to turn the present into the future and the future into the present. Instead, only the present exists; it is what is left in us when we die: "The skin we caressed one day, the sun we saw hide behind the mountain range, the nocturnal aroma of flowering oranges and the music water makes, through its streams, as it flows to the sea,"[4] a sum of all our present times, moments that remain within us as such, places that we once crossed, that do not allow us to give them a meaning, but are potent as present moments, something that happened to us once on our own skin, without any mediation and any shelter, whether it was joy or suffering, fear or relief, pleasure or surprise.

There exists a South with black skin, Africa (a South that Hegel banished outside consciousness and history), that with its rhythms, "the heartbeat of the world,"[5] has delved into the presumptuous body of European music until it made it Other; and there is another South that writes novels and still believes in storytelling, a Latin American South, full of terrible contradictions, but with boundless sensual and oneiric reserves. It is a South that looks at life without the hygienic rules invented by reason; a South that has not sterilized either life or death, land of injustices and great soccer players, of music, telenovelas,[6] and fierceness without shame. A South where the Carnival is a celebration of summer and bodies, and the drunkenness of the party joins together with that of the hot nights; a South where the future struggles to take leave of dreams and of the idea of great redemptions against bullying; a South that cultivates the art of going on walks, too ripe with symbols, allusions, and maledictions to be planned by the surveyors of reason.

There is also a South in the cities of North America: the somewhat perturbed South of young blacks, the rage and exhibitionism that we find in their way of walking, singing, and dancing, in their desire to be recognized and heard. A poor pride, but capable of speaking to all the youth of the world: where the group is the deformed footprint of another idea of wealth, in places where its only proper form seems to be property, fences, well-kept and reserved parks, private police forces, electronic circuits, beautiful women that are blonde as magnificent prey, the adoration of ownership and success.

The Conquest of the Center

There are North-men: those who are hard at work and know how to deserve what they have, made adult by the cold and by contrary winds;

those to whom nothing was given, who believe in constancy and discipline, and prepare for the winter, the ants of the world.

There are West-men, men who are only departures. They are the wrenching away that liberates, the beyond-men; those who escape their Egypts, break through the horizon and have found their home Elsewhere; those for whom the door is always an exit and never an entryway.

There are East-men, those faithful to their roots, the plants of the world; those who do not know the wound of departure and feel they have found their space in the world; those who sit in silence with their thoughts and have found the perfection in the eternal return of the circle.

There are South-men, and they are the ones who lay out in the sun and sing instead of working, the crickets of the world; the ones who waste their time and earn time, envied and disparaged for the same reasons; who live in the here-and-now of the body, never in the before, the after and the beyond.

Each of these types rotates, like the Ptolemaic universe,[7] around its own cardinal point: It looks at the other human types from a different region of the world with sufficiency, disparagement, as an eccentricity of nature or history. Each cultivates the seedling of its fundamentalism and sometimes is choked by its splendid growth. The West looks at the East as tyranny, a community that chokes and represses. The East looks at the West as loss of one's center and uprootedness. The North looks at the South as incontinence, sloth, and whimsy. The South looks at the North as anguished love for the prisons of one's inner self.

How could anyone claim that one of these viewpoints is more correct than the others, deserves to prevail over them, and must become the only one that matters? How could anyone legitimately think that one of these types is closer to perfection and require that all the human beings who live in the others abandon them to become refugees in the first? How could we seriously believe that a takeover by one of the cardinal points, and consequent outlawing of all the others, corresponds to justice? Would it not be a contradiction that points of the compass that gain their meaning from difference and from their relationship with each other must be reduced to a single one?

Yet, this is exactly what is happening, this is the recent history of the world. The North joined with the West, discipline has welded itself to freedom and they have given birth to political economy, to the individualization and disciplining of human beings. This great alliance incorporates a Faustian lack of moderation and wages war against the other cardinal points, raining upon them its extraordinary technological power and its incredibly rich intellectual apparatus. On the other side, there are only totalitarianism and backwardness, whim and fatalism, fundamentalism, deficits, and Mafia. The East and the South are like hardened criminals, outlawed and wanted by every police department.

But as usual this dominion cannot ever completely fulfill itself: The cardinal points are four for all human beings, and each of them speaks to a part of us, revealing itself important to balance us out. This is why the South and the East are peddled on the corners of streets; it is why they are reintroduced to the furthest West, as the Eastern wave of new cults arrives on the coasts of the Pacific; why in all the offices of the spiritual West one works like mad all year long, but dreams of escaping toward the prostituted South, as it is sold by every tourist agency on every square of a West without balance. What had been removed returns with a force directly proportional to the energy it took to remove it. Sometimes this return happens in monstrous shapes, such as the Mafia's trafficking in narcotics and the mass murders in Algeria; at other times, instead, it is the precious voice, the sweeping music, and the idea of a different perfection that one discovers in those women and men who come to our countries looking for work.

Hysterical newspapers and frightened governments see in these arrivals only a problem of public safety, forgetting history and their own migrations. We, instead, know that every arrival not only reminds us of the excesses and the fundamentalism of the North-West, but brings with it someone who helps us fight them.

The cardinal points are four, and they all live inside each of us. We must prevent the establishment of their fundamentalism, the rise of some as criterion and means of evaluation for the others, the ridiculous expectation that one of them might think of itself as the universal cure. We must be the center in the only way this is possible today: as a crossroads, as the ability to play each cardinal point against the fundamentalism of the others.

To those who object that this spiritual topography is Eurocentric, we answer: without a doubt! To those who observe that the East and the South we are talking about are more like idealizations and projections of our ghosts than reality, we answer: certainly! But we also know that we can only meet the Other if we are capable of keeping track of our own ghosts and projections, when the strength that pushes us forward is greater than that of the center of gravity that would have us always quietly gravitate around it. The center is not a fixed and embalmed place, the Ptolemaic rite of a land without landing spots, but a mobile crossing of winds and tides, in the vicinity of contacts, exposed to them. It loves borders, where one does not lock oneself in a circle to celebrate autistic centers, but leans out toward the Other; where one opens doors and crosses thresholds and passageways; where there is attrition, the danger of conflict, but also the possibility of recognition, of a true experience. The center often is not a "where," but a "when": It is when every man leaves autarchy and goes for a stroll with the eyes of the Other. In the center of the world are all the crossroads, all the worlds filled with landing spots, all the lands with welcoming beaches, all those peninsulas, off-kilter and leaning out in the sea.

To the question: "Where is the center?," to the question that asks for directions, we cannot always answer the same way: If we are North, we must point South; if we are South, we must point North; if we are West, we must point East; and if East, West. Today only two of these directions are followed, and it is herein that the lack of moderation lies.

CHAPTER 9

Against All Fundamentalisms: The New Mediterranean

From Unification to a Place in the Sun:
The Third Rome and the Imperialist Mediterranean

Italy becomes a unified State very late, in the second half of the nineteenth century (1859–60), and the problem of national unity monopolizes its political and cultural attention for a long time. Italy arrives to unity after an extremely long period of divisions, without an autonomous presence on the international scene, and very late with respect to the most powerful European countries, which, with the exception of Germany, have already spanned the previous centuries with the great ships of their national states, thus becoming colonial and imperial powers. This "delay" forces the attention of nineteenth-century Italian intellectuals—even the greatest ones, such as Leopardi, Foscolo, Manzoni, and Verdi[1]—to be focused, for the most part, on the theme of Italy's "deliverance" from foreign control.

Even the part of the century that follows national unity is dominated, at least in its early years—when the Historic Right (1861–76) is in power[2]—by the construction and organization of the National State and by the complex problems caused by the unification of the Kingdom: primarily, the emergence of sharp inequalities in the levels of development and standard of living in different areas of the country, and the discovery of the existence of a Southern Question.[3] During this first adjustment period, the restrained and prudent style of the Right prevails: It shows itself capable of managing very harsh repressions in the Mezzogiorno,[4] and, in international affairs, reluctant to aggravate conflicts and situations that would force Italy to clash with stronger nations.

It is only a question of time before the Mediterranean becomes an unavoidable issue for the new State, a knot that sooner or later must be unraveled. As Federico Chabod, one of the most famous scholars of Italian foreign policy, noted, it is the very expansion of the Kingdom of Piedmont southward that forces the ruling classes to adopt a new frame of reference that can no longer be just European or Northern European. Despite the reticence and aversion demonstrated by members of the old Piedmontese ruling class (Balbo, Durando, D'Azeglio), who fear the "Southernization" of the State, the annexation in rapid succession, first of the South and then of Rome, forces them to look differently at the Mediterranean. What prevails, even if slowly, with the rise to power of the Left (1876), is Mazzini's option,[5] the one that attempts to reinterpret, in the age of Nations, the universal mission of Rome. In a very significant document, Mazzini himself outlines Italy's "Mediterranean" calling and the crucial role that Rome plays in it: "Stop and extend your gaze southward, toward the Mediterranean. From within the vastness will arise to your gaze, like a lighthouse, an isolated point, a sign of distant grandeur. Bend your knees and pray! That's where the heart of Italy beats! There lies, solemn and eternal, ROME."[6]

Mazzini's words already help us understand how the Mediterranean will become part of Italy's political and cultural deliberations in the last quarter of the nineteenth century: It is the field of expansion of the *Third Rome*. After the Empire and the Catholic Church, Rome is called to a third great meeting with history, to a new phase of supremacy that the new State cannot elude without sliding into the cowardice of lazy coastal trade. Certainly, for some, at least initially, this new Rome will become the universal capital "of free thought and knowledge"; but soon thereafter the easiest temptation will be the colonial adventure. The Mediterranean is thus destined to become, once more, *mare nostrum* in the narrower sense of the word: the practice and trial grounds for the expansionist aims of the New Italy.

Promoting this turn of events will also be the crossover pressure of two problems the new State must confront: on the one hand, the social question (the rise of socialist movements, but also the worsening of the Mezzogiorno problem as a result of policies that damaged it in favor of Northern industry); on the other, the international question, which reveals that for Italy to overcome its marginality in the European context, it must change its role within the Mediterranean basin. Indeed, the new State has discovered that, among the many aspects of its minority and marginality, it lacks any presence in the sea to which it is bound by geography and history. The oldest European powers occupy this chessboard: Great Britain *in primis*, with its great oceanic empire; but France as well, as it has been consolidating it expansionist aims under the protection of considerable state and military prowess. So, when the new State turns its gaze toward the Mediterranean and intoxicates itself with visions of a great future, it finds itself squeezed and limited in its colonial and expansionist policies.

Colonial expansion is not specifically an Italian pathology, because the European national State has always been, concurrently, a great colonial power. What makes it peculiarly Italian is the delay in reaching unity, the gap between the rhetoric that accompanies the announcement of these ambitions and the harshness of the conflict that they are destined to unleash. The emergence in the heart of Europe of two new, great national States, Germany and Italy, cannot but cause serious problems to any pre-existing balances. For Italy these problems are, on the one side, those of its Northern borders, the so-called "yet-to-be-freed lands" (Trento and Trieste);[7] on the other side, those of the southern borders, and the desire for international relevance pointed toward eastern Africa and the south-eastern shore of the Mediterranean; an expansion that, according to some, would become useful, in conjunction with emigration, to stem and mitigate social issues at least in the Mezzogiorno.

This direction begins to be implemented by the "active" and authoritarian politics of the cabinets of Francesco Crispi (1887–91 and 1893–96), a Sicilian who participated in Garibaldi's expedition; and, though with frequent interruptions and reassessments, it resumes at the turn of the century with a cycle of colonial wars that, while peppered with defeats, leads at the beginning of the twentieth century to the expansion in eastern Africa, with the conquest of Libya and the creation of the Dodecanese, giving Italy a new presence in the Aegean Sea. Italy seeks a *place in the sun* and conquers it in the direction of Greece and of the eastern and northern shores of Africa, sometimes in conflict with, sometimes with the consent of, the other European powers, England, France, and Spain. The Mediterranean is rediscovered, but only in an aggressive context; and the reference to a great past, to Rome and the Empire, to Venice and the sea-faring Republics, is only useful as a means to claim ancient rights on a sea that is no longer *nostrum*, but occupied by others.

In commemorating Giuseppe Garibaldi in 1882,[8] Giosué Carducci, the most authoritative Italian poet of the late nineteenth century, understood this expansionism as the physiological, inevitable consequence of the feat of Garibaldi's "thousand" and the attainment of national unity.

So the red phalanxes overran victoriously the peninsula; and Italy was freed, completely free, along the Alps, all of its islands, and the whole sea. And the Roman eagle returned to spread its wings between sea and mountain, and released raucous cries of joy at the sight of ships that freely sailed the Mediterranean, for the third time property of Italy.[9]

The popular attention toward the Mediterranean, therefore, is connected to the emphasis on the "civilizing mission" of the departing soldiers, the music of marching bands and anthems, and does not carry any real curiosity for the culture of the lands to be conquered and annexed to the empire. The same belatedness of the empire and of the colonial enterprise that lends it both a tragic and comic tone ensures that a tradition of voyages and studies capable of going beyond superficial exoticism cannot get off the ground, as instead had happened in the countries with an older colonial tradition, such as Great Britain and France (Italian anthropology will be born through the work of Ernesto De Martino after World War II and will focus on the study of the "internal" South, the rites and myths of Italy's Mezzogiorno). Italians are parvenus in an improvised enterprise that uses splinters from the past to project the strength and the future it cannot achieve.

For the moment, the consensus in support of the colonial enterprise is fervent and comes even from prominent intellectuals. It is in addressing the "Libyan undertaking" that Giovanni Pascoli coined a phrase about Italy that was destined to be very successful: "The great proletarian has awoken,"[10] clearly illustrating the transformation of the socialist lexicon into the nationalistic one, of class warfare into a clash of nations. The same D'Annunzio, the most representative Italian poet at the turn of the century, who celebrates every exciting and daring experience, will not miss the opportunity to dedicate to the heroes of the African venture the *Canzoni delle gesta d'oltremare*. As for Alfredo Oriani, he had already written in *Fino a Dogali* (1889) very important pages about the civilizing mission of the new State: "The redemption of Africa is not yet that of existing Africans, but the substitution of a higher life for theirs."[11] But, "to penetrate the center of Africa we must therefore conquer all its coastal empires: Europe, and more specifically its nations lying on the Mediterranean have no other mission."[12] As far as Italy is concerned, since it has "twice been the center of the world and is now resurrected to nationhood, it cannot avoid this mission of universal enlightenment, whose tragedies, because they are inevitable, are also without fault."[13] The task is clear: "We must begin Italy's third resurrection!"[14]

Conversely, the colonial enterprises at the beginning of the twentieth century are interlaced with "the fourth war of independence," which wishes to achieve the "liberation" of Trento and Trieste from the Austrian yoke. Italy's intervention in World War I, strongly opposed by Catholics, Socialists and by the prime minister, Giovanni Giolitti, is the result of extraordinary public demonstrations by the interventionists, which have in their front lines, besides Gabriele D'Annunzio, many among the most important and prominent Italian intellectuals. At the end of a victorious war, the nationalistic logic demands the recapture of all Italian territories or those believed to be so. D'Annunzio, who always succeeds in receiving much public attention and traverses the country's tragic history unharmed, heads the conquest of Fiume in September of 1919, thus providing a spectacular spotlight for the polemic about the "mutilated victory," a polemic that questions the peace treaty just signed in Paris. The war and the dramatic postwar events, which lead to the rise to power of Fascism (October 1922), represent the defeat of all the groups (liberals, socialists, Catholics) with limited imperialist ambitions. The new Italy that comes to power has great projects, believes in its civilizing mission, and will follow this direction to its conclusion.

Within this new context, the Mediterranean becomes again the center of attention, because colonial expansionism and the proclamation of Empire are the programmatic aces of the new government's foreign policy. After all, Mussolini is the point of reference for a cultural-political movement that starts at the beginning of the century, moves through interventionism and results in the transformation of some radical tenets of the socialist tradition (i.e., anarcho-syndicalism) into the support for an aggressive nationalism that challenges the world's great powers. Participants in this inter-imperialist conflict are, on the one side, Great Britain, France, and the United States, the great "demo-plutocratic" powers; on the other, Italy, the "proletarian nation," unfairly opposed by the great colonial empires, who disapprove of the newcomer's stirring. Fascism renews and brings to completion the reference to the "glorious past" that had been initiated by the earlier colonial enterprises. The reference to the greatness of imperial Rome becomes the focus of the new aspirations, in a vision of the Mediterranean as a fully Latin world. What is missing, as I have already pointed out, is any real curiosity for the people one wishes to subjugate, as they are mere onlookers in a conflict whose real protagonists are the European States, the only true subjects of history. Just as Tripoli had become, in a famous song, a "pretty land of love," even the *Faccetta nera* is simply that of a young Abyssinian, who waits rapturously for the Italian soldier, for her Duce and her King.[15] As usual, civilizing missions are followed not only by scores of dead, but also by looting and plunder, while the emphasis on great duties and destinies fills the hearts of most Italians with nationalistic pride. The obsessive reference to Rome reduces

Greek tradition to a great premise for the magnificence of the Empire and the "genius of Rome." The recovery of Latin tradition is at the center of what has been called the *"sacralization of politics."* Art that is inspired by the regime (one need only think of urban planning and architecture) abounds in these references, and new cities are named unequivocally (Latina-Littoria, Sabaudia, etc.). Within this framework, the understanding of Roman tradition is subject to unilateral simplifications that support the goals of a national State with great imperial ambitions. In these dangerous simplifications, the emphasis is all on conquest and the warrior spirit of Rome, and becomes functional to the celebration of the new totalitarian State (the fascia are themselves a Roman symbol). The most original creation of Rome, the Law as rational technique for the mediation and monitoring of conflicts which constrains the exercise of power with the observance of its rules, ends in the background and becomes just a qualification one provides to lay claim to leadership. Even the growing cosmopolitanism of the Roman Empire—the impossibility to box it within the schemes of the nation-state, the influence that Hellenistic culture and the provinces had on it, the malleability that the Romans showed in exercising their power (the granting of citizenship, the acknowledgment of local traditions, etc.)—remains in the background, to exalt the epic of a people of farmers and soldiers capable of conquering and dominating the world for many centuries. Cosmopolitan universalism, which Mazzini himself had indicated as the reason for Rome's topicality, degenerates into a biased outlook, as a great and complex experience is drastically reduced to an instrument of legitimization for a Johnny-come-lately imperialism. The one-sidedness of this perspective, which impoverishes the interpretive key to understanding Roman tradition itself, will weigh like a boulder for a long time on the image of Rome.

The great battleship of this effort, which sets sail from Italian ports in the thirties, is, however, destined to shipwreck ruinously, victim of a double delay: The first, mentioned earlier, is the late start of the enterprise with regard to other European states; the second is being tardy with regard to the epoch of colonialism itself, as its end will be decreed by the outcome of World War II.

But the Mediterranean is not only the one portrayed by Fascism. To a minority, it manages to speak in other ways: Small groups of intellectuals, architects, artists, and writers explore in the thirties another path to the Mediterranean, as they attempt to discover its culture, its glory, and its Southern myths. The architectonic debate initiated by Le Corbusier (documented in a short and important book by Benedetto Gravagnuolo),[16] and the work of the De Chirico brothers (especially the varied genius of the youngest, Alberto Savinio), lead us down a different path, where the sea is no longer land of conquest, but master of intelligence.

Usefulness of the sea. "Direct" usefulness. As far as indirect usefulness, it has been considerable and active for millennia. To sharpen the intelligence of human beings. Compare the mind of sea-faring people with that of non sea-faring people. To keep intelligence moving. To make it pass from shore to shore, and from people to people.[17]

Words by the few for the few that will regain currency later on, in the last decade of the century.

The Mediterranean in the Post–World War II Period: The Antimodern Demon

The landscape that opens up in the second half of the twentieth century is characterized by the division of the world into two spheres of influence, a rigid division that does not allow, especially for a border country that came out of the war on the losing side, an autonomous foreign policy. Italy is one of the countries on the southern edge of NATO, on the border with the Soviet empire and with Arab countries, in an extremely delicate area that the United States wishes to keep controlling (the southern command of NATO is in Naples), especially since, within its borders, is housed the most powerful Communist Party in the West.[18]

Though it is situated in the center of the Mediterranean, Italy is forced to enact a foreign policy completely subordinated to Atlantic choices. Thus, its foreign policy is weak, and, if it exists, it is almost below water and clandestine, as Italian governments attempt intermittently to maintain good-neighbor relationships with Arab countries. A segment of Catholic tradition is, to be honest, very watchful of the Mediterranean, from the founder of the Popular Party, the Sicilian Don Luigi Sturzo, to the mayor of Florence in the fifties, Giorgio La Pira: This segment cannot be so easily reduced to the Atlantic policies required of Italian governments. But every attempt to give prominence to an autonomous role that includes collaboration with countries from the southern shore is viewed with suspicion, as a step toward a philo-Arab neutralism, dangerous for the geopolitical balance of the region. In this vein, the political ambitions of Fanfani, and the financial ones of the president of ENI, Enrico Mattei, are suddenly terminated in the early sixties.

Particularly dramatic is the disappearance of Enrico Mattei, who dies when his personal jet explodes taking off from a Sicilian airport. One of the hypotheses that is today openly discussed surrounding the death of Enrico Mattei is that the Mafia killed him, in collusion with financial-political interests that were being harmed by his policy of enacting trade agreements with Arab countries that were completely independent from the cartel of the major oil companies. In the post–World War II years after all, the Mafia has always played a very clear role in protecting American interests in the region, going back to when it encouraged Sicilian separatism in the difficult years right after the war, when the United States feared the victory of the Left in the national elections.

But during the years of the economic boom and the great transformation of Italian society, which go from the middle of the fifties through the sixties, a different, sharper, and more precise image of the Mediterranean emerges: a completely negative image that tends to depict it as something that must be escaped by those who want to become modern, liberal, and fully Westernized. The Mediterranean is no longer a fascinating prey one wants to possess, but something one must distance oneself from as fast as possible. The overall attitude has completely changed. There no longer exists an imperialistic ambition, but the hierarchy between the two shores has not changed: Colonial people have become the underdeveloped ones, those forever condemned to the unsuccessful chase. The Mediterranean is the place where Europe looks onto the South of the world; the counterpart to modernity; the Satan that clashes against the gods of development; the danger that Italy, and specifically its Southern side, faces because it is rooted in it through its history and geography. In this boorish, but deep-seated stereotype, "Mediterranean" takes on different and sometimes contradictory meanings that, nonetheless, as is the case with any strong symbolic representation, are often casually grouped together under the same, single negative sign. On the one hand, the Mediterranean reminds us of the rhetoric of the *ventennio*[19] with its ruinous outcome, and of policies that choose imperial aggression instead of fruitful expansion. On the other, it means backwardness and resistance to modernization; amoral clannishness and nepotism; Mafia and systemic unlawfulness; and the risk of hanging out in the bad company of countries that are unable to develop and fully Westernize. The Mediterranean is a swamp one slides into, a swamp filled with conflicts, terrorists, superstitions, and fundamentalisms: it is antimodernity, the hereditary defect that Italy struggles to free itself from because, as some say, it was never touched by the Protestant reform, the true cure-all that opens every door to modernity.

Even the fact that the South continues to lag behind, regardless of extraordinary interventions,[20] seems to confirm this negative image. As one slowly descends the Italian peninsula, all its pathologies multiply, becoming an insurmountable ball-and-chain. The Mediterranean is the negative counterweight to Europe: While the latter pulls us upward, northward, the Mediterranean drags us down. Within the rhetoric of modernity, the Mediterranean has no way out; it cannot free itself of this negative symbolism. The only acceptable meaning is the one mediated by tourism: wonderful landscapes; hills of olive trees that flow into the sea; and vacation beaches where the disciplined forces of the industrial polis escape to enjoy their moments of freedom and of sun, and rediscover nature and their bodies. In the best of hypotheses, the Mediterranean and the South are the hour of freedom, granted as compensation for a life that is stifled all year long by endless and exhausting work. Cruises, adventure trips, and warm nights under the open sky are the industrialization of that "passion for the South" that had captivated travelers on the Grand Tour.

The Mediterranean as vacation site is the only one that is acknowledged and accepted, as even writers support and describe the perverse complementarity of these two portrayals. Italy's South is a paradise inhabited by demons, where the beauty of the landscapes, experienced as a gift from God, leads Southerners to think of themselves as perfect beings who become progressively worse (this is what the protagonist of *The Leopard*, the prince of Salina, tells a Piedmontese officer in a famous description of the Sicilians).[21] The literary outcomes are successful and praised almost without fail, because they confirm a desperate image and the negative stereotype. Oftentimes, writers leave the tormented but richly creative lands of Campania and Sicily, and continue this dark polemic from afar: "Ulysses," writes Raffaele La Capria, "is the most perfect example of Mediterranean man. . . . In truth, we Mediterranean people, descendants of Ulysses, are, like him, smalltime seafarers: it took him ten years to reach Ithaca!"[22]

The South, with its ancient Mediterranean roots is a lost battle, a place destined to rot. Escape is the only therapy. References to the Mediterranean that are not marked by these negative connotations are few and generic in tone: When one encounters them, especially in poetry, they are always transfigured by elements of the classical tradition or by the nostalgia for one's personal and spiritual infancy (Quasimodo and Saba);[23] or they become one of the many reflections of a twentieth-century "sickness unto life" (Montale),[24] metaphors for the vastness upon which our nothingness reveals itself. Nonfiction writing, whether sponsored by the government or by the opposition, is instead all caught up in the new rhetorical modes of modernity, which it constantly reinvents as experimentation and avant-garde, both in the literary and political field. The Mediterranean captures the attention of public opinion only through the code of the political struggle, whether it is in solidarity with the Algerian Front of National Liberation (FNL) or, at a latter date, with the Palestinians after the Yom Kippur War. However, this solidarity has an internationalist bent, as the Palestinians become close to us like the Vietcong had before them. Beyond these militant connections, which are noble and significant but listless, the Mediterranean continues to be just a negative reference, something from which everybody wants to escape.

Italy and the Mediterranean: Back to the Future

This way of understanding the Mediterranean has dominated for a long time, leading to consequences that I would not hesitate to call devastating. Indeed, the disavowal of the Mediterranean is not simply the disavowal of the Other, of those who live beyond the sea. It is also the disavowal of the Italian South and of Italy itself, a loss of awareness of one's own specificity, a diseased relationship that Italians have with themselves. In Italy, the emphasis on modernity and on the construction of European unity has translated into an authentic "passion for the North"; in the obsessive and repetitive hammering away of the idea that the only right way to be European is to cleanse ourselves of all our "Southern" vices and temptations to become "Northern" European. Wherever the fundamentalism of "the modern" rules, not only are the Mediterranean and the South a black hole, but even Italian identity becomes an illness that must be cured.

Lately, the image of the Mediterranean has begun to change, and we are starting to hear new voices that counter this quasi-unanimous chorus. As is often the case, the change happens first in areas that are far away from official and institutional channels, which are instead about to choke on the rhetoric of modernity. In the intellectual circles that matter, those who have escaped the negative stereotype of the Mediterranean have been few and far between, mainly those who are used to singing outside the chorus. It is not by chance that the first to follow this path were the actor-director Carmelo Bene, who hails from the Salento, and the Sicilian singer-songwriter Franco Battiato: Both are convinced—though they embrace completely different perspectives—that the South and the Mediterranean, far from being negatives, are the site of a more elevated and complex experience than the one offered by modernity.

Another singer-songwriter, the Genoese Fabrizio De André, rediscovered in 1984 with the album *Creuza de Ma* the new power of ancient Southern journeys. Not only do the album's lyrics narrate a variety of beautiful and terrible stories tied to this sea, but the music weaves together rhythms and instruments from many Mediterranean countries. This is not just an escape "elsewhere": "The deciding factor—remembers De André—was our [De André's and Mauro Pagani's, *authorial note*] discovery that the Genoese language has more than two thousand Greek and Turkish words, which are the heredity of the ancient mercantile trade between cities in the Mediterranean region."[25]

A similar frame of mind runs through the dense and rigorous research undertaken by the Sicilian philosopher and author Vincenzo Consolo. Taking as his point of departure the awareness that, in Italy today, "it is very difficult to find a narrative language,"[26] Consolo has decided that the writer's language can only recover its dignity by returning to its origins, where it still occupies a sacred dimension in its oral component, where Sicilian rediscovers the *makamet*, "a rhythmic prose, whose original intent was pedagogical," and which allows for "a transition of prose toward poetic rhythms."[27] Analogous research, but with very different materials and results, is the one undertaken by Raffaele Nigro, who, having started from his own Basilicata with *I fuochi del Basento*, reaches all the way to the Adriatic Sea,[28] laying claim to the independence of Southern means of narration from central-European models. In the desire to reveal these "singers outside the chorus," we must underscore the work performed during these years by Goffredo Fofi, an incessant promoter and editor of anthologies of young Southern writers who are not enslaved by the tastes of mainstream literary circles: The at-times sectarian and unpredictable character of the man should not detract from the merits of a fertile enterprise, which is such precisely because it establishes its autonomy from the rhetoric of officialdom and of academic culture.

What in the beginning was the work of the few is slowly beginning to expand, becoming a widespread movement that is well constructed within, with deep differences both in terms of its quality and in the way one understands the new pivotal role of the Mediterranean. Naples is, as always, the site of cultural experimentation (one need only think of the cinema and theater of Mario Martone), especially as new musical trends are grafted onto a tradition which, understood along guiding principles that diverge from the more stereotyped and celebrated ones, becomes a vehicle to interact with contemporary rhythms, from the blues to rock and roll and rap, but also the Mediterranean music of its Southern shores (such as Roberto De Simone's *Nuova Compagnia di Canto Popolare*, the work of the Bennato brothers, Pino Daniele, the group Almamegretta and many others). This cultural liveliness in the areas of music and theater is not limited to Naples, but is surfacing elsewhere, especially in Apulia, where new groups and initiatives that exceed narrow provincial scopes are coming into existence.

In the cinema, the peripheries of Palermo resurface, in all their desolation, in the movies by Ciprì and Maresco, or in the colorful, deformed and prideful casts of the Milanese director Roberta Torre. While Gianni Amelio has never ceased to narrate the South through harsh and courageous angles, digging deep below any commercial or glossy rhetoric, in Apulia one finds, side by side with nostalgic returns (Sergio Rubini), the emergence of interesting new directors (such as Piva in *Lacapagira*, or Edoardo Winspear, whose *Sangue vivo* continues a lengthy and passionate discussion of the Salento). The Albanian crisis and the war in Kosovo uncover an ancient, but still uncomfortable truth: The ability to narrate interesting stories often depends on our proximity to the traumas of history with all its wounds and tragedies. Traumas shake us from slumber and force us to face the "Other," who suddenly appears without his best clothes or trailing the exotic flavors of spiritual tourism. The Mediterranean is not a tourist's paradise: Its wounds must be discussed, without ever falling prey to anti-Southern indifference, mindful that those tragedies are not the expression of local pathologies, but of problems that pertain to humanity as a whole. Is there anything more violent and vulgar than a world that uproots the weak, turns them into refugees and emigrants, and gives merciless crime new territories to conquer? By remaining aware of this problem, we can uphold a Mediterranean brotherhood and defeat the subtle racism that sometimes hides even behind empathy.

A significant way in which one's sense of Mediterranean affiliation has been recovered is through the experience of new municipal councils, the "republic of cities" that, in revisiting the history of Southern cities, rediscovered the thousand threads that tie them to the history of the Mediterranean. Those who have experienced the thousand facets of this new experience in local home rule know that, in instances when it has been significant and strong, it has centered specifically on the recovery of the cultural and urban relationship with the sea. In many cases, the experience of recovering the history of Southern cities has meant the rediscovery of the sea: Indeed, local municipality had turned their backs to the sea to admire the symbols of industrial modernity, happily welcoming the arrival of big polluting factories that today can no longer provide employment and are ever emptier cathedrals in the desert. All the cities now turn toward their history and, thus, toward the sea; the latter is no longer seen as an unsurpassable frontier, but as an ancient communication pathway between peoples that we must rediscover if we want to make the South central again. It is the beginning of a revolution of the imaginary!

Another interesting, though very different, sign that the South is shedding its long-held negative connotations is the fact that, for more than ten years, the ARCI[29] has organized a biennial festival for young Mediterranean artists, even though the festival often seems just a generic testing ground for beginning artists who do not have a clear relationship to the Mediterranean. But this slippage in meaning is an interesting symptom that allows us to recognize a new dimension in representations of the Mediterranean: the conciliation of its semantic field with the one belonging to the area of creativity, of inventive freedom, of fantasy. The Mediterranean is understood as a freer space because it is further away from the cathedrals of fashion and from the pressures and trends of the market, and because it is the fatherland of a rich arsenal of meanings that should not be pitted, in protectionist fashion, against the great waves of the cultural market, but used as a critical and selective filter in evaluating them, as is befitting a repository of original codes and agreements. When the rhetoric of the modern experiences its first heavy defeats and contemporary theoretical debate starts talking about the postmodern, the Mediterranean sheds the fetters of an exclusively negative configuration and begins to change its meaning; it no longer coincides with the horrors of the premodern that one must avoid, but becomes other, a repository of meanings that creatively interact with the coming era.

The image of the Mediterranean thus is turned upside down: It no longer is something that preceded modernity and its development, as its degraded periphery; instead, it becomes a deformed identity that must be rediscovered and reinvented through its links with the present: no longer an obstacle, but a resource. The Mediterranean interrupts the fundamentalist monolinguism of the modern and the increasingly shallow and flattened language of the media (Pasolini), and it widens the reach of thought and experimentation. It becomes the root that we need to rediscover today: strong, but constitutionally plural, location of clashes and encounters, of victories and losses, of exchanges and invasions. The Mediterranean that emerges is not a monolithic identity, but a multiverse[30] that trains the mind to grasp the complexities of the world: hybridity, crossroads, and identities that do not love purity and cleanliness, but have been mixed for a long time.

The Mediterranean as Horizon of the Future

It is impossible to talk about the Mediterranean in Italy and in the world at large without remembering the opus of Fernand Braudel. His is the true cornerstone for any future work in this area: It is a message in the bottle sent over fifty years ago to human beings who were separated by borders of national states, or lost in the mesh of ideologies that were too hurried and voracious to allow them to stop and hear the voices of places and the long ages of history. In Italy, Braudel was translated by Einaudi in 1976: Since then, his work has traveled slowly and at length throughout, while from France have also arrived the raids of Dominique Fernandez with his returns to the South and to the "mère méditerranéenne."[31]

The 1991 Italian translation of the book by Predrag Matvejevic, *Mediterraneo. Un nuovo breviario*,[32] also marks a turning point. The book, which succeeds in transforming memories, journeys, and odors in precious material for reflection and identity formation, caused a great stir, as it meets, encourages, and accelerates the desire to rediscover the Mediterranean fatherland that had been moving too slowly up to that point.

These new views of the Mediterranean are not the same: The relationship between tradition and modernity is not always experienced in the same way, but this polyphony is the symptom that something has now changed in an irreversible way. On the one hand are the ambitions of *Limes*, the journal supervised by Lucio Caracciolo, which wishes to found an Italian geopolitics. On the other is the chorus of voices constructed in Cosenza around Mario Alcaro (author of *Le identità meridionali*), the passionate work of Giuseppe Goffredo (who recently wrote *Cadmos cerca l'Europa*) through his journal *da Qui*, and the ingenious research project on living in the South by Pietro Laureano.[33] And how could we forget in Sicily the research of Pietro Barcellona, who encounters the South and the Mediterranean on the path to a radical critique of juridical forms and of the anomic individualism of the West; or the ancient yet topical voice of Manlio Sgalambro? And yet, what could we say of the free and creative work of Bruno Amoroso, an economist outside the margins, among the few to bet on the construction of a Mediterranean area of co-development?

This movement also encounters the one that, in the same direction, is started by the most open-minded segment of the Catholic Church, which on the one hand organizes meetings between the various religions, and on the other is committed, through the precious work of Caritas and of volunteerism, to the welcoming of refugees who arrive on the Italian shores from Albania, Tunisia, and Turkey. For its part, the S. Egidio Community carries out the important function of diplomatic contact among Mediterranean countries in the attempt to recompose its most destructive conflicts, or to fight the cultural demonizing of Islam, and its simplification into its most aggressive and fundamentalist versions (it is not by chance that its president, the historian Andrea Ricciardi, has dedicated one of his works to the *Mediterraneo nel Novecento*). Christian universalism, when it is not drawn into fundamentalist temptations, cannot experience but positively this return of the Mediterranean and the fall of these old lines of demarcation. The Mediterranean is a border where Western modernity must confront its "Other" and thus its own shortcomings; it is the privileged location for dialogue and for peace building. For the Catholic Church as well, the Mediterranean is an important challenge that will reveal whether, in its membership, will prevail fear and identity-regression or openness toward the other; whether an identity cemented on rejection will succeed, or we will see Christianity take risks, thus returning to its origins while improving its ability to converse with the future.

The end of a world divided in two blocs enables us to see the "purloined letter," what has always been in front of us, but we were unable to see: the Mediterranean *centrality* of Italy. Not surprisingly, in a recent novel (*Mistero napoletano*), Ermanno Rea narrates the tragic history of the Neapolitan intellectual and political elite caught in the middle of this division, between Stalinism and the cold war. Rea himself, in a recent interview, seems to underscore the beginning of this new phase.

> If our position is experienced as a positive, nowadays we can gain advantages that are as great as the disadvantages we experienced in the recent past. The nail that has been driven in the Mediterranean turns from handicap to wealth: great cultural and commercial exchanges, great understandings between people that number in the millions.[34]

Maybe it is precisely this perspective that dilutes La Capria's pessimism in the last pages of *Napolitan Graffiti* when he fantasizes that Neapolitans might breathe more deeply, and, outside the protective closure of the gulf, might understand themselves as a point "of contact between two civilizations, the Germanic and the Mediterranean, that have always searched for each other, because they knew they were interdependent and indispensable for each other."[35]

On this amalgam, we could build Europe.

Today's Problems

Slowly even governments are heeding this call, though it struggles to assert itself with clarity, constancy, and coherence. Even the higher institutional offices gladly reflect on the Mediterranean as a site of peace and development, a critical theater of operations for Italy: But moving in this direction requires courage instead of suggestive citations and fluffy salutations at conferences.

This is the critical point that the present offers to reflection. The Mediterranean has left the minority; It has entered the cultural debate in a way that was unimaginable even ten years ago; but it remains the topic of conferences, and struggles to find its fulfillment on the political stage. To think the Mediterranean requires an Italian foreign policy that is capable of autonomy and imagination, and is not willing to passively accept decisions made elsewhere. NATO carries even in its name the imprint of North Atlantic hegemony on Europe and the Mediterranean: The recent war in Kosovo is the pure expansion of a Western logic that is unaware of European complexity and which, objectively, stands in opposition to any attempt to build an independent Mediterranean zone. The Mediterranean cannot be the focus of election rallies and good intentions, and then be left out when the actual decisions are taken, remaining at the level of good intentions. If courage and imagination are missing at the political level, a full movement runs the risk of running aground in rhetorical and folkloric shallows, or plunging into the cold and desperate case history of horror and powerlessness.

Certainly, the idea of the Mediterranean has stamina: It will outlast governments and regulate our way of thinking in the next few decades. However, the lack of political courage runs the risk of retroactively and negatively influencing the process that we have attempted to summarily reconstruct here. We thus risk returning to a perverse dualism: on the one side the fundamentalists of modernity, ready to see, in this ebb, the confirmation of their prejudices and return to their well-paid certainties; on the other side a cynical elite that uses the Mediterranean to hide high-risk investments, to celebrate imaginary centralities, a procession of small chiefs who gamble on great destinies, a comedy in which midgets act like giants. If this unfortunate dualism should prevail, it will be difficult to continue to promote the true and honest reasons for a Mediterranean perspective.

Yet, the Mediterranean does not cover solely the Southern part of the peninsula, but characterizes and shapes it in its entirety. Italy is unthinkable outside of its geography and history, outside of its function as a space of mediation between the Mediterranean East and West, its South and North. Either it succeeds in bridging these spaces or it becomes victim of continental drifts, a peripheral offshoot of routes selected elsewhere, with other destinations. The cosmopolitan nature of Italy's tradition and its poor nationalism derive from this vocation, from the country's impossibility to think itself without the Mediterranean, without the construction of a vast *Ecumene* connected by peace relations.[36] *Pontifex* means builder of bridges, and Italy is not itself unless it builds bridges.

The Mediterranean is not nostalgia, but rather an idea of Italy capable of turning it into a meaningful protagonist in building the new Europe. However, if the only road the North wishes to explore is the secession of the rich; if it mutinies to exploit its higher degree of integration and closeness to the heart of Europe; then, the Mediterranean will be the only high road that the South and Italy can practice, the only road for those who want to turn this ancient country not into an unlucky appendix stranded in the middle of the sea, but into a precious and difficult land, the only true bridge between North and South. It is on this suffering that the future will be built.

The Mediterranean does not fear the multiplicity of races and skin colors, the plurality of languages and religions. It is Southern Europe's task to prevent the old continent from perching itself atop Austrian gardens, having become prey of a spiral of fear. The Europe that is slowly being built will be for real only if it is based on the face-to-face meeting between the Mediterranean and the Northern soul. Albert Camus once said, "Europe has never been free of this struggle between darkness and light. It has only degraded itself by deserting the struggle and eclipsing day by night."[37]

We must avoid, now as then, the destruction of this balance between day and night. *The Rebel* was published in 1951, but it is as if Camus wrote these words with the last years of the twentieth century in mind.

CHAPTER 10

Thinking the Mediterranean

Against the Clash of Civilizations

To think the Mediterranean today means, first of all, to deconstruct the perspective of a clash of civilizations and turn this struggle into the goal of a whole historical epoch. The adjective *Mediterranean* contains a cultural and political program, because it describes a sea that unites and divides, that lies *between* lands without belonging exclusively to any of them, that is allergic to all fundamentalisms. In the course of the centuries, this sea has witnessed invasions, forced conversions, and abuses of power; but every time the claims of one land over others has worn itself out and has ebbed, just like the sea's undertow. The Mediterranean, as a sea *between* lands that does not belong to any of them, is a *communal sea*. This belonging to everyone and to no one is an obligation to mediate, to hold lands together. The memory of abuses of power must be transformed into the creation of a common homeland capable of adding to the beauty of places and to the resemblance between places and bodies, a harmony that is strong, self-assured, and capable of translating the knowledge of the border into permanent immunity against all fundamentalisms.

In order to pursue the attempt to fight against all fundamentalisms we must first reflect on and clarify a concept that is crucial to its fulfillment. What is fundamentalism? What forms does it take today? And is it possible to recognize it? At first glance, the answer to these questions seems easy because public opinion considers fundamentalism an exclusive attribute of religion, especially Islam, even though it is now clear that it resides in every faith, including Christianity, and that no religion can claim to be immune from it. But this broader definition, as it is circumscribed to the field of religion, is still too narrow, because it hastily excludes from consideration too many important phenomena and practices that are similar to those it condemns. Those who condemn only some forms of fundamentalism are, in reality, protecting other ones and providing them with some kind of immunity. Either one condemns fundamentalism tout-court, or such condemnation is worthless.

To an unprejudiced gaze, fundamentalism appears indeed as a phenomenon that goes well beyond religion. It constitutes an *activist version of ethnocentrism*, the belief that leads every group to see itself as the center of the world, as an exemplary and privileged form of humanity, and to look down upon others, as if God had assigned them an inferior step on the ladder to perfection. Ethnocentrism is the conjuring trick, dear to every people, that allows it to represent itself as privileged with regards to others, through a narrative that it has written behind the scenes. But in and by itself, ethnocentrism is usually satisfied with celebrating this fake superiority while despising other people from a distance. It becomes fundamentalism only when the diversity of others is no longer something deformed and imperfect to keep at bay, but becomes, through its self-same existence, a danger to one's identity. Fundamentalism suffers from an incurable and unstoppable obsession: It wants to occupy every space; and colonize, convert and render uni-form the entire planet, until it can contain it within itself. In other words, fundamentalism has strong affinities with universalism since it wants to turn the language of its own tribe into the universal idiom. It wants to reduce the many sides of the world to a single one; it wants to export the good, as long as it is, of course, its own concept of good.

If we accept this "broadened" definition of fundamentalism, we cannot but see that the West is not immune from it, but has been its greatest manufacturer, at least starting with the modern era. The first gesture of Columbus, after he lands in the "Indies" and kisses the ground, is to baptize the island he has just touched, foisting on it the name of San Salvador. The metaphor of discovery removes the Other from the stage, along with its gods, names, and rights: This metaphor hides the conquest and the seizure of territories.[1] What was colonialism if not the division of the planet in many provinces of Europe, the contempt for and domination of the other? Who can forget maps from the early twentieth century, where the vast majority of non-European peoples were under the control of Old

World empires? Who can forget that Angola was Portuguese; Congo, Belgian; the Antilles, Dutch; India, British; and Algeria, French? But Western fundamentalism did not end with colonialism. Far from dying out, it has begun to write another page of its long story with the passage of planetary primacy from old Europe to young America. Obviously it had to be another form of fundamentalism, one that was compatible with the demise of colonialism.

When in 1949, Harry Truman, President of the United States, called the world's South "underdeveloped," he was stating a new form of Western supremacy. Instead of the ontological gap between "superior" and "inferior" races, a new hierarchy is created between advanced and backward nations. At first glance, such hierarchy seems mobile and revocable, loose and open: Those who are behind can catch up and are not condemned to remain always among the last. This is the universalism of competition and merit. But it is precisely the gap created between the cultures of "advanced" and "backward" nations that shows the existence of the hierarchy: One culture is the goal while the other is only the starting point. To progress, one must become like the other, and its difference from it coincides with a form of imperfection from which it must reform and free itself as soon as possible. Here recur all the constitutive elements of fundamentalism: The way of life of the West is the exemplary paradigm that must be extended to the entire world.

The cultural imposition is very harsh but hidden behind the pretense of an ineluctable necessity. As Fatima Mernissi writes with exemplary clarity,

> The new imperialism that dominates us, non-Western people, no longer manifests itself via physical occupation. The new imperialism is not even economic, but it is more insidious. . . . The enemy has entrenched itself . . . in our heads: it is how we count, consume, buy, calculate. . . . [I]t has the unreal flavor of the debt and of the so-far-away voices on the phone of experts from the World Bank and the International Monetary Fund.[2]

The entire world must become West and change from being to becoming; and those who remain rooted in being live under the curse of poverty. The clerics of being are replaced by the clerics of becoming: They are educated at the most prestigious Western universities and occupy the seats of the true power, the World Bank and the International Monetary Fund, where the fundamentalism of the market reigns supreme.[3] The clerics with turbans are countered by those of the "city," and the obsessive recitation of prayers is countered by the equally obsessive recitation of Stock Exchange listings. Here too, as in any other fundamentalism, the central premise is beyond doubt: Capitalism is never responsible for the failures, only capitalists are. The purity of the idea is maintained by displacing every sin on the weakness of men. Market and profit are always on the side of the solution, never on the side of problems. And this fundamentalism does not remain in the churches: It speaks every language and knows every university, even the most prestigious ones.

The Trap of Essentialism

To admit that the West has been and still is the largest manufacturer of fundamentalism means to ask immediately one question: What consequences does this continuous and unchallenged domination have on other people? "They will tell him," so affirmed the great British historian Arnold Toynbee, "that the West has been the arch-aggressor of modern times, and each will have their [*sic*] own experience of Western aggression to bring up against him."[4] This experience generates, Toynbee still argues, two kinds of responses: the one of the *Herodians* and the one of the *Zealots*. The Herodians want to imitate the culture of the West, while the Zealots reclaim the "purity" of their tradition and fight against the corruption that comes from the dominant culture. On the one side are those who are more conciliatory and collaborationist; on the other are those who are prouder and more aggressive.

Neither path, claims Toynbee, leads to change. The Herodian perspective is undermined by its mimetic propensity, because it inspires itself to models that it cannot reach. It will always and only be the imperfect, if not grotesque, copy of an original made by others. The Zealot perspective is instead weakened by its own claim to purity and its repulsion of the culture of others. It can find in faith and pride extraordinary surrogates to the technological power of the enemy, but it is very difficult that a substantial change in power relations can ever derive from cultural autarchy.[5]

Toynbee's observations also offer important methodological suggestions. In fact, they always refer to Islamic culture in "contextual" rather than "essentialist" terms. Cultures are never equal to themselves, fixed identities that rotate around an immutable nucleus, but they undergo change. The interpretations that emerge within them are always responses to concrete situations they experience and, thus, before all else, their relationship with other cultures. As a result, it is completely abstract to discuss a culture by attributing to its essence traits that prevail in any given moment and that depend on the reaction to the specific context in which it lives. In doing so, one ignores not only the internal *complexity* of that culture, but also its *power relations with other cultures*, a crucial factor in determining which among its many different interpretations will prevail over the others.

To assign a culture's responses to its presumed essence while neglecting the relationships it is experiencing, allows one to ignore an analysis of power relations. To assign to Islamic culture a single constant essence that has at its core a vocation to war drastically reduces its complexity, a mistake that is useful to all those who, within or outside of this culture, hunger for conflict: Such a representation cancels the culture's internal plurality, and accelerates and paves the way for the clash of civilizations.

To find a clear and clean confirmation for this anti-essentialist hypothesis, all we need to do is go back to the post–World War II years when, with the fall of the colonial system and the rise of nonaligned states, a lay path somewhere between the two outlined by Toynbee seemed to assert itself within the Muslim world. The anticolonial struggle gave the more radical fringes a lay and nationalistic tone in which religion did not play a dominant role. Thanks to nationalism and a strong attraction to socialism, that experience mixed the lay inspiration of Herodianism with the radical one of Zealotism and, even though it originated among small elites (often with military training), it was able to gain a large mass following, often enacting harsh repressions of fundamentalist movements. This lay wave had serious limitations as it often came with the unabashed practice of despotic control and the repression of dissenting voices; but it was certainly driven by a desire to modernize the country that led it to put aside, if not repress, the custodians of religious orthodoxy. These lay and nationalistic elites did not fall only because of their severe internal limits, but also due to the constant and systematic opposition of the West and of its allies in the region. With the defeat of Nasser in the war of 1967, Arab nationalism entered a time of crisis, while fundamentalism began its ascent, which gained center stage with the Iranian revolution of 1979. The hegemony of fundamentalism, therefore, is not born from the *essence* of Islamic culture, but from the systematic hostility of the West, and especially the West's leading nation, toward nationalistic regimes. *We can say, then, that fundamentalism is not the expression of the essence of Islamic culture but is the option that prevails after the defeat of nationalism.* Its prevalence is not the expression of a culture suspicious of modernity, but the *effect of the relationship*, of the deeply asymmetrical nature of the relationship between the West and those nations, and of the refusal to pursue avenues that have ended in failure.

The Mediterranean in Contemporary Theory

At this juncture, it is probably clearer what we mean by thinking the Mediterranean. I have already pointed out that to think of its condition as a border sea allows us to deconstruct any fundamentalist claim. The hybridization of cultures and people weakens all claims of exclusivity, purity, and integrity, as the Mediterranean knows well, having been fraught, from time immemorial, with intertwined stories, mestizos, migrations, and shelters. That it was a sea of different shores not far from each other made it navigable from the start. On this sea between lands, the Other was never a huge distance away, beyond the gap of the Oceans, but could be reached in few days of navigation. In its names and bodies, in its histories, the Other has always been present.

Precisely this insuperable polytheism of the Mediterranean constitutes an effective cure against all fundamentalisms, not only the identity one of closed and "premodern" communities of the Southern shore, but also the modernist and progressively monotheistic one of the Northern shore. In the last few years, it has become a "critical space": It is no longer a "frontier or a barrier between North and South, between East and West, but rather the place of meetings and trends, . . . and continuous transits."[6] A sea, then, that is postmodern and postcolonial, a pluriverse that cannot be brought together by one tongue, under one king, and in the prayers of a single religion. All along, goods and tales have sailed with the ships; all along autarchy has been difficult, and genetic patrimonies have mixed; all along the homicidal traits of the custodians of purity have been visible. But hybridization alone is not enough, because it tells us nothing about the power relations between cultures. Ethnic rape is contamination, but, above all, it is violence, a ferocious asymmetry of power, an affront to women and to the freedom of the other. Those who aim at deconstructing fundamentalisms cannot get around the suffering of the culture that occupies the subaltern position. As long as the asymmetry endures, it is very difficult for more open and tolerant points of view to assert themselves within that culture. If humiliation is not erased, it is very difficult to defeat fundamentalism. Differences can be acknowledged only if among cultures there is a balance of power, reciprocity, and respect, if a certain degree of equality assures the context of justice for the relationship.

Side by side with the postmodern perspective on the Mediterranean, there is another one that sees in its alleged archaism the resistance of alternative principles of social organization and of strong social ties that modernity, dominated by the economy and by utilitarian individualism, is increasingly erasing. The belatedness of the Mediterranean is a precious resource because it preserves, with its networks of communities, a kind of humanity that has stronger bonds and meaning, and is not crushed by the demon of growth. Not everything that belongs to the past has to be thrown away as a useless and dangerous relic: On the contrary, at times it can be a solution rather than a problem. This perspective is fully aware of the inequality in power relations; but it is, at times, inspired by a communitarian nostalgia that makes it difficult to conceive the plurality of the Mediterranean, its ability to overcome borders, multiplying meetings, exchanges, and friendships. In other words, it seems to us that the communitarian perspective, just as the postmodern one, has both merits and flaws.

Therefore, to think the Mediterranean one needs to play both games: the one that acknowledges difference and the one that narrows inequalities; the one that opens to the other and the one that preserves communal relationships of solidarity. The dialogue between cultures cannot remain a simple juxtaposition between them, but must be productive, create new relations, and at once stimulate their friendship and creativity. If we want to deconstruct the perspective that embraces the clash of civilizations, we cannot and should not aim for anything less. It is here that the future is played out, not only in the Mediterranean but in the entire planet. The encounter between cultures is the first item on the agenda of the new millennium.

Amartya Sen has tried to address this issue on two levels. On the one hand, he has underscored the lay, skeptical, and rationalist aspects of Indian tradition in polemic with the image that is dear to *Orientalism* and to the believers in "Asian values" who emphasize the mystical and communitarian traits of that tradition, in opposition to the West.[7] But Sen has also worked productively in the area of Western tradition, reformulating a number of economic notions through a conceptual strategy focused on preventing the economic sphere from becoming autonomous from other social relationships.[8] It is precisely in the wake of this reformulation that Sen, in polemic with Huntington and Kagan, has argued that reducing Islamic tradition to a "sectarian—and belligerent" core forgets "the broader history of the Arab world and of the Muslim people." A dangerous simplification that is exactly symmetrical to the one that restricts love of freedom to the West alone, erasing its presence in other traditions. Sen's targets are "the implicit alliance between Western *parochialism* and Islamic *extremism*" and the tendency common in both to divide humanity in terms of "artificially segmented 'civilizations' defined mainly by religion."[9]

Sen's polemic has great merits, but unfortunately it does not underscore the need to reduce the real asymmetry between subjects. In order to defeat opposite fundamentalisms, the intellectual polemic has to go hand in hand with a rebalancing of power relations. As long as one of the interlocutors is so much stronger than the other one that it can impose the type of government it prefers, it will be difficult to stop the spiral of war.

Like Sen, Mohamed Arkoun also believes that the first goal is to deconstruct the two ideological monsters erected by the theoreticians of the clash of civilizations: "The poles 'Islam' and the 'West', which have been linked by an ideology of reciprocal exclusion since 1945, are reunited in their common resorting to the old theology of warfare." The deconstruction of this logic of reciprocal exclusion between Islam and the West and the reinvention of *l'espace méditerranéen*, a topic that is very dear to Arkoun, are ultimately part of the same process.[10] But Arkoun is also conscious that a fruitful dialogue is difficult in a situation of radical asymmetry between the interlocutors. The defeat of Islamic fundamentalism is possible if the West radically changes its relationships with the nations of the Mediterranean's southern and eastern shores, abandoning the old colonial logic and, in the case of the United States, "the philosophy of Gary Cooper," which contrasts good versus evil and loves to solve conflicts with weapons.

The essential requirement for an effective dialogue, Arkoun argues, is reversing the image of a dogmatic and fundamentalist Islam, which is an unacceptable distortion of the experience of a great civilization, erases phenomena, authors, and periods of intense creativity. Arkoun insists especially on the existence of a large area of convergence between the European and Islamic traditions based on the central value of humanism. The recognition of this area of convergence could give wings to a serious and important discussion between subjects of equal dignity, and would allow a proposal that originates from the Mediterranean to speak even beyond its shores.

Though I value Arkoun's argument, I believe that we must push it even further by asking: What has the West to learn from Islamic culture? Must the West speak only with the part that is homogenous to itself or must it go further? To insist on what unites is necessary but not sufficient, because a meeting as equals between two cultures must succeed in bringing to the table even their heterogeneity without falling into the trap of the incommensurability and impossibility of communicating. The exchange of meaning between two cultures must take place in both directions, aimed both at teaching and learning. *It is neither a universal truth defined by the strongest nor a relativistic closure of cultures within themselves, but the complex construction of a polyphonic universal.* This is where the "intercreativity" discussed by Arkoun can be born, as the cornerstone upon which a Mediterranean space can rest.

New Perspectives

In the last few years, the Islamic world has not only been the stage for confrontations between Herodians and Zealots, pro-Westerners and fundamentalists, but it has also witnessed the emergence of certain phenomena that represent a sign of the creativity internal to Islamic culture that goes beyond the clash of civilizations. Of great interest is, for example, the intellectual and civil movement of scholars that goes by the name of "Islamic Feminism." The value of this movement resides in the fact that, even though unthinkable without the impulses of Western feminism, it is not reducible to one more chapter in the homologation of the dominant culture. The road to the liberation of Muslim women from male power must pass through a new exegesis of the texts of Islamic tradition, capable of individuating and denouncing all those interpolations of the Koran that have built, through time, a patriarchal version of that tradition that places them in contradiction with those passages where the equality of all believers vis-à-vis God is asserted. This is a crucial point: Being permeable to other cultures does not translate into a banal and passive conversion, but initiates a creative process. Tradition cannot be relinquished to radical Islamists, but must be re-read and subjected to new challenges, pushed to look at itself from a different angle, and measure itself with the problems and the challenges of the present. As Leila Ahmed points out, "Muslim women must reject, just as Western women are doing, the androcentrism of whatever culture or tradition to which they belong. In no way does this mean that they need to adopt Western customs and life-styles."[11]

But Islamic feminism is not only the answer of a tradition to the challenges that come from outside, but also a creative contribution to thinking on female difference, since it also looks at the serious forms of subordination that exist even in the "liberated" West. Fatima Mernissi, for example, does not limit herself to denouncing the many forms of misogyny present in Islamic culture, but also takes issues against the tyranny of the "size 6,"[12] the power that, even today, the male gaze exerts on the female body. In an apparently liberated world, the male gaze no longer covers the female body but bares it, demands that it be exhibited in television and advertisements, through strippers to pornography, and all the way to the outskirts of our cities where, in the dark, it offers itself to the power of money. Modesty is not only a repressive cage that those who seek emancipation must escape. It is also a grammar of the relationship between bodies that incites pride and builds opaqueness in a world of windows and shops. Modesty has often been an interdiction decreed by the powerful, a claim of dominion over the body of another; but it can also be a tassel of individual freedom, an interdiction that protects the individual from temptations and the omnivorous pretenses of the market, the safe-keep for a private space rescued from universal commercialization, which forces the latter to wait outside the door.

By reflecting itself in this gaze, the West, so boastful and proud of its achievements, could start looking at its darker side. When two cultures meet on a level plane and in a climate of trust, there is no longer a unilateral response, but an exchange that enriches each of the interlocutors, allowing them to discover, in a different context, qualities that they had thrown out the window, of the train of progress or of the orthodoxy one. The meeting between cultures, therefore, is not the *happy conclusion* of an edifying story, but rather—and especially—the starting point for new perspectives and uncharted courses. Tradition and innovation are not necessarily opposed: Between them there exists only the creative friction that is born with every beginning, when ideas take off and put to sea, to test the present and understand if they will sink with the first storm or land somewhere else.

Another author that can help us in this journey, beyond the ambiguities that at times envelop him, is Tariq Ramadan who, as he pridefully claims the need to construct a European Islam, seems not to be affected by the reverential fear that sometimes plagues the Islamic interlocutors of the West.[13] An authentic dialogue presupposes a discomfort with the other, his ability to tell us, without losing his politeness, even that which clashes with the convictions upon which we stand. Ramadan also moves on two fronts: On the one hand, he urges European Muslims to practice that great invention of the West that is citizenship, and to avoid restricting their experience to the exclusive enclave of religious belonging. On the other hand, however, he never ceases defending the importance of the communal dimension of Islamic religion. From the prohibition against usury to the great importance attributed to assisting other members of the community, Islam has not only something to learn from its encounter with the West, but can offer its interlocutor a mirror, in which it might see those features that it does not love or cannot look at in itself.

The fundamentalism of the market turns the social contract into an archaic mutilation of freedom: By way of a clever and tested mechanism, everything that clashes against the dominant imperatives is hastily assigned to the past. Progress becomes a productive megamachine that crushes as obsolete every institution or behavior that stands in its path. Precisely for this reason we must guard against the partial accusations of nostalgia; in what we call the past, there is much to discard—silent abuses, cruel superstitions, unjustifiable prohibitions—but there is also something else: There are precious suggestions, something that can be useful in the future such as, for example, the "strong notion of responsibility practiced by a vast majority of pre-capitalist cultures on the planet," as discussed by Spivak.[14] We will have to distinguish, then, between the freedom of men and of women, and how it is understood in a world where responsibility toward the Other is seen precisely as an archaic residue; and where the environment and the weakest people are destined to disappear, poisoned in the background. Perhaps it is precisely this transition that allows us to find in the epistemology of the Mediterranean the core of the struggle against the clash of civilizations. If the West wishes to meet up and asks that its interlocutors only listen, it will remain deaf to forms of wisdom present in other traditions, and will continue to repress the fundamental problems of our time: What shape must freedom take to be the prerogative of every human being? Which freedom will allow us to live without destroying the revolving sphere on which life started a long time ago? Are we sure that those customs and behaviors that have never forgotten their original debt to our planet will not come in handy again? From this perspective one can understand the meaning of the critique addressed by Ramadan to the *Social Forum* in Paris in 2003 for not having considered the problem of cultural and religious diversity, and therefore having locked itself into a "completely Eurocentric" discussion.[15] The majority of responses have been contemptuous and have fallen back on the stereotype of hidden authoritarianism, obviously attributing it to the influence of Islamic culture. But the ethnocentrism of the Western Left is a problem and being aware of it is the indispensable condition to overcome it.

The dialectic that the Mediterranean teaches is much more complex than the linear movement of evangelization, even in its lay and secularized form. Its universalism is not dogmatic and a priori, but syncretic and a posteriori; it is a universalism that is always imperfect and lives on translations. It aims at producing a movement on both shores: It does not ask one to burn one's roots, but to renew them through the encounter with the other. For the Arab-Islamic world, it is a matter of learning the vital necessity of an open and pluralistic society; for the West, of recognizing that freedom as the prerogative of the powerful kills brotherhood and equality. The first should realize that the autonomy of lay civil society is not a caving in to the West, but the winning back of an ancient habit of plurality; the second should realize that freedom needs the common good and completes itself with the practice of citizenship.

But to imagine a serious and creative relationship between cultures, without confusing the values of one with its economic and military power, means to put on the agenda the issue of how to rescue technology from the control of power and profit, and place it again into the hands of wisdom, so it can return to its role as instrument that benefits all human beings, not just the more voracious and stronger ones. The two points of pride of the West, citizenship and technology, can play an important role in the future of humanity, but on the condition that they become the common good of humanity, not the instrument of the few, but the wealth of the many. But this acknowledgment will be possible only if it is inhabited by the rediscovery of wisdom and of moderation, by humility toward the Earth and by the return of sobriety, which is the foundation for a different idea of wealth. No culture is asked to renounce its difference, but only to valorize it, to encourage it to offer its wisdom to a shared world. The dialectics of cultures that can originate on the Mediterranean speaks the language of major global issues. When we think rigorously of a place as dense and complex as the Mediterranean, we do not close ourselves in a banal regional ethnocentrism, because inside that complex place, we discover the world. And today more than ever, the world requires that future chapters be written together, drawn from different forms of knowledge and wisdom. The world needs Moderation, that noun that keeps us away from the intoxication that lives within every fundamentalism, intoxication that leads it to forget that where we end the Other begins, and that no one among us can ever claim the exclusive right to God's word.

TRANSLATORS' INTRODUCTION:
ON FRANCO CASSANO'S *SOUTHERN THOUGHT*

1. This statement is translated from private correspondence with the author.

2. See above, note 1.

3. See, for example, the essay "Il gioco della Scienza," *Rassegna italiana di sociologia.* 30, no. 1 (1989): 3–30.

4. Francesco Giacomantonio, "All'origine del pensiero meridiano di Franco Cassano," accessible at http://tiny.cc/oyzzl

5. Michel de Montaigne, "The Profit of One Man Is the Loss of Another," in *Essays of Montaigne*, vol. 1, trans. Charles Cotton (New York: Edwin C. Hill, 1910).

6. Jonathan Morris, "Challenging *Meridionalismo*: Constructing a New History for Southern Italy," in *The New History of the Italian South: The Mezzogiorno Revisited*, ed. Robert Lumley and Jonathan Morris (Exeter, UK.: University of Exeter Press, 1997), 5.

7. The *latifundia* estates were the vast grain-producing land-holdings of Calabria, Apulia, and Western Sicily.

8. See, for example, Salvatore Lupo, "I proprietari terrieri del Mezzogiorno," in *Storia dell'agricoltura italiana*, ed. Piero Bevilacqua, vol. 2 (Venice: Marsilio, 1991); and Marta Petrusewicz, *Latifundium: Moral Economy and Material Life in a European Periphery*, trans. Judith C. Green (Ann Arbor: University of Michigan Press, 1996).

9. We are referring to Ngugi wa Thiong'o's famed *Decolonising the Mind: The Politics of Language in African Literature* (Portsmouth, N.H.: Heinemann, 1986).

10. The reference is to Dipesh Chakrabarty, *Provincializing Europe: Postcolonial Thought and Historical Difference* (Princeton: Princeton University Press, 2000).

11. The reference is to Boaventura de Sousa Santos, ed., *Another Knowledge Is Possible: Beyond Northern Epistemologies* (London: Verso, 2007).

12. Cassano does so in the footsteps of the German philosopher Carl Schmitt, the author of *Land und Meer*, but his understanding of geophilosophical categories is also shaped by the work of Massimo Cacciari, *Geofilosofia dell'Europa* (Milan: Adelphi, 1994). An English translation of *Land und*

Meer is available under the title of *Land and Sea* (Washington, D.C.: Plutarch Press, 1997). While Cacciari's work has not been published in its entirety, an English translation of a chapter from *Geo-filosofia* is included in *The Unpolitical: On the Radical Critique of Political Reason*, ed. Alessandro Carrera (New York: Fordham University Press, 2009), 197–205.

13. Cassano is very aware of the criticism of territorializing-identity politics leveled at his work. Indeed, after the 1996 publication of the first edition of *Southern Thought*, Cassano's call to return to the Mediterranean generated ambivalent responses. While some critics understood the deeper meaning of this work and the context in which it was produced, others merely dismissed it as an imaginary fiction or interpreted it as a reactionary manifesto of "meridionalismo." In 2005, on the occasion of the second edition of the volume, Cassano added "Prologue: Parallels and Meridians" where he clarifies his intent: "Herein lies the main aim of this prologue: to reconstruct the intersection of arguments formulated in *Southern Thought* so as to allow the discussion to continue on more precise foundations. The one who writes has not arrived to the South and to Southern thought from a 'we' or a sudden passion for identity, but from the category of the 'Other,' from a meditation on the shadowy side of every identity. . . . [C]hoosing the South was an attempt to take the side of the *other* even before taking the side of the *self*, a theoretical reaction to a characterization presented in such a negative and caricatured manner that it could not be true." The prologue is included in this translation.

14. Enrique Dussel, "Beyond Eurocentrism: The World-System and the Limits of Modernity," in *The Culture of Globalization*, ed. Fredric Jameson and Masao Miyoshi (Durham: Duke University Press, 1998), 18–19.

15. Friedrich Nietzsche, *The Gay Science*, ed. Bernard Williams (Cambridge: Cambridge University Press, 2001). See, for example, aphorism 124, "In the horizon of the infinite": "We have forsaken the land and gone to sea. We have destroyed the bridge behind us—more so, we have demolished the land behind us! Now, little ship, look out! Beside you is the ocean; it is true, it does not always roar, and at times it lies there like silk and gold and dreams of goodness. But there will be hours when you realize that it is infinite. . . . Oh, the poor bird that has felt free and now strikes against the walls of the cage! Woe, when homesickness for the land overcomes you, as if there had been more *freedom* there—and there is no more 'land'!" (124, 119).

16. Albert Camus, *The Rebel: An Essay on Man in Revolt*, trans. Anthony Bower (New York: Alfred Knopf, 1954), 246–60.

17. For Schulze-Engler's contribution to this debate see Frank Schulze-Engler and Sissy Helff, *Transcultural English Studies: Theories, Fictions, Realities* (Amsterdam: Rodopi, 2009); but also Frank Schulz-Engler, "Theoretical Perspectives: From Postcolonialism to Transcultural World Literature," in *English Literatures across the Globe: A Companion*, ed. Lars Eckstein (Paderborn:

Fink, 2007), 20–32; and "From Postcolonial to Preglobal: Transnational Culture," in *Towards a Transnational Future. Literature and Society in the Postcolonial World*, ed. Geoffrey V. Davis, Peter H. Marsden, Bénédicte Ledent, and Marc Delrez (Amsterdam: Rodopi, 2004), 50–64.

18. We should also mention *Oltre il nulla. Studio su Giacomo Leopardi* (Rome-Bari: Laterza, 2003), a volume which, even though not primarily devoted to the articulation of a southern thought, revisits the famed nineteenth-century poet Giacomo Leopardi's reflection on the past primacy of southern civilization over northern ones. According to Leopardi, such primacy was lost in modernity, when the north overcame unfavorable climate and natural conditions through scientific development, technological innovations, rationalization of work, and so on. However, Cassano also points out that Leopardi tries to think of a time beyond modernity where the limits of reason and progress would be tempered by southern values, chief among them, imagination.

PREFACE TO THE ENGLISH-LANGUAGE EDITION

1. Latin for "the direction of all is against all."—Trans.

2. In Latin, the term *absolutus* means "absolute, done, finished." However, Cassano is pointing out the etymological origin of the word, which suggests that someone/something can be 'freed from ties,' liberated, hence without ties.—Trans.

PROLOGUE: PARALLELS AND MERIDIANS

Most of the texts Cassano cites are, unless he is citing Italian authors, translations of foreign texts. We have given the bibliographical references for these Italian texts, and added notes to provide the original titles and English language translation titles if they exist.—Trans.

1. This objection cannot be moved to the astute observations made by Michel Huysseune in *Modernity and Secession: The Social Sciences and the Political Discourse of the Lega Nord in Italy* (Oxford: Berghahn, 2006).

2. Primo Levi, *The Drowned and the Saved* (New York: Summit Books, 1988). The original title of Levi's work is *I sommersi e i salvati* (1986). However, Levi used the term "Muslim" earlier, in *Se questo è un uomo* (1947, 1958), the narrative of his survival in Auschwitz. English translations of *Se questo è un uomo* are available as *Survival in Auschwitz: The Nazi Assault on Humanity* (New York: Touchstone, 1958–1996), and in the volume *If This Is a Man; and The Truce* (London: Abacus, 1997).—Trans.

3. See my *La certezza infondata. Previsioni ed eventi nelle scienze sociali* (Bari: Dedalo, 1983), *Approssimazione. Esercizi di esperienza dell'altro* (Bologna: Il Mulino, 1989), and *Partita doppia. Appunti per una felicità terrestre* (Bologna: Il Mulino, 1993).

4. For additional discussion, see the chapter on Pasolini in this volume, "Pier Paolo Pasolini: Life as Oxymoron."—Trans.

5. Boaventura de Sousa Santos, *Il Forum Sociale Mondiale: Verso una global-izzazione antiegemonica*. See also *De la mano de Alicia* and *A Crítica da Razão Indolente: Contra o desperdício da experiência*. There are no English translations of de Sousa Santos's works, but selections are available in de Sousa Santos's *Towards a New Common Sense* (New York: Routledge, 1995) and *Towards a New Legal Common Sense* (London: Butterworths, 2002). De Sousa Santos is also the editor of a significant volume in English: *Another Knowledge Is Possible: Beyond Northern Epistemologies* (London: Verso, 2007).—Trans.

6. Walter Mignolo, *Local Histories/Global Designs: Coloniality, Subaltern Knowledges, and Border Thinking* (Princeton: Princeton University Press, 2000) and *The Darker Side of the Renaissance: Literacy, Territoriality, and Colonization* (Ann Arbor: University of Michigan Press, 1995).

7. See Ranajit Guha, ed., *A Subaltern Studies Reader, 1986–1996* (Minneapolis: University of Minnesota Press, 1997), as well as Ranajit Guha and Gayatri Chakravorty Spivak, eds. *Selected Subaltern Studies* (New York: Oxford University Press, 1988).

8. Dipesh Chakrabarty, *Provincializing Europe: Postcolonial Thought and Historical Difference* (Princeton: Princeton University Press, 2000).

9. Cassano uses the term "pietas" with the meaning of 'duty,' 'devotion,' and 'responsibility.'—Trans.

10. Latin for "love of place."—Trans.

11. Cassano's reference to "grande storia," or official history, has been translated as "History."—Trans.

12. Giuseppe Tomasi di Lampedusa, *The Leopard*, trans. Archibald Colquhoun (New York: Pantheon Books, 1960), 212.

13. Ida Dominijanni, "Pensiero a Mezzogiorno," *Il manifesto*, February 14 1996, 24–25.

14. Edward Said, *Orientalism* (New York: Vintage Books, 1979) and *Culture and Imperialism* (New York: Alfred Knopf, 1993).

15. This risk seems to traverse the reflection, lucid and stimulating, of Piergiorgio Giacché on the work of Carmelo Bene. *Carmelo Bene, Antropologia di una "macchina attoriale"* (Milan: Bompiani, 1997).

16. The term "Mezzogiorno" (Italian for the Latin *meridies*) has been used ever since the eighteenth century to describe Southern Italy and the islands. It comprises the regions of Abruzzo, Basilicata, Campania, Calabria, Apulia, Molise, and the islands of Sicily and Sardinia.—Trans.

17. Bruno Amoroso is the scholar who has given the greatest attention to the geopolitical and geoeconomic dimension of this problem. See his *Europa e Mediterraneo. Le sfide del futuro* (Bari: Dedalo, 2000)

18. Praise of slowness can be found in the work of writers such as Milan Kundera, Sten Nadolny, and Robert Pirsig, but also Peter Handke; in the reportages of Paolo Rumiz; in the cinema of Wim Wenders and Werner Herzog, of Theodorus Anghelopoulos and Abbas Kiarostami, and also, unexpectedly, of David Lynch. But reclaiming the slow time of experience brings

together all those who examine the themes of the quality of life, from Ivan Illich to Carlo Petrini, who inspired the food chain Slow Food, from Pierre Sansot to David Le Breton and many others. It also intersects the writing of Erri De Luca and the work of musicians who are not only from the South. It surfaces in some lucid and moving pages of Alex Langer, who juxtaposes to the motto "citius, altius, fortis" from the Olympic games—a motto founded on the model of competition—the rediscovery of the value of the "limit" and therefore of the motto: "lentius, profundius, soavius" (see Alexander Langer, *Il viaggiatore leggero. Scritti 1961–1995* (Palermo: Sellerio, 1996), 328–32; but also the article "Intervento al Convegno giovanile di Assisi," available at www.peacelink.it).

19. Gregory Bateson and M. C. Bateson, *Angels Fear: Towards an Epistemology of the Sacred* (New York: Macmillan, 1987).

20. These two words occur in English in the original.—Trans.

21. Reinhart Koselleck, *Future Past: On the Semantics of Historical Time*, trans. Keith Tribe (Cambridge: MIT Press, 1985).

22. Niklas Luhmann, "The Future Cannot Begin. Temporal Structures," in *The Differentiation of Society* (New York: Columbia University Press, 1982), 271–88.

23. Zygmunt Bauman, *Liquid Modernity* (Cambridge: Polity, 2000) and Zygmunt Bauman and Keith Tester, *Conversations with Zygmunt Bauman* (Cambridge: Polity, 2001)

24. Cassano is citing from the Italian translation of Marc Augé, *Rovine e macerie. Il senso del tempo* (Turin: Bollati Boringhieri, 2004, 137). The original title of the work is *Le Temps en ruines* (Paris: Galilée, 2003). No English translation of this work exists.—Trans.

25. Richard Sennett, *The Corrosion of Character: The Personal Consequences of Work in the New Capitalism* (New York: W. W. Norton, 1998).

26. Regarding the "rationalization of behavior" see Max Weber's *The Protestant Ethic and the Spirit of Capitalism* (New York: Scribner's, 1958), and *Economy and Society: An Outline of Interpretive Sociology* (New York: Bedminster Press, 1968).

27. Zaki Laîdi, *La tyrannie de l'urgence* (Montreal: Editions Fides, 1999). But see also by the same author *Le sacre du present* (Paris: Flammarion, 2000).

28. Bauman, *Liquid Modernity*, and *Conversations with Zygmunt Bauman*. See also Ulrich Beck, *Risk Society: Towards a New Modernity* (London: Sage, 1992), and *I rischi della libertà. L'individuo nell'epoca della globalizzazione* (Bologna: Il Mulino, 2000).

29. Robert Jackall, *Moral Mazes: The World of Corporate Managers* (New York : Oxford University Press, 1988).

30. See Guido Rossi, *Il conflitto epidemico* (Milan: Adelphi, 2003). Of interest are also the observations of Alessandro Pizzorno in "L'ordine giuridico e statale nella globalizzazione," in *Globalizzazione e movimewnti sociali*, ed.

Donatella Della Porta and Lorenzo Mosca (Rome: Manifestolibri 2003), 221–37.

31. On the question of *Acceleration Society* a debate has begun in our country that includes interventions from Paul Virilio and David Harvey to Zaki Laîdi, James Gleick, Lothar Baier, Thomas H. Eriksen, Michel Blayr, and Carl Honoré. See also the issue of *Constellations* 10, no. 1 (2003): 3–52 on the thesis of Hartmuth Rosa. Of particular interest in this same issue is the contribution by Carmen Leccardi, "Revisiting 'Acceleration Society,'" 34–41.

32. Agnes Heller, "Cultural Memory, Identity, and Civil Society," in *Politik und Gesellschaft*, 1–6 (available online at http://www.fes.de/ipg/ipg2_2001/artheller.htm).

33. Sennett, *Corrosion of Character*, 62.

34. Ibid., 117.

35. Zygmunt Bauman, *Globalization: The Human Consequences* (New York: Columbia University Press, 1998), 18.

36. Peter Handke, *Gedicht an die Dauer* (Frankfurt: Suhrkamp, 1986).

37. Albert O Hirschman, "Melding the Public and the Private Spheres: Taking Commensality Seriously," in *Crossing Boundaries: Selected Writings* (New York: Zone Books, 2001), 11–32.

38. W. E. B. Du Bois, "Dusk of Dawn," in *W. E. B. Du Bois Writings* (New York: Library of America, 1986), 586–87.

39. By Edgar Morin, see "Mère Méditerranée," *Le monde Diplomatique*, August 1995, and "Penser la Méditerranée et Méditerranéiser la pensée," *Confluences Méditerranée* 28 (Winter 1998–99). By Matvejevic, see *Breviario mediterraneo* (Milan: Garzanti, 1991) and *Il Mediterraneo e l'Europa. Lezioni al Collège de France* (Milan: Garzanti, 1998). A short version of *Breviario mediterraneo* is available in English as *Mediterranean: A Cultural Landscape* (Berkeley: University of California Press, 1999).—Trans.

40. The reference is to Derrida's *Margins of Philosophy* (Chicago: University of Chicago Press, 1982). The philosopher's entire work is a constant and sustained interrogation on the themes of the border.

41. Cassano's reference is to Ludwig Wittgenstein, *Remarks on Frazer's Golden Bough*, ed. Rush Rhees, trans. A. C. Miles, rev. Rush Rhees (Atlantic Highlands, N.J.: Humanities Press, 1979).

42. *Vallum* derives from the Latin *vallus*, or "stake." It refers to a type of Roman fortification that included a palisade and, at times, a moat.—Trans.

43. Edouard Glissant, *Poetics of Relation* (Ann Arbor: University of Michigan Press, 1990), but see also "Métissage et créolisation," in *Discours sur le métissage, identités métisses: en quête d'Ariel*, ed. Sylvie Kandé (Paris: L'Harmattan, 1999), 47–53.

44. See Homi K. Bhabha, *Nation and Narration* (London: Routledge, 1990) and *The Location of Culture* (London: Routledge, 1994).

45. Among Spivak's perceptive works of deconstruction see *Critique of Postcolonial Reason* (Cambridge: Harvard University Press, 1999), and the essay "Subaltern Studies Deconstructing Historiography," in *Selected Subaltern Studies*,

Other Words: Essays in Culture Politics, and Outside in the Teaching Machine, ed. Guha and Spivak (New York: Oxford University Press, 1988), 3–32. Of interest also is Donna Landry and Gerald McLean, eds., *The Spivak Reader: Selected Works of Gayatri Chakravorty Spivak* (London: Routledge, 1996).

46. Samuel Huntington, *The Clash of Civilizations and the Remaking of the World Order* (New York: Simon and Schuster, 1996), especially the section "Bounding the West," 157–63.

47. *Hospes* is Latin for "guest," and *hostis* means "stranger" or "enemy.'—Trans.

48. Joseph Brodsky, "Flight from Byzanthium," in *Less Than One: Selected Essays* (New York: Farrar, Straus and Giroux, 1986), 413.

49. Joseph Brodsky and Vaclav Havel, " 'The Post-Communist Night-mare': An Exchange," trans. Paul Wilson, *New York Review of Books*, vol. 11, no. 4, February 17, 1994.

50. Raimundo Panikkar, *The Intrareligious Dialogue* (New York: Paulist Press, 1978).

51. *Hic et nunc* is Latin for "here and now."—Trans.

52. Amartya Sen, *Laicismo indiano* (Milan: Feltrinelli, 1998). A few of the essays in the Italian volume are contained in Sen, *The Argumentative Indian: Writings on Indian History, Culture, and Identity* (London: Allen Tate, 2005).—Trans.

53. Luce Irigaray, *Between East and West* (New York: Columbia University Press, 2002).

54. See especially the chapter "Un altro Occidente. Riflessioni sull'Europa," from my *Homo civicus: La ragionevole follia dei beni comuni* (Bari: Dedalo, 2004), 85–114.

55. See Flavia Monceri, *Altre globalizzazioni. Universalismo liberale e valori asiatici* (Soveria Manelli: Rubettino, 2002) but also by the same author the bibliography on Asian values for *Jura Gentium. Centro di filosofia del diritto internazionale e della politica globale* (www.juragentium.unifi.it).

56. Salman Rushdie, *Imaginary Homelands: Essays and Criticism, 1981–1991* (London: Penguin Books, 1992), 16.

57. See, in particular, Enrique Dussel, "Europa, Modernidad y Eurocentrismo," 41–53, and Aníbal Quijano, "Colonialidad del poder. Eurocentrismo y América Latina," 401–46, both in *La colonialidad del saber; eurocentrismo y ciencia sociales. Perspectivas latinoamericana.* ed. Edgardo Lander (Buenos Aires: Clacso, 1993).

58. Only here, in the original, Cassano uses the italicized English term.—Trans.

59. Wole Soyinka, *Myth, Literature, and the African World* (Cambridge: Cambridge University Press, 1976), 38.

60. "Micromégas" is a short story by Voltaire. Written in 1752, it narrates the journey to Earth of the title character, a giant from a planet that orbits

Sirius. Usbek is a character from Montesquieu's *Lettres persanes* (*Persian Letters*). Published in 1721, this work provides a satirical commentary on Western culture and society from the perspective of Usbek and Rica, Persian noblemen who travel through France.—Trans.

61. Cassano's reference is to themes that traverse Italian poet Giacomo Leopardi's entire oeuvre but are perhaps best illustrated in the canto "La ginestra," or "The Flower of the Desert" (1836). Cassano has devoted a monograph to the study of Leopardi titled *Oltre il nulla. Studio su Giacomo Leopardi* (Bari: Laterza, 2003)—Trans.

62. Ryszard Kapuściński, *The Shadow of the Sun* (New York: Alfred A. Knopf, 2001). Cassano's quotations are on pages 3 and 323, respectively. The first quotation is from the chapter "The Beginning: Collision, Ghana, 1958" (3–13); the second quotation is from "In the Shade of a Tree, in Africa" (314–25).—Trans.

63. Ngugi wa Thiong'o, *Moving the Centre: The Struggle for Cultural Freedoms* (London: James Currey, 1993).

INTRODUCTION: FOR A THOUGHT FROM THE SOUTH

1. The Latin translates as "according to its own principles." The reference is to Bernardino Telesio's *De rerum natura iuxta propria principia*, a philosophical treatise published in 1563, which claimed that the principles that governed the functioning of the world should be investigated through observation, rather than by reason alone.—Trans.

2. Literally "different words." The *dissòi lógoi* was an ancient rhetorical practice, initiated in sophistic writing, to argue both sides of an argument. The first reference to its use was made in the third century A.D. by Iamblichus in his *Exhortation to Philosophy*.—Trans.

3. See in this regard what Cassano says in the essay "Pier Paolo Pasolini: Life as Oxymoron."—Trans.

4. *Omertà r*efers to the Mafia practice of keeping one's silence to protect the "clan" from discovery. When a mafioso is caught either by the police or by a rival clan, it behooves him or her to keep the silence, in order to protect his immediate and extended family from reprisals on the part of its enemies.—Trans.

5. Cassano is referring to the original version of *Southern Thought*. Therefore, his reference to the composition of these essays is 1994 to 1996.—Trans.

1. GOING SLOW

1. In Italian, verbs all end in three suffixes: *-are, -ere, -ire.* Cassano is here playing on the rhyming quality between "*mare*" (sea) and "*-are*."—Trans.

2. Fantozzi is a literary and cinematic stock character created by the Genoese comedian Paolo Villaggio. Very popular in the seventies, to the point that a number of movies and vignettes had him as protagonist, Fantozzi is the epitome of the middle-class bourgeois trying to keep up with the Joneses and,

in the process, making a fool of himself, his origins, and an entire way of life.—Trans.

3. Here Cassano is referring to the Italian translation (*Il rovescio e il dritto*, Milan: Bompiani, 1988), 37–41, of Albert Camus's first book, *L'envers et l'endroit*, published in 1937. Translated into English either as *Betwixt and Between* or *The Wrong and the Right Side*, it is Camus's first attempt to theorize a coherent philosophy of life. An English translation is available in *The Wrong and the Right Side*, collected in Camus, *Lyrical and Critical Essays*, trans. Ellen Conroy Kennedy (New York: Alfred A, Knopf, 1969), 50–61. The text cited by Cassano, however, is from "Helen's Exile," in *Lyrical and Critical Essays*, 148.—Trans.

2. OF LAND AND SEA

The epigraph that begins this chapter is a citation from one of Dylan Thomas's youth poems titled "No Thought Can Trouble My Unwholesome Pose," now collected in *The Notebooks of Dylan Thomas*, ed. Ralph Maud (New York: New Directions, 1967), 69.

1. Arnold Toynbee, *Hellenism: The History of Civilization* (Oxford: Oxford University Press, 1959), 19–21.

2. C. Jacob Burckhardt, *Force and Freedom: Reflections on History*, trans. James Hastings Nichols (New York: Pantheon, 1943). 211–14.

3. Cassano's original citation is from Gilles Deleuze and Félix Guattari, *Geofilosofia. Il progetto nomade e la geografia dei saperi* (Sesto San Giovanni: Mimesis Editrice, collana Millepiani, 1993), 12. As a collection of texts by Gilles Deleuze and Félix Guattari, this book exists only in Italian. The English quotation is from the chapter "Geophilosophy," in *What Is Philosophy?* trans. Hugh Tomlinson and Graham Burchell (New York: Columbia University Press, 1994), 87.—Trans.

4. Helmut Berve, *Storia greca* (Bari: Laterza, 1959), 7. The original, titled *Griechische Geschichte*, is available in three volumes (Freiburg im Breisgau: Herder, 1963).—Trans.

5. G. W. F. Hegel, *Lectures on the Philosophy of World History*, trans H. B. Nisbet (New York: Cambridge University Press, 1975), 195–96.

6. Spyros Asdrachas, "Una città liquida: l'Arcipelago greco," in *La salvaguardia delle città storiche in Europa e nell'area mediterranea: atti del convegno internazionale di studi* (Bologna: Nuova Alfa Editoriale, 1983), 139–45.

7. Carl Schmitt, *Terra e mare*, a cura di A. Bolaffi (Milan: Giuffrè, 1986). The Italian translates *Land und Meer. Eine weltgeschichtliche Betrachtung* (Leipzig: Reclam, 1942). In English it has appeared as *Land and Sea*, trans. Simona Draghici (1954; Washington, D.C.: Plutarch Press, 1997). Unfortunately, there seem to be some passages in the English translation that do not correspond to passages in the Italian translation, so we occasionally translated passages cited by Cassano from the Italian version.—Trans.

8. Plato, *The Laws*, IV, trans. Trevor Saunders (Baltimore: Penguin Books, 1970), 158–62. In this passage, Plato discusses the transformation of foot soldiers into sailors as a negative one, since he believed that foot soldiers face battle directly, while sailors and seamanship teach human beings deceit and cowardice by allowing them to dodge and tack direct fights with the enemies.—Trans.

9. Martin Heidegger, *What Is Philosophy?* (New Haven, Conn: College and University Press, 1956), 31.

10. Jacques Derrida, *Writing and Difference*, trans. Alan Bass (Chicago: University of Chicago Press, 1978), 81.

11. Ibid., 153.

12. Friedrich Nietzsche, *Philosophy in the Tragic Age of the Greeks*, trans. Marianne Cowan (Chicago: Henry Regnery, 1962), 32.

13. Ibid., 33.

14. Massimo Cacciari, *Geo-filosofia dell'Europa* (Milan: Adelphi, 1994). No English translation is available, with the exception of a chapter titled "Geophilosophy of Europe," included in *The Unpolitical: On the Radical Critique of Political Reason*, ed. Alessandro Carrera (New York: Fordham University Press, 2009) 197–205.

15. Plutarch, "The Obsolescence of Oracles," in vol. 5 of Plutarch's *Moralia*. Loeb Classical Library Edition (London: Heinemann, 1939), 351.

16. Karl R. Popper, *The Open Society and Its Enemies* (Princeton: Princeton University Press, 1963); and Eric A. Havelock, *The Liberal Temper in Greek Politics* (New Haven: Yale University Press, 1964).

17. Santo Mazzarino, *Il pensiero storico classico*, vol. 1 (Bari: Laterza, 1966), 245–99.

18. Here and in the following few paragraphs, Cassano discusses Thucydides' famous Melian Dialogue (or Melian Debate) found in chapter 17 of his *History of the Peloponnesian War* (New York: Penguin Books, 1954).—Trans.

19. In Sophocles' *Antigone*, Creon upholds the law of Thebes, which declared that traitors could not be given proper burial, against Antigone's plea to allow her to bury her brother Polyneices, who had fought against their brother Eteocles to become ruler of Thebes. Creon's opposition results in the death of every member of his family, including his wife, Eurydice, and son, Haemon.—Trans.

20. Protagoras and Gorgias were two of the most famous Sophist philosophers of the mid-to-late fifth century B.C. Protagoras was famous for his "Antilogies," which stated that every argument to establish a truth had a correspondent and contrary argument. The Sicilian Gorgias equally believed in antinomies to negate the possibility of reaching certain and definitive truths.—Trans.

21. Antonio Capizzi, *I sofisti ad Atene: L'uscita retorica dal dilemma tragico* (Bari: Levante, 1990), 65.

22. Federico Chabod, *Storia dell'idea d'Europa* (Rome-Bari: Laterza, 1995), 23.

23. Capizzi, *Sofisti*, 65.

24. Paul Valéry, *The Collected Works of Paul Valéry*, vol. 10, trans. Jackson Mathews, ed. Denise Folliot (New York: Pantheon Books, 1962), 23–36.

25. Chabod, *Storia dell'idea d'Europa*, 23.

26. Herodotus, *The Histories*, trans. Robin Waterfield (Oxford: Oxford University Press, 1998), 68. Cyrus tells the Greeks: " 'I have never yet found occasion to fear the kind of men who set aside a space in the middle of their town where they can meet and make false promises to one another. If I remain healthy, their tongues will be occupied with events at home rather than those in Ionia.' This was intended by Cyrus as a slur against Greeks in general, because they have town squares where they buy and sell goods, whereas it is not a Persian practice to use such places at all and the town square is entirely unknown among them."—Trans.

27. Jacob C. Burckhardt, *Storia della civiltà greca*, vol. 1 (Florence: Sansoni, 1955), 96–98; and Santo Mazzarino, *Fra Oriente e Occidente. Ricerca di storia greca arcaica* (Florence: La Nuova Italia, 1947), 206–13. A much abridged English translation of Burckhardt's *Storia* appeared as *History of Greek Culture* (New York: Ungar, 1963). However, references to the plurivocality of the Greek world can be found in chap. 2, "The Polis and Its Historical Development," 18–97; chap. 3, "Objective Consideration of the Forms of the State," 98–103, and chap. 4, "The Unity of the Greek Nation," 104–23.

28. G. W. F. Hegel, *Lectures on the Philosophy of World History*, trans. H. B. Nisbet (London: Cambridge University Press, 1975), 196.

29. Alberto Savinio, *Opere. Scritti dispersi. Tra guerra e dopoguerra (1943–1952)*. Introduction by Leonardo Sciascia; ed. Sciascia and De Maria (Milan: Bompiani, 1989), 1285.

30. Ibid., 1279.

31. Ibid., 1027.

32. Michel Mollat du Jourdin, *Europe and the Sea*, trans. Teresa Lavander Fagan (Oxford: Blackwell, 1993), 4, 230, 231.

33. Valéry, *La crisi del pensiero*, 44; "The European," in *The Collected Works of Paul Valéry*, trans. Jackson Mathews, ed. Denise Folliot (New York: Pantheon Books, 1962), 312.—Trans.

34. Jacques Derrida, *The Other Heading: Reflections on Today's Europe*, trans. Anne Brault and Michael B. Naas (Bloomington: Indiana University Press, 1992), 20–22.

35. Alberto Savinio, *Nuova enciclopedia*. (Milan: Adelphi, 1977), 64.

36. Paul Valéry, *Sguardi sul mondo attuale* (Milan: Adelphi, 1994), 145–46. This is a collection of essays partially based on the French original entitled *Regards sur le monde actuel* (Paris: Stock, 1931. Since the English version,

Reflections on the World Today, trans. Francis Scarfe (New York: Pantheon Books, 1948), does not contain several passages cited by Cassano, the translators are citing their own version.—Trans.

37. Valéry, *Sguardi sul mondo attuale*, 146; see n. 36.—Trans.

38. Valéry, *Sguardi sul mondo attuale*, 276; *Reflections on the World Today*, trans. Francis Scarfe (New York: Pantheon Books, 1948), 169.—Trans.

39. Valéry, *La crisi del pensiero*, 65; "The European," in *The Collected Works of Paul Valéry*, 319.

40. Valéry, *Sguardi sul mondo attuale*, 148; see n. 36.—Trans.

41. Ibid., 149; see n. 36.—Trans.

42. Schmitt, *Land and Sea*, 1.

43. Schmitt, *Terra e mare*, 103. This passage is not included in the English translation.—Trans.

44. Ibid., 109. Again, this passage is not included in the English translation.—Trans.

45. The V2 is a long-range ballistic missile. It was originally developed by Germany at the beginning of World War II.—Trans.

46. Stefano Levi Della Torre, *Essere fuori luogo. Il dilemma ebraico tra diaspora e ritorno* (Rome: Donzelli, 1995). No English translation exists of this book.—Trans.

47. Martin Heidegger was born and later buried in the town of Messkirch, a rural town between Freiburg and Ulm. Cassano is here referring to the fact that Heidegger roots much of his philosophy "inland," away from the antagonistic sea.—Trans.

48. Martin Heidegger, "The Fundamental Question of Metaphysics," in *An Introduction to Metaphysics* (New Haven: Yale University Press, 1959), 38.

49. Ibid., 38–39.

50. Ibid., 50.

51. Alberto Savinio, *Alcesti di Samuele. Alcesti di Samuele e atti unici* (Milan: Adelphi, 1991), 47–48. In this tragedy, Savinio reinvents the myth of Alcestes, the queen who descended to Hades, by turning her into a Hebrew woman who kills herself so as to not stand in the way of her Nazi husband's career. In the original myth, Alcestes is saved and brought back to life by Heracles; here, instead, it is President Roosevelt who tries to rescue her. However, faced with the choice of returning among the living and staying in Hades, she chooses the latter.—Trans.

52. Savinio, *Opere*, 62.

53. Martin Heidegger and Erhart Kästner, *Briefwechsel: 1953–1974* (Frankfurt am Main: Insel, 1986), 51.

54. Martin Heidegger, *Saggi e discorsi* (Milan: Mursia, 1991). Heidegger himself collected the essays and presentations found in this volume around 1954. A current edition of the volume in the original is *Vorträge und Aufsätze* (Stuttgart: Verlag Klett-Cotte, 2000).—Trans.

55. George Steiner, *Martin Heidegger* (Florence: Sansoni, 1980), 142.

56. Ibid.,143.

57. Remo Bodei, in Theodor W. Adorno, *Il gergo dell'autenticità. Sull'ideologia tedesca*, introduction by Remo Bodei (Turin: Bollati Boringhieri, 1980), xxxiv. The citation is taken from the introduction, and thus occurs originally in Italian and is not present in the German, *Jargon der Eigentlichkeit. Zur Deutschen Ideologie* (Frankfurt am Main: Suhrkamp Verlag, 1964), or English version, *The Jargon of Authenticity* (New York: Routledge, 2003).—Trans.

58. Friedrich Nietzsche, *The Gay Science* (Cambridge: Cambridge University Press, 2001), 289, 163.

59. Ibid., 283, 161.

60. Ibid., 240, 147.

61. Ibid., 124, 119.

62. Ibid., 343, 199.

63. Ibid., 310, 176.

64. Ibid., 337, 190–91.

65. Ibid., 382, 246.

66. Friedrich Nietzsche, *Thus Spoke Zarathustra: A Book for All and None*, trans. Adrian Del Caro, ed. Adrian Del Caro and Robert Pippin (New York: Cambridge University Press, 2006), 186.

67. Ibid., 194.

68. Roberto Calasso, "Monologo fatale," in *Ecce homo. Come si diventa ciò che si è*, by Friedrich Nietzsche (Milan: Adelphi, 1981), 165.

69. Savinio, *Nuova enciclopedia*, 250–52.

70. Martin Heidegger, "Why Poets?" in *Off the Beaten Track*, trans. Julian Young and Kenneth Haynes (Cambridge: Cambridge University Press, 2002), 200–241.

71. Henrik Ibsen, *The Lady from the Sea* (London: R. Hart-Davis, 1960).

72. Gilles Deleuze and Félix Guattari, *Anti-Oedipus* (Minneapolis: University of Minnesota Press, 1983).

73. Burckhardt, *History of Greek Culture*, 104.

74. Burckhardt, *Force and Freedom: Reflections on History* (New York: Pantheon Books, 1943), 211.

75. Jacques Derrida, *Of Spirit: Heidegger and the Question* (Chicago: University of Chicago Press, 1989).

76. Heidegger, "The Fundamental Question of Metaphysics," 38.

77. Carlo Diano, *Forma ed evento. Principi di un'interpretazione del mondo Greco*, preface by Remo Bodei (Venice: Marsilio, 1993).

78. Emmanuel Lévinas, "The Trace of the Other," in *Deconstruction in Context: Literature and Philosophy*, ed. Mark C. Taylor (Chicago: University of Chicago Press, 1986), 348.

79. In Canto XXVI of the *Inferno*, Dante meets Ulysses in the circle of the deceivers. But he retells a myth of Ulysses that is neither in the *Iliad* nor the

Odyssey. Indeed, what Ulysses recounts, when prompted by Virgil, is how he died. An important component of the story is his crossing the columns of Hercules that lead out of the Mediterranean into the Atlantic Ocean, in open defiance of God's will. For this arrogance, God condemns him and his crew to death. In a famous tercet ("Consider your birth:/you were not made to live like brutes/
but to follow virtue and knowledge"), Ulysses summarizes the argument he used to convince his men to explore and pursue their leader's desire to expand his knowledge of the world.—Trans.

80. Schmitt, *Terra e mare*, 43; *Land and Sea*, 13. The second cited passage, however, is not present in the English version, so we have translated the passage ourselves.—Trans.

81. Max Horkheimer and Theodor Adorno, *The Dialectic of Enlightenment*, by Edmund Jephcott was published in 2002 (Stanford: Stanford University Press).

82. Moses Finley, *The World of Odysseus* (New York: Viking, 1954), 25.

83. Gabriel Audisio, "Vues sur Ulysse, ou l'ambivalence des Méditerranéens," in *Cahiers du Sud*, special number titled *Le genie d'oc et l'Homme méditerranéen* (February 1943), 281.

84. Ibid., 273.

85. Alain Corbin, *The Lure of the Sea: The Discovery of the Seaside in the Western World, 1750–1840*, trans. Jocelyn Phelps (Berkeley: University of California Press 1994), 8.

86. Roberto Calasso, *The Marriage of Cadmus and Harmony*, trans. Tim Parks (New York: Knopf, 1993), 351.

87. Ibid., 366.

88. Piero Boitani, *L'ombra di Ulisse. Figure di un mito* (Bologna: Il Mulino), 1992.

89. Raffaele La Capria, *L'occhio di Napoli* (Milan: Mondadori, 1994), 9.

90. Alberto Savinio, *Capitano Ulisse* (Milan: Adelphi, 1989).

3. THINKING THE FRONTIER

1. Georges Simenon, "Frontiere," *Limes*, no. 2 (1994): 289–96.

2. Cassano engages in an intricate game with the Latin word *frons*, "forehead," and the many derivatives that occur in the Italian language. If the reader understands the English "front" to mean "forehead," as well as to hold similar meanings in compound nouns and verbs, it is possible to follow the wordplay in English as well.—Trans.

3. G. W. F. Hegel, *The Phenomenology of Spirit*, most recently by A. V. Miller (with foreword by J. N. Findlay [Oxford: Clarendon Press, 1977]). The citation refers to a small chapter by this subheading. See the link at http://www.marxists.org/reference/archive/hegel/works/ph/phba.htm.—Trans.

4. Cassano is here referring to *Il deserto dei tartari*, a famous book by Dino Buzzati that narrates the unending wait of a garrison on the borderlands for

the arrival of the enemy Tatars. It was made into a 1976 movie by the same title (in English, *The Desert of the Tatars*), starring Vittorio Gassman, Philippe Noiret, Max Von Sydow, and Jacques Perrin. An English translation of the book is available as *The Tartar Steppe* (Manchester: Carcanet, 1985).—Trans.

5. The Latin term *limes* corresponds to "boundary" or "threshold," and is the origin for the English "limit."—Trans.

6. René Girard, *Violence and the Sacred* (Baltimore: Johns Hopkins University Press).

7. Georg Simmel, *Sociology: Inquiries into the Construction of Social Forms*, trans. and ed. Anthony J. Blasi, Anton K. Jacobs, and Mathew Kanjirathinkal, with introduction by Horst J. Helle (Leiden: Brill, 2009).

8. We have taken a few liberties to maintain the original meaning and wordplay. The only exception is "transgressors in disguise" for the original "trasgressori travestiti." We have lost the alliterative power of the original, because by translating "travestiti" as "tranvestites," we would have achieved a very different meaning from the one suggested in the original.—Trans.

9. Cassano is talking, here and below, about the movie by the Greek director, Theodoros Angelopoulos, titled *Το Μετέωρο βήμα του πελαργού* (1991), also known in French as *Le pas suspendu de la cigogne* and in English as *The Suspended Step of the Stork*.—Trans.

10. The original plays on the alliterative value of "polizie" (police forces) and "pulizie" (cleansings). Cassano has confirmed that the word "pulizie" which means "cleaning" or "cleansings" should be understood to mean "ethnic cleansings," as they had occurred in Bosnia at the time Cassano was writing.—Trans.

11. Constantine Cavafy, *Cinquantacinque poesie* (Turin: Einaudi, 1968), 39. The original poems, in Greek, were published in a variety of venues.—Trans.

12. Cassano uses the English terms "news" in opposition to the preceding Italian "notizie," which we have translated as "national reporting." What Cassano is underscoring is the difference between local, national reporting and reporting from international agencies such as ANSA, UPI or AP, whereby the latter are supposedly less biased in collecting their information.—Trans.

13. Jacques Le Goff, *Time, Work, and Culture in the Middle Ages*, trans. Arthur Goldhammer (Chicago: University of Chicago Press, 1980).

14. "Fungibility" is a term used to define the properties of those market goods whose units can be mutually substituted among themselves (and not, erroneously, with different market goods).—Trans.

15. Karl Marx, *Economic and Philosophic Manuscripts of 1844*, ed. Dirk J. Struik, trans. Martin Milligan (New York: International, 1964).

16. The Latin "Deus absconditus" (literally: "hidden God") refers to a religious and philosophical concept, whereby God creates the world and life, but then refrains from participating in this life by "hiding" and allowing life to proceed without his intervention (see in particular St. Thomas Aquinas for such a concept of God).—Trans.

17. Joshua Meyrowitz, *No Sense of Place: The Impact of the Electronic Media on Social Behavior* (New York: Oxford University Press, 1986).—Trans.

18. Karl Polanyi, *The Great Transformation* (New York: Farrar and Rinehart, 1944).

19. Here Cassano refers to the Latin "ius excludendi omnes alios" ("the right to exclude all others"), a Latin and Italian concept of property that is exclusionary, exclusivist, and extensive (indeed, the original Latin suggests that it extends "usque ad inferos et usque ad sidera," "all the way to hell and to the stars").—Trans.

20. Eric Hobsbawm and Terence Ranger, eds., *The Invention of Tradition* (New York: Cambridge University Press, 1983).

21. Simone Weil used the term "uprooting" repeatedly in her writings, especially in *L'enracinement*. *"Prélude à un declaration des devoirs envers l'être humain"* (Paris: Gallimard, 1949). In this regard, see Betty McLane-Iles, *Uprooting and Integration in the Writings of Simone Weil*. (New York: Lang, 1987).—Trans.

22. The italicized words appear in English in the original, just as a few lines later *born to lose* also appears in English.—Trans.

23. Robert K. Merton, *Social Theory and Social Structure* (Glencoe, Ill.: Free Press, 1957), 447–64.

24. Isaiah Berlin, *Le origini della violenza e del nazionalismo*. Interview with Giancarlo Bosetti in *Reset*, no. 5 (1994): 38–42.

25. Edgar Morin and Anne Brigitte Kern, *Homeland Earth: A Manifesto for the New Millennium*, trans. Sean Kelly and Roger LaPointe (Cresskill, N.J.: Hampton Press, 1999).

4. THE FUNDAMENTALISM OF THE RAT RACE

1. Serge Latouche, *The Westernization of the World*, trans. Rosemary Morris (Cambridge: Polity Press, 1996), 54.

2. Arnold J. Toynbee, *Civilization on Trial* (Oxford: Oxford University Press, 1948), 188.

3. Ibid., 198–99.

4. Hubert Prolongeau, *La vita quotidiana in Colombia al tempo del cartello di Medellín* (Milan: Rizzoli, 1994), 122. The original was published in French as *La Vie quotidienne en Colombie au temps du cartel de Medellin* (Paris: Hachette Litteratures, 1992). No English translation is available.

5. Paul Valéry, *Sguardi sul mondo attuale* (Milan: Adelphi, 1994), 148. As mentioned in a previous essay in this book, this is a collection of essays originally published in French with the title *Regards sur le monde actuel* (Paris: Stock, 1931). Cassano refers to an essay that is not included in the English translation by Francis Scarfe, *Reflections of the World Today* (New York: Pantheon, 1948).

5. ALBERT CAMUS: THE NEED FOR SOUTHERN THOUGHT

1. Albert Camus, *Notebooks, 1935–1942*, trans. Philip Thody (New York: Alfred A. Knopf, 1963), *Notebooks, 1942–1951*, trans. Justin O'Brien (New

York: Alfred A. Knopf, 1965), and *Notebooks, 1951–1959,* trans. Ryan Bloom (Chicago: Ivan R. Dee, 2008). Here Cassano is quoting from *Notebooks, 1942–1951,* 120.

2. Albert Camus, *Lyrical and Critical Essays,* trans. Ellen Conroy Kennedy (New York: Alfred A. Knopf, 1969), 352.

3. Camus, *Lyrical and Critical Essays,* 351; *Notebooks, 1942–1951,* 124.

4. Camus, *Notebooks. 1942–1951,* 124.

5. Ibid., 158.

6. Ibid., 151–52.

7. Ibid., 152.

8. Ibid.

9. Ibid., 141.

10. Unlike ethical virtues, which are tied to ethical principles and imply a commitment to the state, the family, and other institutions, formal virtues respond to contingent and particular commitments only. The beautiful soul, or *schöne Seele,* is a spirit that lacks criteria for moral judgment and therefore does not act in a morally significant way.—Trans.

11. *Pantragism* refers to a prehistorical view of reality as tragic. *Panlogism* is the belief that rational thought realizes the world. In Hegel's dialectical system, *pantragism* is integrated into *panlogism* with the victory of the logos over the irrational of reality.—Trans.

12. Albert Camus, *The Rebel: An Essay on Man in Revolt,* trans. Anthony Bower (New York: Alfred Knopf, 1954), 115.

13. Ibid., 190.

14. Ibid., 203–4.

15. Ibid., 207.

16. Ibid., 234.

17. Fyodor Dostoevsky, *The Brothers Karamazov,* trans. Constance Garnett (Mineola, N.Y.: Dover, 2005), 221–22.

18. Grenier's quotation, which translates as "Camus was Ivan Karamazov," is reported by Cassano in French.—Trans.

19. Jean Grenier, *Albert Camus soleil et ombre. Une biographie intellectuelle* (Paris: Gallimard, 1987), 137.

20. Albert Camus, *The Plague,* trans. Stuart Gilbert (New York: A. A. Knopf, 1948).

21. Paul Nizan, *Aden Arabie,* trans. John Pinkham (New York: Columbia University Press, 1987), 65.

22. Camus, *Rebel,* 236.

23. Camus, *Essais,* 380. The passage is not included in the English version *Lyrical and Critical Essays.* Cassano's reference is to an interview with Camus by Emile Simon. The French edition of *Essais* (Paris: Gallimard, 1967) anthologizes three interviews, "Trois interviews" (377–87), which include the interview by Simon, originally published in *Revue du Caire* (1948), 378–83. It is likely that Cassano refers to these pages.—Trans.

24. Albert Camus, *Reflections on the Guillotine*, trans. Richard Howard (Michigan City, Ind.: Fridtjof Karla, 1959), 44.

25. Camus, *Plague*, 121.

26. Camus, *Lyrical and Critical Essays*, 357.

27. Camus, *Notebooks, 1942–1951*, 213.

28. Cassano is referring to Camus's *The Fall*, trans. Justin O'Brien (New York: Alfred A. Knopf, 1959). Through the main character of Jean-Baptiste Clamence, Camus expounds his ideas of universal guilt and lack of innocence.

29. Camus, *Reflections on the Guillotine*, 5.

30. *Albert Camus and Jean Grenier: Correspondence, 1932–1960*, trans. Jan F. Rigaud (University of Nebraska Press, 2003), 112.

31. Camus, *Notebooks, 1942–1951*, 156.

32. Camus, *Rebel*, 161.

33. Camus, *Lyrical and Critical Essays*,192.

34. Camus, *Rebel*, 161.

35. Ibid., 161–62.

36. G. W. F. Hegel, *Lectures on the Philosophy of World History*, trans. H. B. Nisbet (London: Cambridge University Press, 1975), 171.

37. Ibid., 197.

38. Ibid.

39. Camus, *Notebooks, 1942–1951*, 136.

40. Camus, *Rebel*, 265.

41. Ibid.

42. Ibid., 266.

43. Ibid.

44. Cassano's reference is to the West as "Abend-land" or the land of the sunset.—Trans.

45. Camus, *Rebel*, 267.

46. Friedrich Nietzsche, *Beyond Good and Evil*, trans. R. J. Hollingdale (London: Penguin Books, 1973), 188.

47. Ibid.

48. Camus's foreword to Jean Grenier, *Islands: Lyrical Essays*, trans. Steve Light (Copenhagen and Los Angeles: Green Integer, 2005), 7.

49. Gide's *Les Nourritures terrestres* (1897) is a lyrical prose poem. It is translated as *The Fruits of the Earth*, trans. Dorothy Bussy (New York: Alfred Knopf, 1949).—Trans.

50. Grenier, *Islands: Lyrical Essays*, 8.

51. Camus, *Lyrical and Critical Essays*, 357.

52. Cassano refers to Camus's *Il rovescio e il diritto* (Milan: Bompiani, 1988). We have chosen to use the English title, *The Wrong Side and the Right Side* (though the book has also been translated as *Betwixt and Between*). The title of the French original is *L'envers et l'endroit* (1937). References are to the text of *The Wrong Side and the Right Side* contained in *Lyrical and Critical Essays*, 5–61.

53. Camus, *Lyrical and Critical Essays*, 13.

54. Camus, *Essais*, 1835. Cassano is referring to the text "Présentation du desert," 1834–35. The text is not included in the English version.—Trans.

55. Camus, *Lyrical and Critical Essays*, 79.

56. Ibid., 102, 104.

57. Albert Camus, *Théâtre, Récits, Nouvelles* (Paris: Gallimard, 1962), 1910. Cassano is referring to the essay "Herman Melville," in *Théâtre, Récits, Nouvelles, 1907–1911*. In the English translation, it is part of *Lyrical and Critical Essays*, 288–94. Citation is on 293.—Trans.

58. Albert Camus, *A Happy Death*, trans. Richard Howard (New York: Alfred Knopf, 1972), 130–36.

59. Camus, *Notebooks, 1951–1959*, 21.

60. Camus, *Rebel*, 268.

61. Camus, *Notebooks, 1951–1959*, 56.

62. Ibid., 45–46.

63. Albert Camus, *The Myth of Sisyphus and Other Essays*, trans. Justin O'Brien (New York: Alfred A. Knopf, 1957). 137.

64. Camus, *Il rovescio e il diritto*, 51. The passage in not included in the English version, *Lyrical and Critical Essays*.—Trans.

65. Camus, *Lyrical and Critical Essays*, 349.

66. Ibid., 7.

67. Ibid.

68. Ibid., 8.

69. Ibid., 9.

70. Simone Weil, *The Need for Roots* (Boston: Beacon Press, 1952) is the English version of *L'Enracinement*, Simone Weil's last essay, published posthumously (Paris: Gallimard, 1949).—Trans.

71. Camus, *Essais*, 1700. Cassano refers to a passage from *Essais* corresponding to the section *Textes complémentaires d'Albert Camus. Commentaires, Notes et Variantes*, ed. Roger Quilliot and Louis Faucon, 1167–1930. The text is not included in the English translation.

72. Jean-Claude Brisville, *Camus* (Paris: Gallimard, 1959), 223.

73. Jean Grenier, *Albert Camus Souvenirs* (Paris: Gallimard, 1968), 11.

74. Ibid.

75. Camus, *Notebooks, 1942–1951*, 211.

76. *The Stranger* was published as *L'Etranger* in 1942. It is among Camus's best-known novels.—Trans.

77. Grenier, *Albert Camus*, 133.

78. Camus, *Notebooks, 1942–1951*, 20.

79. Mucius Scaevola was a legendary Roman aristocrat who volunteered to murder Porsenna, an Etruscan commander who laid siege to Rome in 508 B.C. Mucius, however, stabbed a servant of Porsenna instead of the commander himself and when confronted with his error decided to burn his right hand as

a punishment. Legend has it that he placed it in a caldron until the fire completely consumed it. Porsenna, impressed by the resolve and courage of Mucius, freed him).—Trans.

80. Camus, *Notebooks, 1951–1959*, 193.

81. The original italicizes *omertà*, a term that was originally as is still associated with the Mafia's code of silence. Since the term has now been incorporated in English dictionaries, we have maintained it in the translation.—Trans.

82. Camus, *Essais*, 1899–1900. Cassano refers to the interview "La pari de notre génération," originally published in *Demain*, October 24–30, 1957, and included in *Essais*, section *Textes complémentaires d'Albert Camus. Commentaires, Notes et Variantes*, 1898–1904. It is not included in the English translation, so we have translated the passage ourselves—Trans.

83. Camus, *Lyrical and Critical Essays*, 14.

84. Cassano's reference is to Camus's *State of Siege*. The English translation is in *Caligula and Three Other Plays*, trans. Stuart Gilbert (New York: Vintage Books, 1962), 135–232.—Trans.

85. Ibid., 143, 154, 164, 190.

86. Camus, *Notebooks, 1942–1951*, 95.

87. Ibid., 68.

88. Ibid., 70.

89. Camus, *Essais*, 1906. Cassano refers to a speech titled "Ce que je dois à l' Espagne," contained in the section *Textes complémentaires. Commentaires, Notes et Variantes*, 1905–8. It has not been translated into English.—Trans.

90. Camus, *Notebooks, 1951–1959*, 18.

91. Camus, *Notebooks, 1942–1951*, 226.

92. Camus, *Essais*, 1901–2. See note 89. The text has not been translated into English.—Trans.

93. Albert Camus, "L'Espagne et le donquichottisme," *Le Monde libertaire* 12 (November 1955), anthologized in *Volonté anarchiste 26, Albert Camus et les libertaires*, 22.

94. Camus, *Plague*, 237.

95. Ignazio Silone, *Severina* (Milan: Mondadori, 1990), 58.

96. Ignazio Silone, *Bread and Wine*, translated by Eric Mosbacher (New York: Penguin, 1962), 228. But see also: Gustav Herling, *Diario scritto di notte* (Milan: Feltrinelli, 1992).—Trans.

97. Camus, *Essais*, 1901. See note 89. The text is untranslated.—Trans.

98. Ibid.,1925. Cassano is referring to the text "Dernière interview d'Albert Camus," included in the section *Textes complémentaires. Commentaires, Notes et Variantes*, 1925–1928. It has not been included in the English version.—Trans.

99. Camus, *Théâtre, Récits, Nouvelles*, 1724. Cassano is referring to the text "Pourquoi je fais du théâtre?" 1720–28. It is not included in the English version.—Trans.

100. Camus, *Notebooks 1942–1951*, 126.

101. The reference is to Italian poet Giacomo Leopardi's best-known poems, "La ginestra o il fiore del deserto" (1836).—Trans.

102. Camus, *Notebooks, 1942–1951*, 245.

6. PIER PAOLO PASOLINI: LIFE AS OXYMORON

1. Pier Paolo Pasolini, *Volgar' eloquio*, edited and with a preface by Gian Carlo Ferretti (Rome: Editori Riuniti, 1987), 51.

2. The reference here is to Pasolini's *Le ceneri di Gramsci* (Milan: Garzanti, 1976), a collection of eleven poems Pasolini wrote between 1951 and 1956 that reveal a conflicted relationship with Marxism and that were published for the first time in 1957. A limited selection of English translations is contained in the volumes Pasolini, *Poems*, selected and translated by Norman Macafee with Luciano Martinego, foreword by Enzo Siciliano (New York: Random House, 1982), and Pasolini, *The Ashes of Gramsci*, trans. David Wallace (Peterborough, Cambs, UK: Spectacular Diseases, 1982). It should be noted that *The Ashes of Gramsci* contains only the eponymous poem and omits the other texts that were included in the original collection.—Trans.

3. In Italian the pronoun "you" is translated as "tu" or "Lei." "Tu" is used for colloquial address whereas "Lei" is for formal communication.—Trans.

4. Franco Fortini, *Nuovi saggi italiani*, 2 vols. (Milan: Garzanti, 1987), 1:144. Fortini, a literary critic, translator, and poet, was a very influential figure in Italian post-war culture, up to his death in 1994. With regard to "prosa d'arte," or "artistic prose," the latter has a long tradition in Italy and is characterized by crafted syntax, elegant diction, and other rhetorical refinements.—Trans.

5. Fortini was the son of Dino Lattes, a Jewish lawyer from Leghorn, and Emma Fortini del Giglio, a nonpracticing Catholic.—Trans.

6. Fortini, *Nuovi saggi italiani*, 1:132.

7. See Giorgio Barberi Squarotti, *Poesia e narrativa del secondo Novecento* (Milan: Mursia, 1961); Guido Santato, *Pier Paolo Pasolini. L'opera* (Vicenza: Neri Pozza,1980); Luigi Martellini, *Pier Paolo Pasolini* (Florence: Le Monnier, 1983), and *Introduzione a Pasolini* (Rome-Bari: Laterza, 1989); and Giuseppe Zigaina, *Pasolini tra enigma e profezia* (Venice: Marsilio, 1989). Zigaina's volume has been translated as *Pasolini between Enigma and Prophecy* (Toronto: Exile Editions, 1991).

8. Pier Paolo Pasolini, *Lettere 1955–1975*, ed. Nico Naldini (Turin: Einaudi, 1988), 442.

9. Ibid., 445. Since only one volume of Pasolini's letters has been translated into English as *The Letters of Pier Paolo Pasolini*, ed. Nico Naldini, trans. Stuart Hood (London: Quartet Books, 1992), the reference in English is not available.—Trans.

10. Occasionally, Cassano cites passages from Pasolini's poetic, journalistic and essayistic output without identifying the source. Although we have tried

to fill the gaps, the author himself does not always recollect the sources for these citations.—Trans.

11. These verses are from the poem "Ogni giorno è l'ultimo," now collected in Pier Paolo Pasolini, *Tutte le poesie* (Milan: Mondadori, 2003). The collection *Poems* (see note 2) does not contain the text of "Ogni giorno è l'ultimo" to which Cassano refers.—Trans.

12. These verses are also from "Ogni giorno è l'ultimo."—Trans.

13. Enzo Siciliano, *Vita di Pasolini* (Milan: Rizzoli, 1978), 161; Siciliano, *Pasolini: A Biography*, trans. John Shepley (New York: Random House, 1982), 121.

14. Cassano is referring to a difficult time in Pasolini's relationship with the Italian Left. In 1947 Pasolini made a public declaration in favor of Communism, and by 1949 he had joined the Italian Communist Party (PCI). In October 1949, however, he was expelled from the Udine section of the party on grounds of moral unworthiness following charges of obscenity and corruption of minors.—Trans.

15. Pier Paolo Pasolini, *Lettere 1940–1954*, ed. Nico Naldini (Turin: Einaudi, 1986), 389; *Letters of Pierpaolo Pasolini*, 324.

16. Cassano's reference is to the incipit of Pound's Canto 80, from the Pisan Cantos: "Amo ergo sum, and in just that proportion. . . ."—Trans.

17. Pier Paolo Pasolini, *L'usignolo della Chiesa cattolica* (Turin: Einaudi, 1976), 67. This work collects poems published between 1943 and 1948, and appeared originally through the Bolognese editor Longanesi in 1958. The overarching theme is the contradiction of Pasolini's soul.—Trans.

18. See Walter Siti, "Postfazione in forma di lettera," in *Desiderio di Pasolini*, ed. Stefano Casi (Turin: Sonda, 1990), 183–87.

19. Pasolini, *Lettere 1940–1954*, 389–90; *Letters of Pierpaolo Pasolini*, 324.

20. We have found this expression in a review that Pasolini wrote of Calvino's *Invisible Cities*, though it seems to have been taken out of context. It is now available in Pasolini, *Descrizioni di descrizioni* (Milan: Garzanti, 2006), 58–64.—Trans.

21. The citations are taken from Pasolini's prose poem "Versi da testamento" in *Scritti corsari* (Milan: Garzanti, 1975).—Trans.

22. Sandro Penna was an openly homosexual Italian poet who lived his sexuality as a state of marginalization. Some of his love poems have been translated into English. See *This Strange Joy* (Columbus: Ohio State University Press, 1982) and *Remember Me, God of Love* (Manchester: Carcanet, 1993).—Trans.

23. Pier Paolo Pasolini, *Passione e ideologia* (Milan: Garzanti, 1977), 392. Originally published in 1960 by Garzanti, this work contains a number of essays on the Italian poetic tradition in the Italian language and in dialect. It was dedicated to the writer Alberto Moravia.—Trans.

24. Ibid., 403.

25. Pier Paolo Pasolini, *Trasumanar e organizzar* (Milan: Garzanti, 1976), 5. This was the author's last collection of poetry and was originally published in 1971. In it Pasolini expresses the difficulties of "trasumanar," that is, of transcending the human condition in its relationship with social and collective life.—Trans.

26. Ibid., 14.

27. Roland Barthes, *Roland Barthes by Roland Barthes*, trans. Richard Howard (New York: Hill and Wang, 1977), 47.

28. "The Tears of the Excavator" is a poem from *The Ashes of Gramsci*. In it, Pasolini recalls his departure from Friuli following charges of obscenity and concludes with the tears of a woman digger. For the texts, see *Poems*, 25.—Trans.

29. Pasolini, *Le ceneri di Gramsci*, 93. See note 2.

30. Ibid., 42.

31. Ibid., 91.

32. Pier Paolo Pasolini, *Il portico della morte*, ed. Cesare Segre (Rome: Quaderni Pier Paolo Pasolini, 1988), 191.

33. Cassano uses the Italian titles of three movies by Pasolini: *Teorema* (1968), *Edipo re* (1967), and *Porcile* (1969). We have used the titles of the English releases. *Teorema* is also the title of one of Pasolini's novels.—Trans.

34. Pier Paolo Pasolini, *Il sogno del centauro*, with a preface by Gian Carlo Ferretti, ed. Jean Duflot (Rome: Editori Riuniti, 1983), 50.

35. Ibid., 51.

36. Nico Naldini, *Pasolini, una vita* (Turin: Einaudi, 1989), 305.

37. Ibid., 306.

38. The Italian title, as cited by Cassano, is *La religione del mio tempo* (Milan: Garzanti, 1976). It was first published in 1961 and contains a section titled "Poesie incivili," or "Uncivil Poems."—Trans.

39. Ibid., 156.

40. Ibid., 161. The title of the poem in Italian, as quoted by Cassano, is "La rabbia."

41. Ibid., 162.

42. Pier Paolo Pasolini, *Il caos*, ed. Gian Carlo Ferretti (Rome: Editori Riuniti, 1981), 56.

43. Pasolini, *Il sogno del centauro*, 177.

44. Cassano's reference is to the already mentioned *Scritti corsari*, a collection of articles from 1973 to 1975, where Pasolini critiques the degradation of Italian society and culture while addressing issues that were very important at that time, including abortion and divorce.—Trans.

45. Ibid., 21.

46. Alexander Mitscherlich, *Society without the Father*, trans. Eric Mosbacher (New York: Harcourt, Brace, and World, 1969), 269–70.

47. Pasolini, *Trasumanar e organizzar*, 39.

48. Pasolini, *Scritti corsari*, 24.

49. See the poem dedicated to Rudy Dutschke in *Trasumanar e organizzar*, 23–24.

50. Pasolini, *Lettere 1955–1975*, 2:675. The second volume of Pasolini's letters has not been translated.

51. Ibid., 2:710.

52. Pier Paolo Pasolini, *Lutheran Letters*, trans. Stuart Hood (Manchester: Carcanet, 1983), 15.

53. Pasolini, *Il sogno del centauro*, 81.

54. Remo Bodei, *Geometria delle passioni* (Milan: Feltrinelli, 1991), 13.

55. Pasolini, *Lutheran Letters*, 20–21.

56. The title of the original is "Abiura della Trilogia della vita," from *Trilogia della vita*. The letter was written June 5, 1975.—Trans.

57. In Italian the titles are *Il Decamerone* (1971); *I racconti di Canterbury* (1972); and *Il fiore delle mille e una notte* (1974).—Trans.

58. Pier Paolo Pasolini, *Trilogia della vita* (Milan: Mondadori, 1990), 7.

59. Ibid., 7.

60. Ibid., 8.

61. Michel Foucault, *The History of Sexuality*, vol. 1 (New York: Pantheon, 1978).

62. Pasolini, *Il sogno del centauro*, 82.

63. Pasolini, *Scritti corsari*, 120.

64. Ibid., 154.

65. Ibid., 155.

66. Pasolini, *Il sogno del centauro*, 82.

67. Pier Paolo Pasolini, *San Paolo* (Turin: Einaudi, 1977), 91. Pasolini worked on the screenplay between 1968 and 1974 but never brought it to completion; only notes and dialogues are available.—Trans.

68. Pasolini, *Trasumanar e organizzar*, 27.

69. Ibid., 28.

70. Ibid., 10.

71. Ibid., 28.

72. Ibid., 197.

73. Ibid., 181.

74. Ibid., 180.

75. Ludwig Wittgenstein, *Remarks on Frazer's Golden Bough*, ed. Rush Rhees, trans. A. C. Miles (Atlantic Highlands, N.J.: Humanities Press, 1979), 28.

7. EUROPE AND SOUTHERN THOUGHT

This essay was first published in *Paeninsula: L'Italia da ritrovare* (Bari: Editori Laterza, 1998), 75–90. We are thankful to Editrice Laterza (Bari) for granting us the permission to publish it here.—Trans.

1. The reference is to Nietzsche's *Birth of Tragedy*, where the German philosopher discusses Athenian classical tragedy as a balancing between two different ways of perceiving and understanding reality, the Dionysian and the Apollonian. The Dionysian represented the reality of revelry and elementary forces, whereas the Apollonian was centered on an idealized and almost formal view of reality. *The Birth of Tragedy and Other Writings*, ed. Raymond Geuss and Ronald Speirs, trans. Ronald Speirs (Cambridge, UK: Cambridge University Press, 1999).—Trans.

2. After the early years of the Roman Empire, many of the emperors were chosen from among the army's generals, who often came from the provinces of the Roman empire, rather than the patrician families of Rome. This was the result of Rome's attribution of citizenship to many of the people it conquered and annexed to its territories.—Trans.

3. G. W. F. Hegel, *Lectures on the Philosophy of World History*, trans. H. B. Nisbet (New York: Cambridge University Press, 1975), 196.

4. Cassano is here referring to Paul Valéry's comment that Europe can be considered the "appendix" or a "promontory" of Asia, as he discusses it in "The Crisis of the Mind," in Paul Valéry, *History and Politics*, trans. Denise Folliot and Jackson Mathews (New York: Bollingen, 1962), 31.

5. Hegel, *Lectures on the Philosophy of World History*, 196.

6. Ibid., 202.

7. Ibid., 161.

8. Karl Löwith, *The Theological Implications of the Philosophy of History* (Chicago: University of Chicago Press, 1949).

9. Carl Schmitt, *Land and Sea*, trans. Simona Draghici (1954; Washington, D.C.: Plutarch Press, 1997).

10. William Gibson, *Neuromancer* (New York: Ace Books, 1984).

11. Here and below, Cassano is citing Gilles Deleuze and Félix Guattari's work. For the model of the sea as "smooth space," see Gilles Deleuze and Félix Guattari, *A Thousand Plateaus: Capitalism and Schizophrenia*, trans. Hurley, Seem, and Lane (London: Athlone Press, 1987), 478–82. See also Gilles Deleuze and Félix Guattari, *Anti-Oedipus: Capitalism and Schizophrenia*, trans. Brian Massumi (Minneapolis: University of Minnesota Press, 1983), 184–262.—Trans.

12. Massimo Cacciari, *L'arcipelago* (Milan: Adelphi, 1997).

13. Cesare Musatti was an Italian twentieth-century politician, philosopher, and psychoanalyst. After having introduced Gestalt psychology to Italy, he worked as a psychoanalyst and in 1947 was awarded the first Italian Chair of Psychology at the Università Statale of Milan.—Trans.

14. James Hillman, *Re-Visioning Psychology* (New York: Harper Paperbacks, 1977).

15. Gregory Bateson, *Mind and Nature: A Necessary Unity* (Cresskill, N.J.: Hampton Press, 1979).

16. Cassano is here referring to Martin Heidegger's reflections on abandonment in *Being and Time*, translated by Joan Stambaugh (New York: State University of New York Press, 1996).—Trans.

8. CARDINAL KNOWLEDGE

This text first was published in *Paeninsula: L'Italia da ritrovare* (Bari: Editori Laterza, 1998), 45–58. We are thankful to the editor for allowing us to publish it in this volume.—Trans.

1. Jean-Baptiste Colbert was the first controller general of French finances under King Louis XIV and later secretary of state. He gave a structure to the French taxation system, and reorganized most business and industry ventures to run more smoothly. Known for his harshness and direct manners, he helped make France the most powerful country in Europe during his time.—Trans.

2. Cassano uses the Italian name for the movie, *Le ali della libertà* ("Wings of Freedom"). At the end of the movie, after escaping from jail, the main character, Andy Dufresne, escapes to Mexico, where he is eventually reunited with Red, another prisoner who had befriended him during his time in prison.—Trans.

3. *Homo ierarchicus* literally means "man of hierarchies." As a famous book by the same title written by Louis Dumont (1967) suggests, it refers to the system of castes and to an almost innate impulse of man to establish hierarchies of valuation in social constructs.—Trans.

4. Alvaro Mutis, *La neve dell'ammiraglio* (Turin: Einaudi, 1990).

5. The reference is to Italian jazz critic Marcello Piras and an article he wrote titled "Africa: il battito cardiaco del mondo," *da Qui*, March 1997, 181–94.—Trans.

6. *Telenovelas* are the equivalent of American soap operas, though slightly more prone to melodrama. They originated in South America, especially in Brazil and Argentina, and then migrated to European countries such as Italy.—Trans.

7. In astronomy, the viewpoint promoted by Ptolemy (a Roman astronomer of Egyptian ethnicity who lived in the second century A.D.) was essentially "geocentric," claiming that the Earth was at the center of the universe and all other celestial bodies rotated around it.—Trans.

9. AGAINST ALL FUNDAMENTALISMS: THE NEW MEDITERRANEAN

This essay was first published as "Contro tutti i fondamentalismi: Il nuovo Mediterraneo," in a collection of essays edited by Franco Cassano and Vincenzo Consolo titled *Rappresentare il Mediterraneo. Lo sguardo italiano* (Messina: Mesogea, 2000) 37–69. We are thankful to the author and the publisher for the permission to publish it here.—Trans.

1. Although the cultivation of the idea of "Italy" on the basis of a shared linguistic and cultural patrimony dates back to the Middle Ages, during the

eighteenth and nineteenth centuries this idea was revisited by poets, musicians, writers, and painters who began to promote the vision of an independent and unified Italian nation whose achievements would match the glory reached by the Italian city-states during the Renaissance. Cassano alludes here to the writers Giacomo Leopardi (1798–1837), Ugo Foscolo (1778–1827), and Alessandro Manzoni (1785–1873), and the composer Giuseppe Verdi (1813–1901).—Trans.

2. The Historic Right governed the country between 1866 and 1876. It was mainly composed of governmental people influenced by Victor Emmanuel II's main political adviser, Camillo Benso, count of Cavour, the diplomat most responsible for attaining Italy's unification through diplomatic channels. Among its policies were heavy taxation of the whole country (including the newly annexed regions and some of its less wealthy populations); centrally administered fiscal and social decrees, which created the premises for a massive bureaucratic infrastructure; and the abolition of internal tolls, which allowed northern industry to expand southward at a time when most of the south was recovering from a semifeudal system still operating in many of its regions.—Trans.

3. The Southern Question came about after the unification of 1860, with the denunciations of the conditions of the South issued by Pasquale Villari, Leopoldo Franchetti, and Sydney Sonnino in the mid-1870s. It would later solidify around the concept of *Blocco storico*, or historic bloc, whose early articulations date from the end of the nineteenth century, in the work of Antonio De Viti De Marco and Francesco Saverio Nitti, but would be fully explored by Gaetano Salvemini and Antonio Gramsci. The *Blocco storico* would eventually facilitate the solidification of a binary conceptual framework of two Italies: a Northern Italy identified with the modern nation and worthy of belonging to the constellation of leading European nations; and a Southern one seen as a historical, cultural, moral, and political pathology to be remedied before it could reach the developmental state of the North.—Trans.

4. The term *Mezzogiorno* (literally, midday) refers generically to the regions of Southern Italy. It eventually became a political term with very similar connotations to those attached to the *Southern Question*. In fact, in the second part of the twentieth century, the "questione del Mezzogiorno" was often used as a synonym for the Southern Question (see note 3).—Trans.

5. Giuseppe Mazzini (1805–72) is considered one of the most important, if controversial, figures of nineteenth-century Italian democratic nationalism. Mazzini's political vision for Italy entailed the end of Austrian hegemony and the creation of an Italian democratic republic with Rome as the capital.—Trans.

6. Giuseppe Mazzini, as cited in Federico Chabod, *Storia della politica estera italiana dal 1870 al 1896* (Rome and Bari: Laterza, 1976), 226. The cited passage is from Mazzini's exhortation "Ai giovani d'Italia." Here and elsewhere,

when the original text is in Italian, we have taken the liberty to translate it ourselves.—Trans.

7. The "yet-to-be-freed lands," or "terre irredente," refers to territories that belonged to the Austro-Hungarian Empire but were considered "Italian" by the movement for national independence.—Trans.

8. In the spring of 1860, Giuseppe Garibaldi (1807–82), who had refined his military skills in the fight for the independence of the South American republics, agreed to lead an expedition of Northern volunteers to help Sicilian rioters. With his army of a "thousand" men, he sailed from Quarto, landing in Marsala on the western Sicilian coast. From here, the expedition advanced into the mainland, and, on September 7, 1860, Garibaldi reached Naples. Following a popular vote, or "plebiscito," for a unitary state, the Piedmontese administration was extended to the entire peninsula. The new Kingdom of Italy was proclaimed in March 1861 and Victor Emmanuel II assumed the title of King of Italy.—Trans.

9. Giosué Carducci, *Per la morte di Giuseppe Garibaldi* (Bologna: Zanichelli, 1907), 23–24.

10. Cassano's reference here is to the famous speech by the same title that Giovanni Pascoli gave in November of 1911 at the theater of his hometown of Barga.—Trans.

11. Alfredo Oriani, *Fino a Dogali* (Milan: Editrice Galli, 1889), 117. The text is now available on line through a special project of the Biblioteca Braidense of Milan at http://www.liberliber.it/biblioteca/o/oriani/fino_a_dogali/pdf/fino_a_p.pdf.—Trans.

12. Ibid.

13. Ibid., 118.

14. Ibid.

15. Cassano is referring to two songs popular at the time of the colonial conquest. The first, titled "A Tripoli" (Arona and Corvetto were the songwriters), was popular in 1911, during the time of the Libyan conquest. The second, "Faccetta nera" (Micheli and Ruccione were the songwriters), was famous in 1935, at the time of the Abyssinian conquest.—Trans.

16. Benedetto Gravagnuolo, *Le Corbusier e l'antico: Viaggi nel Mediterraneo* (Napoli: Electa, 1997).

17. Alberto Savinio, "Senza mare davanti l'intelligenza non cammina," in A. Savinio, *Opere. Scritti dispersi. Tra guerra e dopoguerra (1943–1952)* (Milan: Bompiani, 1989), 1027.

18. The PCI (Partito Comunista Italiano) emerged from World War II as the strongest leftist party in Western Europe. It often challenged the Christian Democrats for control of the country and, in some regions (Tuscany, Emilia-Romagna, Umbria) it actually governed for most of the second half of the twentieth century. With the scandal of Tangentopoli in the early nineties, like many other traditional parties it disbanded and was reconstituted into smaller parties, never to regain the kind of influence it had previously.—Trans.

19. Cassano is alluding to the two decades between Mussolini's ascent to power in 1922 and the fall of the regime in July 25, 1943.—Trans.

20. Following World War II, the Italian State intervened heavily in an attempt to develop Southern infrastructures for agriculture and industry. One of these interventions was the "Cassa per il Mezzogiorno," established by the De Gasperi government in 1950 with partial funding from the World Bank.—Trans.

21. The reference is to Giuseppe Tomasi di Lampedusa's *Il gattopardo*, a novel published posthumously in 1958. In it, Lampedusa chronicles the events that led to the unification of Italy in 1860 from the perspective of a Sicilian aristocrat, Prince Fabrizio di Salina. The reference can be found in the English translation, *The Leopard* (New York: Pantheon Books, 1960), 212.—Trans.

22. Raffaele La Capria, *L'occhio di Napoli* (Milan: Mondadori, 1994), 9.

23. See the poetry of Salvatore Quasimodo (1901–68), especially *Acque e terre* (1930); and *Autobiografia* (1924) by Umberto Saba (1883–57).—Trans.

24. The reference is to Eugenio Montale's poem, from his first poetry collection, *Ossi di Seppia*, that begins with the line "I have often met the evil of living," *Cuttlefish Bones (1920–1927)*, trans. William Arrowsmith (New York: W. W. Norton, 1992), 53.—Trans.

25. Cesare Romana, *Amico fragile. Fabrizio De André si racconta a Cesare G. Romana* (Milan: Sperling and Kupfer Editori, 1991), 135.

26. Vincenzo Consolo, *Fuga dall'Etna* (Rome: Donzelli, 1993), 53.

27. Ibid.

28. Cassano is referring to two novels by Raffaele Nigro: *I fuochi del Basento* (Milan: Camunia, 1987) and *Adriatico* (Florence: Giunti, 1998).—Trans.

29. ARCI stands for Associazione Ricreativa e Culturale Italiana (Italian Recreational and Cultural Association). It is an organization that promotes social and cultural interactions especially among youths, in the name of solidarity and social engagement. Almost every major Italian city has an ARCI group that organizes a number of activities and events on behalf of its citizens.—Trans.

30. Cassano uses the term "multiverse" as a counter to "universe." In scientific theory, "multiverse" refers to "universes" that operate outside our time-space continuum in parallel dimensions. The term is also used to describe those areas where no one idea dominates, but where a multiplicity of them seem to interact and affect each other.—Trans.

31. Fernand Braudel wrote extensively on the Mediterranean and the influences of capitalism on civilization. His most famous works are *Memories of the Mediterranean*, trans. Siân Reynolds (New York: Random House, 2001), and *Civilization and Capitalism, 15th–18th Centuries*, 3 vols., trans. Siân Reynolds (Berkeley: University of California Press, 1979). The reference to Dominique Fernandez is to his book *Mère Méditerranée* (Paris: Grasset, 1965).—Trans.

32. The original, *Mediteranski brevijar*, was published in Croatian and then translated into a number of European languages. Matvejevic has since acquired Italian citizenship and teaches both at the Univerity of Rome (La Sapienza) and the University of Paris III (New Sorbonne). An English version of this book appeared in abbrievated form under the title *Mediterranean: A Cultural Landscape*, trans. Michael Henry Heim (Berkeley: University of California Press, 1999).—Trans.

33. We have left the titles of these works and of the journals Cassano mentions in Italian, since none have been translated into English.—Trans.

34. Aldo Varano, *Il divario che non c'è. Nord e sud visti da Bevilacqua, Cassano, Consolo, Desantis, Lupo, Rea, Reichlin, Trigilia* (Cosenza: Memoria, 1998), 94.

35. Raffaele La Capria, *Napolitan Graffiti. Com'eravamo* (Milan: Rizzoli, 1998).

36. The term "ecumene" derives from the Greek term *oikoumene*, corresponding to the land "inhabited and known" to man. In ancient times, this used to define Greece, as a land that was central to the conception of the Mediterranean as the known inhabited world. It then extended its meaning to the religious valence of all those gathered together under the umbrella of the Christian religion.—Trans.

37. Albert Camus, *The Rebel: An Essay on Man in Revolt*, trans. Anthony Bower (New York: Alfred Knopf, 1954), 266.

10. THINKING THE MEDITERRANEAN

1. On this point see the excellent work of Walter Mignolo, *The Darker Side of the Renaissance: Literacy, Territoriality, and Colonization* (Ann Arbor: University of Michigan Press, 1995).

2. Fatima Mernissi, *The Veil and the Male Elite: A Feminist Interpretation of Women's Rights in Islam* (Reading, Mass.: Addison-Wesley, 1991), 18.

3. Joseph E. Stiglitz, *La globalizzazione e i suoi oppositori* (Turin: Einaudi, 2002), 34–36. The original was published in English as *Globalization and Its Discontents* (New York: Norton, 2002).—Trans.

4. Arnold Toynbee, *The World and the West* (London: Oxford University Press, 1953), 2.

5. See Arnold Toynbee, *Civilization on Trial* (New York: Oxford University Press, 1948), but also *A Study of History* (Oxford: Oxford University Press, 1962).

6. Ian Chambers, "The Mediterranean: A Postcolonial Sea." *Third Text* 18 (2004): 423–33.

7. Cassano is referring to Amartya Sen's *L'altra India. La tradizione razionalistica e scettica della cultura Indiana*. Some of the essays of this volume are found in *The Argumentative Indian: Writings of Indian History, Culture, and Identity* (New York: Farrar, Straus and Giroux, 2005).—Trans.

8. See the following by Amartya Sen: *Capability and Well-Being* (New York: United Nations Press, 1991), and *The Standards of Living: Lecture 1. Concepts*

and Critiques, and *Lecture 2. Lives and Capabilities* (Salt Lake City: University of Utah Press, 1992).

9. The discussion between Sen and Kagan is in an exchange of letters regarding the military intervention of the United States in Iraq. It can be read at the following site: http://www.slate.com/id/2140932/entry. See also Amartya Sen, *Identity and Violence: The Illusion of Destiny* (New York: Norton, 2006).

10. Mohamed Arkoun, "(Ré)inventer l'espace méditerranéen," a long and dense interview published in *Courrier de la planète*: http://www.courrierde-laplanete.org/73/article1.html, 10.

11. Leila Ahmed, *Women and Gender in Islam: Historical Roots of a Modern Debate* (New Haven: Yale University Press, 1992), 245.

12. See "Size 6: The Western Women's Harem," in Fatima Mernissi, *Scheherazade Goes West, or the European Harem* (New York: Washington Square Press, 2000), 208–20.

13. See Tariq Ramadan, *To Be a European Muslim: A Study of Islamic Sources in the European Context* (Leicester, UK: Islamic Foundation, 1999) and *Western Muslims and the Future of Islam*, trans. Carol Bebawi (New York: Oxford University Press, 2004).

14. Gayatri Chakravorty Spivak, "Righting Wrongs," in *Human Rights, Human Wrongs*, ed. Nicholas Owen (Oxford: Oxford University Press, 2003), 168–227. See also *Imperative zur Neuerfindung des Planeten/Imperatives to Re-Imagine the Planet*, ed. Willi Goetschel, trans. Bernard Schweizer (Vienna: Passagen Verlag, 1999).

15. Tariq Ramadan, "Les défis du pluralisme," *Politis* 756, June 19, 2003. The debate that followed Ramadan's intervention is now at http:www.aidh.org.dial.

Adorno, Theodor W. *The Jargon of Authenticity*. New York: Routledge, 2003.

Ahmed, Leila. *Women and Gender in Islam: Historical Roots of a Modern Debate*. New Haven: Yale University Press, 1992.

Amoroso, Bruno. *Europa e Mediterraneo. Le sfide del futuro*. Bari: Dedalo, 2000.

Angelopoulos, Theodoros. *The Suspended Step of the Stork*. 1991.

———. *Το Μετέωρο βήμα του πελαργού*. 1991.

Arkoun, Mohamed. "(Ré)inventer l'espace méditerranéen." *Courrier de la planète*: http://www.courrierdelaplanete.org/73/article1.html, 2004.

Asdrachas, Spyros. "Una città liquida: l'Arcipelago greco". *La salvaguardia delle città storiche in Europa e nell'area mediterranea: Atti del convegno internazionale di studi*, 130–45. Bologna: Nuova Alfa Editoriale, 1983.

Audisio, Gabriel. "Vues sur Ulysse, ou l'ambivalence des Méditerranéens." *Cahiers du Sud*, special number *Le génie d'oc et l'Homme méditerranéen* (February 1943): 271–82.

Augé, Marc. *Le Temps en ruines*, Paris: Galilée 2003.

———. *Rovine e macerie. Il senso del tempo*. Turin: Bollati Boringhieri, 2004.

Barberi Squarotti, Giorgio. *Poesia e narrativa del secondo Novecento*. Milan: Mursia, 1961.

Barthes, Roland. *Roland Barthes by Roland Barthes*. Translated by Richard Howard. New York: Hill and Wang, 1997.

Bateson, Gregory. *Mind and Nature: A Necessary Unity*. Cresskill, N.J.: Hampton Press, 1979.

Bateson, Gregory, and M. C. Bateson. *Angels Fear: Towards an Epistemology of the Sacred*. New York: Macmillan, 1987.

Bauman, Zygmunt. *Globalization: The Human Consequences*. New York: Columbia University Press, 1998.

———. *Liquid Modernity*. Cambridge: Polity Press, 2000.

———. *Società, etica, politica*. Cortina: Milan, 2002.

Bauman, Zygmunt, and Keith Tester. *Conversations with Zygmunt Bauman*. Cambridge: Polity Press, 2001.

Beck, Ulrich. *Risk Society: Towards a New Modernity*. London: Sage, 1992.

Berger, Peter L., and Thomas Luckmann. *The Social Construction of Reality*. Garden City, N.Y.: Anchor Books, 1966.

Berlin, Isaiah. "Le origini della violenza e del nazionalismo." Interview with Giancarlo Bosetti. *Reset* 5 (1994): 38–42.

Berve, Helmut. *Storia greca*. Bari: Laterza, 1959.

Bhabha, Homi K. *The Location of Culture*. New York: Routledge, 1994.

———, ed. *Nation and Narration*. London: Routledge, 1990.

Bodei, Remo. *Geometria delle passioni*. Milan: Feltrinelli, 1991.

Boitani, Piero. *L'ombra di Ulisse. Figure di un mito*. Bologna: Il Mulino, 1992.

Braudel, Fernand. *Civilization and Capitalism, 15th–18th Centuries*. 3 vols. Translated by Siân Reynolds. Berkeley: University of California Press, 1979.

———. *Memories of the Mediterranean*. Translated by Siân Reynolds. New York: Random House, 2001.

Brisville, Jean-Claude. *Camus*. Paris: Gallimard, 1959.

Brodsky, Joseph. "Flight From Byzantium." In *Less Than One: Selected Essays*. New York: Farrar, Straus and Giroux, 1986.

Brodsky, Joseph, and Vaclav Havel. "'The Post-Communist Nightmare': An Exchange." Translated by Paul Wilson. *New York Review of Books* 11, no. 4 (1994): 4–7.

Burckhardt, C. Jacob. *Force and Freedom: Reflections on History*. Translated by James Hastings Nichols. New York: Pantheon, 1943.

Buzzati, Dino. *The Tartar Steppe*. Manchester: Carcanet, 1985.

Cacciari, Massimo. *L'arcipelago*. Milan: Adelphi, 1997.

———. "Geophilosophy of Europe." In *The Unpolitical: On the Radical Critique of Political Reason*, edited by Alessandro Carrera. New York: Fordham University Press, 2009, 197, 205.

Calasso, Roberto. *The Marriage of Cadmus and Harmony*. Translated by Tim Parks. New York: Knopf, 1993.

———. "Monologo fatale." In Friedrich Nietzsche, *Ecce homo. Come si diventa ciò che si è*, 151–98. Milan: Adelphi, 1981.

Camus, Albert. *La caduta*. Milan: Bompiani, 1990.

———. *Caligula and Three Other Plays*. Translated by Stuart Gilbert. New York: Vintage Books, 1962.

———. "L'Espagne et le donquichottisme." *Le Monde libertaire* 12 (November 1955), anthologized in *Volonté anarchiste* 26, *Albert Camus et les libertaires* (1984): 22–24.

———. *Essais*. Paris: Gallimard, 1967.

———. *The Fall*. Translated by Justin O' Brien. New York: Alfred A. Knopf, 1959.

————. *A Happy Death*. Translated by Richard Howard. New York: Alfred Knopf, 1972.

————. "Helen's Exile." In *Lyrical and Critical Essays*, translated by Ellen Conroy Kennedy. New York: Alfred A. Knopf, 1969.

————. *Il rovescio e il diritto*. Milan: Bompiani, 1988.

————. *Lyrical and Critical Essays*. Translated by Ellen Conroy Kennedy. New York: Alfred A. Knopf, 1969.

————. *The Myth of Sisyphus and Other Essays*. Translated by Justin O'Brien. New York: Alfred A. Knopf, 1957.

————. "The New Mediterranean Culture." In *Lyrical and Critical Essays*, translated by Ellen Conroy Kennedy. New York: Alfred Knopf, 1969.

————. *Notebooks, 1935–1942*. Translated by Philip Thody. New York: Alfred A. Knopf, 1963.

————. *Notebooks, 1942–1951*. Translated by Justin O'Brien. New York: Alfred A. Knopf, 1965.

————. *Notebooks, 1951–1959*. Translated by Ryan Bloom. Chicago: Ivan R. Dee, 2008.

————. *Opere (Romanzi, racconti, saggi)*. Edited and with an introduction by R. Grenier. Milan: Bompiani, 1988.

————. *The Plague*. Translated by Stuart Gilbert. New York: A. A. Knopf, 1948.

————. "Prometheus in the Underworld." In *Lyrical and Critical Essays*, translated by Ellen Conroy Kennedy. New York: Alfred Knopf, 1969.

————. *The Rebel: An Essay on Man in Revolt*. Translated by Anthony Bower. New York: Knopf, 1954.

————. *Reflections on the Guillotine*. Translated by Richard Howard. Michigan City, Ind.: Fridtjof Karla Publications, 1959.

————. *Théâtre, Récits, Nouvelles*. Paris: Gallimard, 1962.

————. *Tutto il teatro. Il malinteso, Caligula, I giusti, Lo stato d'assedio*. Milan: Bompiani, 1988.

Camus, Albert, and Jean Grenier. *Albert Camus and Jean Grenier: Correspondence, 1932–1960*. Translated by Jan F. Rigaud. Lincoln: University of Nebraska Press, 2003.

Capizzi, Antonio. *I sofisti ad Atene: L'uscita retorica dal dilemma tragico*. Bari: Levante, 1990.

Carducci, Giosué. *Per la morte di Giuseppe Garibaldi*. Bologna: Zanichelli, 1907.

Casi, Stefano, ed. *Desiderio di Pasolini*. Turin-Milan: Sonda, 1990.

Cassano, Franco. *Approssimazione. Esercizi di esperienza dell'altro*. Bologna: Il Mulino, 1989, 2003.

————. *Autocritica della sociologia contemporanea. Weber, Mill, Habermas*. Bari: De Donato, 1971.

———. *La certezza infondata. Previsioni ed eventi nelle science sociali.* Bari: Dedalo, 1983.

———. "Il gioco della Scienza." *Rassegna italiana di Sociologia* 30, no. 1 (1989): 3–30.

———. *Il pensiero meridiano.* Bari: Laterza, 1996, 2005.

———. *Il teorema democristiano.* Bari: De Donato, 1979.

———. *Paeninsula. L'Italia da ritrovare.* Bari: Editori Laterza, 1998.

———. *Partita doppia. Appunti per una felicità terrestre.* Bologna: Il Mulino, 1993.

———. "Un altro Occidente. Riflessioni sull'Europa." In *Homo civicus. La ragionevole follia dei beni comuni,* 85–114. Bari: Dedalo, 2004.

———. *Homo civicus. La ragionevole follia dei beni comuni.* Bari: Dedalo, 2004.

———. *Marxismo e filosofia. 1958–1971.* Bari: De Donato, 1973.

———. *Oltre il nulla. Studio su Giacomo Leopardi.* Bari: Laterza, 2003.

Cassano, Franco, and Remo Bodei. *Hegel e Weber. Egemonia e legittimazione.* Bari: De Donato, 1977.

Cassano, Franco, and Danilo Zolo, eds. *L'alternativa mediterranea.* Milan: Feltrinelli, 2007.

Cavafy, Constantine. *Cinquantacinque poesie.* Turin: Einaudi, 1968.

Chabod, Federico. *Storia della politica estera italiana dal 1870 al 1896.* Rome-Bari: Laterza, 1976.

———. *Storia dell'idea d'Europa.* Rome-Bari: Laterza, 1995.

Chakrabarty, Dipesh. *Provincializing Europe: Postcolonial Thought and Historical Difference.* Princeton: Princeton University Press, 2000.

Chambers, Ian. "The Mediterranean: A Postcolonial Sea." *Third Text* 18 (2004): 423–33.

Consolo, Vincenzo. *Fuga dall'Etna.* Rome: Donzelli, 1993.

Corbin, Alain. *The Lure of the Sea: The Discovery of the Seaside in the Western World, 1750–1840.* Translated by Jocelyn Phelps. Berkeley: University of California Press, 1994.

de Sousa Santos, Boaventura. *Another Knowledge Is Possible: Beyond Northern Epistemologies.* London: Verso, 2007.

———. *A Crítica da Razão Indolente: Contra o desperdício da experiência.* Porto: Edições Afrontamento, 2000.

———. *De la mano de Alicia.* Universidad de los Andes: Santafé de Bogotá, 1998.

———. *Il Forum Sociale Mondiale: Verso una globalizzazione antiegemonica.* Troina: Città aperta, 2003.

———. *Towards a New Common Sense.* New York: Routledge, 1995.

———. *Towards a New Legal Common Sense.* London: Butterworths, 2002.

Deleuze, Gilles, and Félix Guattari. *Anti-Oedipus: Capitalism and Schizophrenia.* Translated by Brian Massumi. Minneapolis: University of Minnesota Press, 1983.

———. "Geophilosophy." In *What Is Philosophy?* Translated by Hugh Tomlinson and Graham Burchell. New York: Columbia University Press, 1994.

———. *A Thousand Plateaus: Capitalism and Schizophrenia.* Translated by Robert Hurley, Mark Seem, and Helen R. Lane. London: Athlone Press, 1987.

Derrida, Jacques. *Margins of Philosophy.* Chicago: University of Chicago Press, 1982.

———. *The Other Heading: Reflections on Today's Europe.* Translated by Anne Brault and Michael B. Naas. Bloomington: Indiana University Press, 1992.

———. *Writing and Difference.* Translated by Alan Bass. Chicago: University of Chicago Press, 1978.

Diano, Carlo. *Forma ed evento. Principi di un'interpretazione del mondo greco.* Preface by Remo Bodei. Venice: Marsilio, 1993.

Dick, Philip K. *The Man in the High Castle.* New York: Putnam, 1962.

Dominijanni, Ida. "Pensiero a Mezzogiorno." *Il manifesto*, February 14, 1996, 24–25.

Dostoevsky, Fyodor. *The Brothers Karamazov.* Translated by Constance Garnett. Mineola, N.Y.: Dover, 2005.

Du Bois, W. E. B. "Dusk of Dawn." In *W. E. B. Du Bois Writings.* New York: Library of America, 1986.

Dussel, Enrique. "Beyond Eurocentrism: The World-System and the Limits of Modernity." In *The Culture of Globalization*, edited by Fredric Jameson and Masao Miyoshi, 3–31. Durham: Duke University Press, 1998.

———. "Europa, Modernidad y Eurocentrismo." In *La colonialidad del saber: eurocentrismo y ciencias sociales. Perspectivas latinoamericanas*, edited by Edgardo Lander, 41–53. Buenos Aires: Clacso, 1993.

Elias, Norbert. *Time: An Essay.* Oxford: Blackwell, 1991.

Fernandez, Dominique. *Mère Méditerranée.* Paris: Grasset, 1965.

Ferretti, Gian Carlo. *Pasolini. L'universo orrendo.* Rome: Editori Riuniti, 1967.

Finley, Moses. *The World of Odysseus.* New York: Viking, 1954.

Fortini, Franco. *Nuovi saggi italiani.* 2 vols. Milan: Garzanti, 1987.

Foucault, Michel. *The History of Sexuality*, vol. 1. New York: Pantheon, 1978.

Gallino. Luciano. *Dizionario di Sociologia.* Turin: Utet, 2004.

Giacché, Piergiorgio. *Carmelo Bene. Antropologia di una "macchina attoriale."* Milan: Bompiani, 1997.

Giacomantonio, Francesco. "All'origine del pensiero meridiano di Franco Cassano." http://vulgo.org/index.php?view=article&catid=81%3Are censione&id=544%3Aallorigine-del-pensiero-meridiano-di-franco-cassano&format=pdf&option=com_content&Itemid=44.

Gibson, William. *Neuromancer*. New York: Ace Books, 1984.

Girard, René. *Violence and the Sacred*. Translated by Patrick Gregory. Baltimore: Johns Hopkins University Press, 1977.

Glissant, Edouard. "Métissage et créolisation." In *Discours sur le métissage, identités métisses: en quête d'Ariel*, edited by Sylvie Kandé, 47–53. Paris: L'Harmattan, 1999.

———. *Poetics of Relation*. Ann Arbor: University of Michigan Press, 1990.

Gravagnuolo, Benedetto. *Le Corbusier e l'antico: Viaggi nel Mediterraneo*. Naples: Electa, 1997.

Grenier, Jean. *Albert Camus soleil et ombre. Une biographie intellectuelle*. Paris: Gallimard, 1987.

———. *Albert Camus. Souvenirs*. Paris: Gallimard, 1968.

———. *Islands: Lyrical Essays*. Translated by Steve Light. Copenhagen and Los Angeles: Green Integer, 2005.

Guha, Ranajit, ed. *A Subaltern Studies Reader, 1986–1996*. Minneapolis: University of Minnesota Press, 1997.

Guha, Ranajit, and Gayatri Chakravorty Spivak, eds. *Selected Subaltern Studies*. New York: Oxford University Press, 1988.

Handke, Peter. *Gedicht an die Dauer*. Frankfurt: Suhrkamp, 1986.

Havelock, Eric A. *The Liberal Temper in Greek Politics*. New Haven: Yale University Press, 1964.

Hegel, G. W. F. *Lectures on the Philosophy of World History*. Translated by H. B. Nisbet. New York: Cambridge University Press, 1975.

———. *The Phenomenology of Spirit*. Translated by A. V. Miller. Oxford: Clarendon Press, 1977.

Heidegger, Martin. *Being and Time*. Translated by Joan Stambaugh. New York: State University of New York Press, 1996.

———. *An Introduction to Metaphysics*. Translated by Ralph Manheim. New Haven: Yale University Press, 1959.

———. *Saggi e discorsi*. Milan: Mursia, 1991.

———. *Sentieri interrotti*. Florence: La Nuova Italia, 1984.

———. *What Is Philosophy?* Translated by Jean T. Wilde and William Kluback. New Haven, Conn.: New College and University Press, 1956.

———. "Why Poets?" In *Off the Beaten Track*, translated by Julian Young and Kenneth Haynes, 200–241. Cambridge: Cambridge University Press, 2002.

Heidegger, Martin, and Erhart Kästner. *Briefwechsel: 1953–1974*. Frankfurt am Main: Insel, 1986.

Heller, Agnes. "Cultural Memory, Identity, and Civil Society." *Politik und Gesellschaft Online, International Politics and Society* 2 (2001): 1–6. http://www.fes.de/ipg/ipg2_2001/artheller.htm.

Herling, Gustaw. *Volcano and Miracle: A Selection from the Journal Written at Night.* New York: Penguin USA, 1997.

Herodotus. *The Histories.* Translated by Robin Waterfield. Oxford: Oxford University Press, 1998.

Hillman, James. *Re-Visioning Psychology.* New York: Harper, 1977.

Hirschman, Albert O. "Melding the Public and the Private Spheres: Taking Commensality Seriously." In *Crossing Boundaries. Selected Writings.* New York: Zone Books, 2001.

Hobsbawm, Eric, and Terence Ranger, eds. *The Invention of Tradition.* New York: Cambridge University Press, 1983.

Huntington, Samuel. *The Clash of Civilizations and the Remaking of the World Order.* New York: Simon and Schuster, 1996.

Huysseune, Michel. *Modernity and Secession: The Social Sciences and the Political Discourse of the Lega Nord in Italy.* Oxford: Berghahn, 2006.

Ibsen, Henrik. *The Lady from the Sea.* London: R. Hart-Davis, 1960.

Irigaray, Luce. *Between East and West.* New York: Columbia University Press, 2002.

Jackall, Robert. *Moral Mazes: The World of Corporate Managers.* Oxford: Oxford University Press, 1988

Kagan, Robert. *Identity and Violence: The Illusion of Destiny.* New York: Norton, 2006.

———. "Is There a Clash of Civilizations?" http://www.slate.com/id/2140932/entry.

Kapuściński, Ryszard. *Ebano.* Milan: Feltrinelli, 2000.

———. *The Shadow of the Sun.* Translated by Klara Glowczewska. New York: Knopf, 2001.

Koselleck, Reinhart. *Future Past: On the Semantics of Historical Time.* Cambridge: MIT Press, 1985.

La Capria, Raffaele. *Napolitan Graffiti. Com'eravamo.* Milan: Rizzoli, 1998.

———. *L'occhio di Napoli.* Milan: Mondadori, 1994.

Laîdi, Zaki. *Le sacre du present.* Paris: Flammarion, 2000.

———. *La tyrannie de l'urgence.* Montreal: Editions Fides, 1999.

Landry, Donna, and Gerald McLean, eds. *The Spivak Reader: Selected Works of Gayatri Chakravorty Spivak.* New York: Routledge, 1996.

Langer, Alexander. *Il viaggiatore leggero. Scritti 1961–1995.* Palermo: Sellerio, 1996.

———. "Intervento al Convegno giovanile di Assisi (1994)." *Rocca* (Agosto 1995). http://www.peacelink.it.

Latouche, Serge. *L'Autre Afrique, entre don et marché.* Paris: Albin Michel, 1998.

————. *The Westernization of the World.* Translated by Rosemary Morris. Cambridge: Polity Press, 1996.

Leccardi, Carmen. "Revisiting 'Acceleration Society.'" *Constellations* 10, no. 1 (2003): 34–41.

Le Goff, Jacques. *Time, Work, and Culture in the Middle Ages.* Translated by Arthur Goldhammer. Chicago: University of Chicago Press, 1980.

Levi, Primo. *The Drowned and the Saved.* New York: Summit Books, 1988.

————. *If This Is a Man; and The Truce.* London: Abacus, 1997.

————. *Survival in Auschwitz: The Nazi Assault on Humanity.* New York: Touchstone, 1958.

Levi Della Torre, Stefano. *Essere fuori luogo. Il dilemma ebraico tra diaspora e ritorno.* Rome: Donzelli, 1995.

Lévinas, Emmanuel. "The Trace of the Other." In *Deconstruction in Context: Literature and Philosophy,* edited by Mark C. Taylor, 345–59. Chicago: University of Chicago Press, 1986g.

Löwith, Karl. *The Theological Implications of the Philosophy of History.* Chicago: University of Chicago Press, 1949.

Luhmann, Niklas. "The Future Cannot Begin: Temporal Structures." In *The Differentiation of Society,* 271–88. New York: Columbia University Press, 1982.

Lupo, Salvatore. *Il giardino degli aranci: il mondo degli agrumi nella storia del Mezzogiorno.* Venice: Marsilio, 1990.

Martellini, Luigi. *Introduzione a Pasolini.* Rome-Bari: Laterza, 1989.

————. *Pier Paolo Pasolini.* Florence: Le Monnier, 1983.

Marx, Karl. *Economic and Philosophic Manuscripts of 1844.* Edited by Dirk J. Struik. Translated by Martin Milligan. New York: International, 1964.

————. *Manoscritti economici-filosofici del 1844.* Edited by Norberto Bobbio. Turin: Einaudi, 1968.

Matvejevic, Predrag. *Breviario mediterraneo.* Milan: Garzanti, 1991.

————. *Mediterranean: A Cultural Landscape.* Berkeley: University of California Press, 1999.

————. *Il Mediterraneo e l'Europa. Lezioni al Collège de France.* Milan: Garzanti, 1998.

Mazzarino, Santo. *Fra Oriente e Occidente. Ricerca di storia greca arcaica,* Florence: La Nuova Italia, 1947.

————. *Il pensiero storico classico,* vol. 1. Bari: Laterza, 1966.

Mernissi, Fatima. *Scheherazade Goes West, or the European Harem.* New York: Washington Square Press, 2000.

————. *The Veil and the Male Elite: A Feminist Interpretation of Women's Rights in Islam.* Reading, Mass.: Addison-Wesley, 1991.

Merton, Robert K. *Social Theory and Social Structure.* Glencoe, Ill.: Free Press, 1957.

Meyrowitz, Joshua. *No Sense of Place: The Impact of the Electronic Media on Social Behavior.* New York: Oxford University Press, 1985.

Mignolo, Walter. *The Darker Side of the Renaissance: Literacy, Territoriality, and Colonization.* Ann Arbor: University of Michigan Press, 1995.

———. *Local Histories/Global Designs: Coloniality, Subaltern Knowledges, and Border Thinking.* Princeton: Princeton University Press, 2000.

Mitscherlich, Alexander. *Society without the Father.* Translated by Eric Mosbacher. New York: Harcourt, Brace, and World, 1969.

Mollat du Jourdin, Michel. *Europe and the Sea.* Translated by Teresa Lavander Fagan. Oxford: Blackwell, 1993.

Monceri, Flavia. *Altre globalizzazioni. Universalismo liberale e valori asiatici.* Soveria Mannelli: Rubettino, 2002.

———. *Jura Gentium Centro di filosofia del diritto internazionale e della politica globale.* http://www.juragentium.unifi.it.

Montaigne, Michel de. "The Profit of One Man Is the Loss of Another." In *Essays of Montaigne,* vol. 1. Translated by Charles Cotton. New York: Edwin C. Hill, 1910.

Montale, Eugenio. *Cuttlefish Bones (1920–1927).* Translated by William Arrowsmith. New York: W. W. Norton, 1992.

Morin, Edgar. *Homeland Earth: A Manifesto for the New Millennium.* Translated by Sean Kelly and Roger LaPointe. Cresskill, N.J.: Hampton Press, 1999.

———. "Mère Méditerranée." *Le monde Diplomatique,* August 1995.

———. "Penser la Méditerranée et Méditerranéiser la pensée." *Confluences Méditerranées* 28 (Winter 1998–99).

Morris, Jonathan. "Challenging *Meridionalismo:* Constructing a New History for Southern Italy." In *The New History of the Italian South: The Mezzogiorno Revisited,* edited by Robert Lumley and Jonathan Morris, 1–29. Exeter, UK.: University of Exeter Press, 1997.

Mutis, Alvaro. *La neve dell'ammiraglio.* Turin: Einaudi, 1990.

Naldini, Nico. *Pasolini, una vita.* Turin: Einaudi, 1989.

Negri, Antimo. *Nietzsche. La scienza del Vesuvio.* Rome and Bari: Laterza, 1994.

Nietzsche, Friedrich. *Beyond Good and Evil.* Translated by R. J. Hollingdale. London: Penguin Books, 1973.

———. *The Birth of Tragedy and Other Writings.* Edited by Raymond Geuss and Ronald Speirs. Translated by Ronald Speirs. Cambridge: Cambridge University Press, 1999.

———. *Ecce homo. Come si diventa ciò che si è.* Milan: Adelphi, 1981.

———. *La filosofia nell'epoca tragica dei Greci e scritti 1870–1873.* Milan: Adelphi, 1991.

———. *La gaia scienza.* Milan: Adelphi, 1979.

————. *The Gay Science.* Edited by Bernard Williams. Cambridge: Cambridge University Press, 2001.

————. *Philosophy in the Tragic Age of the Greeks.* Translated by Marianne Cowan. Chicago: Henry Regnery, 1962.

————. *Thus Spoke Zarathustra: A Book for All and None.* Edited by Adrian Del Caro and Robert Pippin. Translated by Adrian Del Caro. New York: Cambridge University Press, 2006.

Nigro, Raffaele. *Adriatico.* Florence: Giunti, 1998.

————. *I fuochi del Basento.* Milan: Camunia, 1987.

Nizan, Paul. *Aden Arabie.* Translated by John Pinkham. New York: Columbia University Press, 1987.

Oriani, Alfredo. *Fino a Dogali.* Milan: Editrice Galli, 1889. As cited at http://www.liberliber.it/biblioteca/o/oriani/fino_a_dogali/pdf/fino_a_p .pdf.

Panikkar, Raimundo. *The Intrareligious Dialogue.* Paulist Press, 1978.

Pasolini, Pier Paolo. *The Ashes of Gramsci.* Translated by David Wallace. Peterborough, Cambs, UK: Spectacular Diseases, 1982.

————. *Descrizioni di descrizioni.* Milan: Garzanti, 2006.

————. *Il caos.* Edited by Gian Carlo Ferretti. Rome: Editori Riuniti, 1981.

————. *Il portico della morte.* Edited by Cesare Segre. Rome: Quaderni Pier Paolo Pasolini, 1988.

————. *Il sogno del centauro.* Edited by Jean Duflot. With a preface by Gian Carlo Ferretti. Rome: Editori Riuniti, 1983.

————. *Lettere 1940–1954,* Edited by Nico Naldini. Turin: Einaudi, 1986.

————. *Lettere 1955–1975.* Edited by Nico Naldini. Turin: Einaudi, 1988.

————. *The Letters of Pierpaolo Pasolini.* Edited by Nico Naldini. Translated by Stuart Hood. London: Quartet Books, 1992.

————. *Lutheran Letters.* Translated by Stuart Hood. Manchester: Carcanet, 1983.

————. *Passione e ideologia.* Milan: Garzanti, 1977.

————. *Poems.* Selected and translated by Norman Macafee with Luciano Martinego. Foreword by Enzo Siciliano. New York: Random House, 1982.

————. *La religione del mio tempo.* Milan: Garzanti, 1976.

————. *San Paolo.* Turin: Einaudi, 1977.

————. *Scritti corsari.* Milan: Garzanti, 1975.

————. *Trasumanar e organizzar.* Milan: Garzanti, 1976.

————. *Trilogia della vita.* Milan: Mondadori, 1990.

————. *Tutte le poesie.* Milan: Mondadori, 2003.

————. *L'usignolo della Chiesa cattolica.* Turin: Einaudi, 1976.

————. *Volgar' eloquio.* Edited by Gian Carlo Ferretti. Rome: Editori Riuniti, 1987.

Petrusewicz, Marta. *Latifundium: Moral Economy and Material Life in a European Periphery.* Translated by Judith C. Green. Ann Arbor: University of Michigan Press, 1996.

Piras, Marcello. "Africa: il battito cardiaco del mondo." *da Qui,* March 1997, 181–94.

Pizzorno, Alessandro. "L'ordine giuridico e statale nella globalizzazione." In *Globalizzazione e movimenti sociali,* edited by Donatella Della Porta and Lorenzo Mosca, 221–37. Rome: Manifestolibri, 2003.

Plato. *The Laws, IV.* Translated by Trevor Saunders. Baltimore: Penguin, 1970.

Plutarch. "The Obsolescence of Oracles." In *Moralia,* vol. 5. Loeb Classical Library. London: Heinemann, 1939.

Polanyi, Karl. *The Great Transformation.* New York: Farrar and Rinehart, 1944.

Popper, Karl R. *The Open Society and Its Enemies.* Princeton: Princeton University Press, 1963.

Prabhu, Anjali. *Hybridity. Limits, Transformations, Prospects.* Albany: State University of New York Press, 2007.

Prolongeau, Hubert. *La vita quotidiana in Colombia al tempo del cartello di Medellín.* Milan: Rizzoli, 1994.

Quijano, Anibal. "Colonialidad del poder. Eurocentrismo y América Latina." In *La colonialidad del saber: eurocentrismo y ciencias sociales. Perspectivas latinoamericanas,* edited by Edgardo Lander, 401–46. Buenos Aires: Clacso, 1993.

Ramadan, Tariq. Les défis du pluralisme," *Politis* 756, June 19, 2003.

———. *Les musulmans d'Occident et l'avenir de l'Islam.* Arles: Actes Sud, 2003.

———. *To Be a European Muslim: A Study of Islamic Sources in the European Context.* Translated by C. Dabbak. Leicester, UK: Islamic Foundation, 1999.

———. *Western Muslims and the Future of Islam.* Translated by Carol Bebawi. New York: Oxford University Press, 2004.

Romana, Cesare. *Amico fragile. Fabrizio De André si racconta a Cesare G. Romana.* Milan: Sperling and Kupfer Editori, 1991.

Rossi, Guido. *Il conflitto endemico.* Milan: Adelphi, 2003.

Rushdie, Salman. *Imaginary Homelands: Essays and Criticism, 1981–1991.* London: Penguin, 1992.

Said, Edward. *Culture and Imperialism.* New York: Knopf, 1993.

———. *Orientalism.* New York: Vintage, 1979.

Santato, Guido. *Pier Paolo Pasolini. L'opera.* Vicenza: Neri Pozza, 1980.

Savinio, Alberto. *Alcesti di Samuele e atti unici.* Milan: Adelphi, 1991.

———. *Capitano Ulisse.* Milan: Adelphi, 1989.

———. *Nuova enciclopedia*. Milan: Adelphi, 1977.

———. *Opere. Scritti dispersi. Tra guerra e dopoguerra (1943–1952)*. Introduction by Leonardo Sciascia. Edited by Leonardo Sciascia and De Maria. Milan: Bompiani, 1989.

———. "Senza mare davanti l'intelligenza non cammina." In Alberto Savinio, *Opere. Scritti dispersi. Tra guerra e dopoguerra (1943–1952)*. Milan: Bompiani, 1989.

Schmitt, Carl. *Land and Sea*. Translated by Simona Draghici. Washington, D.C.: Plutarch Press, 1997.

Schultze-Engler, Frank. "From Postcolonial to Preglobal: Transnational Culture." In *Towards a Transnational Future. Literature and Society in the Postcolonial World*, edited by Geoffrey V. Davis, Peter H. Marsden, Bénédicte Ledent, and Marc Delrez, 50–64. Amsterdam: Rodopi, 2004.

———. "Theoretical Perspectives: From Postcolonialism to Transcultural World Literature." In *English Literatures across the Globe: A Companion*, edited by Lars Eckstein, 20–32. Paderborn: Fink, 2007.

Schulze-Engler, Frank, and Sissy Helff. *Transcultural English Studies: Theories, Fictions, Realities*. Amsterdam: Rodopi, 2009.

Sen, Amartya. *L'altra India. La tradizione razionalistica e scettica della cultura Indiana*. Milan: Mondadori, 2005.

———. *The Argumentative Indian: Writings on Indian History, Culture, and Identity*. London: Allen Tate, 2005.

———. *Capability and Well-Being*. New York: United Nations Press, 1991.

———. *Identity and Violence: The Illusion of Destiny*. New York: Norton, 2006.

———. *Laicismo indiano*. Edited by Armando Massarenti. Milan: Feltrinelli, 1998.

———. *The Standards of Living: Lecture 1: Concepts and Critiques*, and *Lecture 2: Lives and Capabilities*. Salt Lake City: University of Utah Press, 1992.

Sennett, Richard. *The Corrosion of Character: The Personal Consequences of Work in the New Capitalism*. New York: W. W. Norton, 1998.

Siciliano, Enzo. 1981. *Pasolini: A Biography*. Translated by John Shepley. New York: Random House, 1982.

Silone, Ignazio. *Bread and Wine*. Translated by Eric Mosbacher. New York: Penguin, 1962.

———. *Severina*. Milan: Mondadori, 1990.

Simenon, Georges. "Frontiere." *Limes* 2 (1994): 289–96.

Simmel, Georg. *Sociology: Inquiries into the Construction of Social Forms*. Translated and edited by Anthony J. Blasi, Anton K. Jacobs, and Mathew Kanjirathinkal. With an introduction by Horst J. Helle. Leiden: Brill, 2009.

Siti, Walter. "Postfazione in forma di lettera." In *Desiderio di Pasolini*, edited by Stefano Casi, 183–87. Turin: Sonda, 1990.

Soyinka, Wole. *Myth, Literature, and the African World*. Cambridge: Cambridge University Press, 1976.

Spivak, Gayatri Chakravorty. *Critique of Postcolonial Reason*. Cambridge: Harvard University Press, 1999.

———. *Imperative zur Neuerfindung des Planeten/Imperatives to Re-Imagine the Planet*. Edited by Willi Goetschel. Translated by Bernard Schweizer. Vienna: Passagen Verlag, 1999.

———. *Other Words. Essays in Culture Politics*. New York: Routledge, 1988.

———. *Outside in the Teaching Machine*. New York: Routledge, 1998.

———. "Righting Wrongs." In *Human Rights, Human Wrongs*, edited by Nicholas Owen, 168–227. Oxford: Oxford University Press, 2003.

———. "Subaltern Studies: Deconstructing Historiography." In *Selected Subalterrn Studies*, edited by Ranajit Guha and Gayatri Chakravorty Spivak, 3–32. New York: Oxford University Press, 1988.

Steiner, George. *Martin Heidegger*. Chicago: University of Chicago Press, 1978.

Stiglitz, J. E. *Globalization and Its Discontents*. New York: Norton, 2002.

Thiong'o, Ngugi wa. *Decolonising the Mind: The Politics of Language in African Literature*. London: J. Currey; Portsmouth, N.H.: Heinemann, 1986.

———. *Moving the Centre: The Struggle for Cultural Freedoms*. London: James Currey, 1993.

Thomas, Dylan. *Dylan Thomas: The Notebook Poems, 1930–34*. Edited by Ralph Maud. London: Everyman, 1999.

Tomasi di Lampedusa, Giuseppe. *Il gattopardo*. Milan: Feltrinelli, 1958.

———. *The Leopard*. Translated by Archibald Colquhoun. New York: Pantheon Books, 1960.

Toynbee, Arnold J. *Civilization on Trial*. New York: Oxford University Press, 1948.

———. *A Study of History*. Oxford: Oxford University Press, 1962.

———. *The World and the West*. London: Oxford University Press, 1953.

Valéry, Paul. "The Crisis of the Mind." Translated by Denise Folliot. In Paul Valéry, History and Politics, translated by Denise Folliot and Jackson Mathews, 10:23–36. New York: Bollingen, 1962.

———. "The European." In *The Collected Works of Paul Valéry*, vol. 10, edited by Denise Folliot and translated by Jackson Mathews, 307–23. New York: Pantheon, 1962.

———. *History and Politics*. Translated by Denise Folliot and Jackson Mathews. New York: Bollingen, 1962.

———. *Reflections on the World Today*. Translated by Francis Scarfe. New York: Pantheon, 1948.

Varano, Aldo. *Il divario che non c'è. Nord e sud visti da Bevilacqua, Cassano, Consolo, Desantis, Lupo, Rea, Reichlin, Trigilia.* Cosenza: Memoria, 1998.

Venturi, Franco. *L'Italia fuori d'Italia, Dal primo Settecento all'Unità. Vol. 3. Storia d'Italia.* Edited by Ruggiero Romano and Corrado Vivanti, 1385–1481.Turin: Einaudi, 1973.

Weber, Max. *Economy and Society: An Outline of Interpretive Sociology.* New York: Bedminster Press, 1968.

———. *The Protestant Ethic and the Spirit of Capitalism.* New York: Scribner's. 1958.

Weil, Simone. *L'enracinement: Prélude à un declaration des devoirs envers l'être humain.* Paris: Gallimard, 1949.

Wittgenstein, Ludwig. *Remarks on Frazer's Golden Bough.* Edited by Rush Rhees. Translated by A. C. Miles. Atlantic Highlands, N.J.: Humanities Press, 1979.

Zigaina, Giuseppe. *Pasolini between Enigma and Prophecy.* Translated by Jennifer Russel. Toronto: Exile Editions, 1991.